Alternative Work Schedules

Jon L. Pierce
University of Minnesota, Duluth

John W. Newstrom
University of Minnesota, Duluth

Randall B. Dunham
University of Wisconsin, Madison

Alison E. Barber
University of Minnesota, Minneapolis

Allyn and Bacon, Inc.

Boston   London   Sydney   Toronto

Library of Congress Cataloging-in-Publication Data

Alternative work schedules / Jon L. Pierce . . . [et al.].
    p. cm.
  Includes index.
  ISBN 0-205-11163-7 :
  1. Hours of labor, Flexible. 2. Compressed work week. 3. Part-
time employment. 4. Shift systems. I. Pierce, Jon L. (Jon
Lepley)
HD5109.A39 1989
658.3'121—dc19   88–6522
                                          CIP

Series Editor: Jack Peters
Senior Editorial Assistant: Dottie Bibbo
Production Coordinator: Susan Freese
Editorial-Production Service: Helyn Pultz
Manufacturing Buyer: Bill Alberti
Cover Administrator: Linda K. Dickinson

Printed in the United States of America

10 9 8 7 6 5 4 3 2 1   93 92 91 90 89 88

Dedicated, with deep appreciation, to these scholars, who have made a significant contribution to our professional careers—

Larry Cummings
Keith Davis
Andre Delbecq
Randy Dunham

Dick Gaumnitz
Harve Rawson
Allen Solem
George Zirkle

Contents

Preface

Many employees now work under some form of alternative work schedule. The reasons for the popularity of these schedules are many and diverse, but they generally include a combination of personal benefits and organizational gains. However, much of the literature on why alternative schedules are implemented and beneficial consists of unsubstantiated folklore. This has, unfortunately, contributed to confusion regarding the nature of these systems.

The overall purpose of this book is to identify and clarify the current state of knowledge on alternative work schedules. Its specific objectives are to (1) present a comprehensive and current review of the research and conceptual literature on flexible hours, compressed work weeks, permanent part-time employment, and shift work; (2) suggest to practitioners how to systematically assess the acceptability of various schedules; (3) provide guidelines for the implementation and evaluation of a selected schedule; and (4) document the development and application of evaluation instruments for assessing the social-psychological effects associated with a particular schedule. Given these diverse objectives, various readers will undoubtedly have differential interest in (and experience differential intellectual challenge from) different parts of the book.

Overall, the literature on alternative work schedules has been neither guided by integrative models nor characterized by consistently solid research designs. As a result, most conclusions about them must be stated with a certain degree of caution. Practitioners, in particular, are urged not to conclude automatically that a system that allegedly worked for another organization will necessarily work for theirs. We strongly urge the serious practitioners who are interested in the adoption of alternative work schedules to engage in a careful diagnosis of the work environment, employ a participative development strategy, and carefully implement, monitor, and fine-tune the adopted system. This book has been prepared to serve these ends.

Intended Audience and Nature of Content

There are many individuals and groups of individuals who, for different reasons, are interested in alternative work schedules. The content of the book varies in terms of the type of materials presented as well as level and style of presentation. These differences serve the educational needs of the student, undergraduate as well as graduate; fill the informational and intellectual curiosities of practicing managers; and serve the work-schedule selection, design, and implementation needs of those who act as organizational change agents.

We wrote this book, first, to provide you with a detailed portrait of several alternative work schedules. We look closely at the conceptual and/or theoretical explanations for how and why a particular schedule should have social-psychological and behavioral consequences, thereby affecting employee attitudes, motivation, and behavior. In addition to a review of the conceptual arguments for a particular work schedule, we provide the reader with an extensive review of the theoretical and empirical research literature on various work schedules. This review provides the reader with an encyclopedic understanding of the current state of knowledge that surrounds each schedule. The reader who wants a detailed and comprehensive insight into this literature should read Chapters Two through Five. The reader who wants only a quick overview of the literature, its summary, and conclusions can selectively read some of the chapters or some sections of each chapter. The summary or conclusion section in each chapter outlines the state of knowledge and predicts the social-psychological and behavioral effects of the alternative work schedule.

Second, we wrote this book for consultants, change agents, and managers who would like to institute an alternative work schedule. For them, we have included two chapters, Six and Seven, that are very basic, descriptive, and prescriptive in nature. These chapters, unlike the previous four, present the details of how to proceed in a step-by-step fashion. They carefully describe the processes through which an alternative schedule might be selected, implemented, and evaluated.

Finally, Appendices A and B are scientific in nature. These appendices were written for the intellectually curious reader interested in the technical aspects of developing instruments for the measurement of employee attitudes and the assessment of an organization's experiences with an alternative schedule. Appendix A reports on the development of a set of measurement instruments that can be employed to identify an appropriate work schedule and evaluate its effectiveness. Appendix B illustrates a systematic evaluation of an alternative work schedule implemented in an organization.

Organization of the Book

The book is organized into five parts. Part One is retrospective in nature and provides an overview of the meaning of work and the scheduling of work in people's lives. The historical review concludes with contemporary experimentation with alternatives to the traditional five-day, forty-hour work week.

Part Two focuses attention on alternatives to the traditional work week. The alternatives discussed are flexible working hours (Chapter Two), shortened or compressed work weeks (Chapter Three), permanent part-time employment (Chapter Four), and shift work (Chapter Five). Each of these four chapters introduces the particular work-schedule concept; reviews the existing theoretical and/or conceptual reasons why this particular work schedule should have an impact upon employee work-related attitudes, motivation, and behavior; presents an extensive review of the empirical literature; and summarizes the effects of that work schedule.

Part Three consists of two chapters that are application oriented. Chapter Six, "Exploring and Selecting Work Schedules," describes the step-by-step process by which the manager, consultant, or organizational change agent might go about identifying a work schedule that fits the social-psychological climate of an organization. Chapter Seven, "Implementing and Evaluating Work Schedules," presents the step-by-step process for implementing an alternative work schedule. As part of the process we recommend that the effects produced by the schedule be monitored so that it can be evaluated later.

In Part Four, Chapter Eight reviews and summarizes the state of knowledge that is derived from theory and observation of alternative work schedules in operation. An integrative model portrays the complex linkages through which an alternative work schedule may lead to general worker reactions and/or organizational effectiveness.

There are five appendices in the book. Appendix A describes the development of a set of instruments that can be employed by researchers, change agents, and managers for measuring employee attitudes toward alternative work schedules. These instruments can be employed in both the selection and evaluation of an alternative work schedule. Appendix B illustrates one field experiment in which we studied an organization's experiment with an alternative work schedule. The report serves to illustrate a systematic approach that can be taken in order to observe and evaluate an organizational experience with an alternative work schedule. Appendices C, D, and E present the survey instrument, scoring information, and tables for summarizing results, respectively. Viewed collectively, the appendices provide helpful tools and models upon which an organization can base its design and evaluation approaches.

In conclusion, we have several dreams. We hope that you will learn something from our review of the literature about the social-psychological and behavioral effects associated with a variety of work schedules. There is nothing inherently magical about the traditional five-day, forty-hour work week. We believe that many organizations use this schedule solely as a result of tradition. We also believe that managers can design organizationally and humanly functional schedules if they engage in a systematic examination of various options. Thus, we hope that this book stimulates your thinking about what alternative schedules might be designed and implemented in the organizations of today and tomorrow. We believe that much remains to be learned about the process through which these work schedules produce their effects. And we hope that this book stimulates additional experimentation with different work schedules. Finally, we hope that you enjoy reading and thinking about the ways in which hours of work are and can be structured.

Acknowledgments

Many managers have been willing to experiment with and implement alternatives to the traditional five-day, forty-hour work week. To them we express our gratitude, for it has enabled researchers like ourselves to study the important social-psychological conditions associated with the pattern of hours that people work. Experimentation in organizations has also provided many employees with new work schedules. In many cases, this has given them an opportunity to choose a schedule that provides greater harmony between the demands of their work and nonwork lives. We are grateful to the managers who paved the way so that other managers can now learn from their successes and failures.

It has been fascinating to study and experiment with alternative work schedules. To those organizations that allowed us to conduct our studies, we express our appreciation. They helped us learn about the dynamics of the relationship between work schedules and employee work attitudes, motivation, and behaviors. We have written this book so that other students and practitioners alike can share in the knowledge we have gained.

We wish to express our thanks to a number of individuals who played key roles in the development of this book. Jean Jacobson, Randi K. Huntsman, Connie Johnson, Lori Bielawski, and Kora Cavanaugh typed the manuscript. We thank them for their expertise, interest, and patience throughout the process. They, too, had the opportunity to experience alternatives to their regular work schedules, with our early-morning, late-night, and weekend demands to type this, change that, and rush to meet our deadlines. We also wish to thank the reviewers of the manuscript, Stanley D. Nollen of Georgetown University and Richard T. Mowday of the University of Oregon, for their helpful comments. And we especially appreciate the stong encouragement and editorial support we received from Jack Peters, without whose faith in us this book would never have been completed.

About the Authors

Jon L. Pierce is a Professor of Management and Organization in the School of Business and Economics at the University of Minnesota, Duluth. He received his Ph.D. in management and organizational studies at the University of Wisconsin, Madison. He is the author of more than forty papers that have been published or presented at various professional conferences. His work has appeared in the *Academy of Management Journal, Academy of Management Review, Journal of Management, Journal of Occupational Behaviour, Journal of Applied Behavioral Sciences, Personnel Psychology*, and also *Organization Behavior and Human Decision Processes*. His research interests include alternative work schedules, job design, organizational commitment, and organization-based self-esteem. He has served on the editorial review board for the *Academy of Management Journal* and the *Journal of Management*.

John W. Newstrom is a Professor of Human Resource Management in the School of Business and Economics at the University of Minnesota, Duluth. He completed his doctoral degree in management and industrial relations at the University of Minnesota and then taught at Arizona State University for several years. He is the author of over fifty articles and professional papers and his work has appeared in publications such as *Personnel Psychology, California Management Review, Journal of Management, Academy of Management Journal*, and *Journal of Occupational Behaviour*. He has served on the editorial review boards for the *Academy of Management Review, Academy of Management Journal, Personnel Administrator*, and *Journal of Management Development*. He is the coauthor of six other books, including *Human Behavior at Work: Organizational Behavior* (with Keith Davis) and *The Manager's Bookshelf* (with Jon Pierce). His primary research interests lie in the areas of transfer of training, alternative work schedules, and group dynamics.

Randall B. Dunham received both his master's degree and Ph.D. in industrial-organizational psychology from the University of Illinois in 1975 and has since taught at the University of Wisconsin, Madison. He is the author of over forty articles in professional journals and more than thirty-five presentations at professional conferences. His major fields of interest are job design, job satisfaction, work scheduling, compensation, and stress management. He is the author of four other books, including *Organizational Surveys* and *Organizational Behavior*. He is a Fellow in the American Psychological Association and has served on the editorial board of the *Academy of Management Journal*.

Alison E. Barber has a master's degree in industrial relations from the University of Wisconsin, Madison. She previously worked as a personnel generalist for both the Chevron and General Mills companies. She is currently completing her doctorate in industrial relations at the University of Minnesota, where her research interests lie in the areas of staffing and compensation.

Part One

Work and the Hours of Work— A Look Back

Chapter One

←————————————————————————→

Work through the Ages

▶ The philosophical meaning of work has changed dramatically through the ages. Accompanying these philosophical changes has been an evolutionary decrease in the total hours worked, followed by a number of major innovations in the way in which these hours are scheduled. Concurrent with this evolution, the societal acceptance and pursuit of leisure time have made a complete swing of the pendulum. These developments are briefly traced prior to introducing the alternative work schedules employed in a variety of organizations today.

The Meaning of Work

Differing perspectives abound on the role of work in the primitive world. There was a time when "to work" meant "to live," and the day was traditionally filled with various forms of work such that it consumed much of the time of both men and women. For example, early people secured a living by gathering the bounties of the earth. Spare time, if available, was spent in rest and play. Anthropologists suggest that for many, enjoyment of leisure and the success of the hunt were both valued activities.[1] However, work really began for the human race with the domestication of animals.[2] It appears that the availability of food determined the amount of time devoted to work and nonwork activities in these simple societies. Work of this nature was undoubtedly seen as synonymous with survival, and it clearly played a major role in everyone's life.

Negative Views

To the early Greeks (around 400 B.C.), work was seen as a virtual curse. For them, work meant sorrow, fatigue, and burden. In work they saw neither inherent value nor dignity. Greek ideology saw labor as an activity that contaminated the mind and drew the soul away from the roots of virtue. The Greeks believed that the gods hated the human race and therefore, instead of providing it with plenty, forced it to work. Any activity that brought people into contact with the material world and away from truth was a painfully humiliating necessity, one to be minimized or reduced altogether. To enable the few to avoid this humiliation, the majority of people in the Greek world were forced to labor so that the elite could engage in the pure exercise of the mind. The Greek elite took leisure—being free from the necessity of labor—very seriously.[3] Plato and Aristotle justified slavery so that there would be production of the things necessary to sustain life. If the majority engaged dutifully in this sorrowful activity then the minority in the Greek society could carry on with the pure activities of the spirit in art, philosophy, and politics. Influenced by the writings of Plato and Aristotle, the Romans embraced many of the same ideas.

The early Hebrews basically shared the Greek and Roman view of work. They too saw it as painful drudgery, but they reasoned that it was an atonement activity people must engage in to make amends for the original sin of their forebears. However, labor achieved a certain measure of dignity for some, since they reasoned that God had worked for six days in the creation of the earth.

Conflicting Perspectives

In early times, the Jewish world's lack of enduring distinctiveness probably contributed to diverse schools of thought regarding the meaning of work. According to some historians, within the Jewish world there were in fact two conflicting attitudes toward the place of work.[4] In one, work was condemned as taking time that rightfully belonged to the spiritual life. In the other, work was thought of as a meaningful way of cooperating with God.

The contemporaneous Persians' perspective was the antithesis of the Greek view of work, for their doctrine valued labor. To work was to collaborate with the will of Ahuramazda (the spirit of good). The Persian doctrine was an ideology that prized labor, thrift, and property, and gave them ethical value. Work was regarded as an honorable activity, and one that was not to be confused with punishment.

Jesus, on the other hand, defined the real purpose of life as knowing, loving, and serving God. The work-related ideas given by Jesus are difficult to interpret, yet it appears that Jesus rebelled against the concept of work. Clearly there is no mention of the blessedness of work in the Beatitudes. It seems as though Jesus did not define work and wealth as wicked per se, but as folly. The real enemy is not work, but the neglect of the work of God when human work and its associated wealth fills the mind. The Greeks had seen leisure as an opportunity for contemplation. It was the highest and most godlike of all activities distinguishing people from animals, their beasts of burden. Likewise, early Christian thought viewed contemplative leisure as important (though not an end in itself), and even divine if it was directed toward God. Simultaneously, in many ways, early Christianity followed the Jewish view casting work as a form of God's punishment.

Positive Views

After the fall of Rome in the fifth century, monastic influence recast the view of work in Western culture. Manual work became an instrument for self-purification if it was done to help others. Work and wealth accumulation took on positive value when coupled with acts of charity, and resulted in the receipt of God's blessing.

Early medieval Christianity also advocated work as a means to avoid falling prey to the evil thoughts and deeds that might accompany idleness. Thus work was seen as a necessity for a healthy body and soul. Saint Augustine (fifth c. A.D.) approved handicraft, tilling the soil, and commerce on a small scale. These activities follow the greatly honored activities of meditations on the divine in virtue. Saint Benedict and other monks of his time (sixth c. A.D.) advocated mixing work and prayer. These views and behaviors can be seen and interpreted as a legitimization of work.

During the eleventh to fourteenth centuries, numerous sects in Europe scorned wealth, preached work as punishment for the pride of the flesh, and exalted poverty as religious sanctity. Toward the end of this period, the Roman Catholic Church drew closer and closer to the secular world around it and began to grant increasing legitimacy to both labor and its fruits. Saint Thomas Aquinas (thirteenth c.) believed that work was a necessary part of life. He drew up a hierarchy of professions and trades based on their value to society. Work took on the role of a natural right and duty. Ecclesiastical labor and contemplation, however, still ranked above all other forms of labor. Aquinas also argued that once people achieved a surplus of produce there was no further obligation to toil. Contemplation enabled people to see the divine, and, as long as there was a surplus, this was a good activity.

The Roman Catholic Church, under the influence of Aquinas, St. Antoninus of Florence, and St. Gernandion of Siena, condemned idleness and extravagance while praising activity and industry. Morality, it was said, must guide activity directed toward personal enrichment; charity was encouraged as a worthy end toward which to place wealth.

By the end of the nineteenth and the beginning of the twentieth centuries, the Orthodox movements of Christian Democracy and Christian Socialism broke with St. Thomas Aquinas and proclaimed work as the foundation of all human progress. Work was seen as a duty imposed by divine and human law. Society must ensure the "right to work" for all of its citizens, coupled with the "right to be cared for" for those unable to work. Yet work was still to be guided by natural and divine law. This meant that work as an end in itself could not be allowed by the Church. The ultimate goal is the life hereafter, and present activities must be focused toward this end.

Protestantism was the catalyst that established work as the base and key of life. Martin Luther (d. 1546), like many before him, saw work as having both penal and educational values. He also saw work as an activity in which all should engage. Idleness, according to Luther, was unnatural. Charity should only be directed toward those who cannot work. He attacked the monastic and contemplative life as an outgrowth of egotism and lack of human affection. It was through Luther's influence that work took on a religious dignity.

John Calvin (d. 1564) built upon Luther's philosophy of work. A primary Calvinist doctrine stated that it is God's will that all people work. Although work is the will of God, however, lusting after the fruits of labor could not be accepted. With this new creed came a new man. He was strong-willed, austere, hard-working out of religious conviction. Idleness was seen as softening the soul and it was therefore shunned as a deadly sin.[5] This ideology stressed that work pleases God. Intermittent and occasional labor could not be tolerated; it must be continuous (six days per week), disciplined, rational, and specialized. Thus Calvin's command was to work and to succeed at it, for it is the way by which people can serve God. This philosophy carries with it an abhorrence of rest and pleasure.

There were, however, competing pressures during this period. For example, Sir Thomas More (d. 1535) talked about utopia as a place where people labor for six hours then turn to rest and pleasure in the remaining hours of the day.

From the time of Calvin well into the 1950s, the perceived value and importance of work stood firm. Work appeared to lose its connection with religion and came to stand as having value and authority in its own right—work for the sake of work. Labor was seen as the cause of all human progress— material and intellectual, as well as spiritual. It was acknowledged as a factor controlling success and failure. Outside of the context of Protestantism, sport and play simultaneously achieved valued roles in human existence. Sport introduced pauses and relaxation from the tensions derived from work. Play put light and cheerfulness into life, relieving the weight and seriousness that stem from a life totally filled with work. Nevertheless, ties with the Protestant work ethic remained in place and, according to this new ideology, play and sport remained a pause in the difficult and serious affair between people and labor.

The Pendulum Swings Again

Building upon the ideology that encouraged the mixing of labor with play and sport, and moving beyond the Protestant ethic's stress on a life filled with work, the religion of work in the United States gave way to a new religion of its exact opposite. This new religion values rest, relaxation, recreation, amusement, and other activities that serve personal pleasure.[6]

One writer expressed this new ideology when he said,

> Our ideas about work are undergoing considerable change. . . . It is no longer necessary to work six days a week to make a living. . . . What is needed is a new philosophy of work. . . . We must learn from the butterfly not the bee. . . . Work must be recognized, not as a virtue, but as an intrinsic evil, the only justification for which is in its product.[7]

It is clear from this overview that there have been varied beliefs about work throughout the ages. In spite of sharply different philosophical meanings attached to the concept throughout time, members of the human race have always found it necessary to devote some portion of the week to it. The ways in which that work week has changed in structure is reviewed next.

The Historical Structure of Work Time

In addition to changing definitions of the meaning of work, the structuring of time devoted to work has also changed through the centuries. Anthropologists report that obtaining food was the single most important activity in the lives of hunter-gatherers as well as small-scale agricultural and pastoral societies.[8] The actual amount of time people directed toward getting food is not known, but recent studies provide suggestive evidence about life during these early periods. The contemporary Dobe Bushmen of Africa, despite their harsh environment, devote twelve to nineteen hours a week to food getting. Women gather enough food in one day to feed their families for three days. The rest of their time is spent resting, doing embroidery, visiting other camps, and entertaining visitors. This rhythm of work and leisure appears to be maintained throughout the year. The (male) hunters work more frequently than the women, but with a more uneven schedule. They may hunt for a week and then not again for two or three weeks. In the meantime rest, visiting, and dance are common leisure-time activities.

It is intuitively obvious that the amount of time given by primitive people to meeting their survival needs varied with the difficulty of finding food. As a result, some societies lacked the leisure time necessary to build cultures; in other societies, considerable amounts of time were available for leisure. Thus the structure of the earliest work day and week was based on the availability of food. When food was scarce, a seven-day search from dawn to dusk was common; when food was plentiful, a twelve- to twenty-hour week was not uncommon. Similarly, the totality of the Dobe Bushman's existence revolves simultaneously around two separate goals: first, the desire to live well with adequate leisure time; and second, the desire to enjoy the rewards (social and nutritional) afforded by the killing of game.

The first major change in the work week occurred with the development of agriculture and the domestication of animals. For those raising the crops and keeping animals the work week was from before sunrise to after sunset, seven days a week. The development of agriculture and the domestication of animals eventually brought with it a modest surplus of food. This in turn provided the opportunity for the introduction of differentiated labor. Some people could now devote all of their time to specialties such as the manufacture of weapons, tools, clothing, and other life-sustaining necessities.

The first division of labor, coupled with the shift to agrarian ways of living, set the stage for the emergence of the so-called great irrigation societies, around 3000 B.C. in the Near, Middle, and Far East. Labor in these civilizations remained relatively unchanged until the eighteenth-century arrival of industrial machine power.

With the growth and development of irrigation societies came the emergence of the first organized and institutionalized forms of state government. A leadership class, with laws, armies, and clergy, orchestrated the growth and distribution of foodstuffs. Other occupational specializations soon proliferated.

A major result in these developing societies, in countries like Egypt and Mesopotamia, was the emergence of a highly stratified class system with the elites at the top; craftsmen, merchants, and agriculturalists in the middle; and a mass of slaves at the bottom. As noted earlier, manual labor was an abhorred activity. During this period the vast majority of laborers worked in the fields in a sunrise-to-sunset, seven-day work-week framework. The bottom stratum of these societies consisted of extremely large numbers of people, and this slave class labored almost continuously (like the farmer). Their work schedule was basically an all-day, seven-day-week affair.

Work Hours in More Recent Times

In 1791 Philadelphia carpenters pressed for and achieved a reduced and standardized 6 A.M. to 6 P.M. work day. This work schedule replaced the more flexible and nebulously defined sun-up-to-sun-down work schedule that had frequently resulted in fourteen to sixteen hours, six days per week. By 1822, Philadelphia mill workers and machinists passed a resolution stating that ten hours of labor on any single day was long enough. Following the lead taken by the Philadelphia carpenters, they asked for a 6 A.M. to 6 P.M. work day, coupled with one-hour breaks for breakfast and dinner.

When the Philadelphia carpenters pressed for a 6 to 6 workday, however, public opinion did not support them. Idleness was regarded as a vice and their demand for a shorter work day seemed to be an argument for idle time. The general public saw this as a step toward moral decay and therefore a request that should not be granted. When the Boston carpenters struck for a ten-hour day in 1825, their employers argued that idleness would afflict the well-being of society. Moral and economic arguments were used in an attempt to counter these demands. In spite of the push for a shorter work week, the prevailing hours in many occupations and cities in the United States remained twelve or thirteen hours per day, six days a week, well into the 1830s.

The primary movement for shorter working hours was led by the building-trades unions. This industry generally had a work week already shorter than that of other industries. The builders' continued push for a shorter week enabled them to be the first labor group to secure the ten-hour work day. By 1835 this goal had been achieved for building unions in many of the large eastern cities.

In most other industries, however, the average hours of work per day remained as high as eleven or twelve in 1840 and did not begin a marked decrease until the middle of the 1850s. By 1890 the ten-hour day was well established in the majority of occupations and industries. The major exception to this trend was in the cotton mills, the sawmills, the iron and steel plants, and on the railroads. In fact, the iron and steel industry remained the major business resisting the shorter work-week movement. It was not until as late as 1932 that the steel industry abandoned its twelve-hour, seven-day schedule.

In 1850 the average weekly scheduled hours of work (versus actual hours worked) in the United States was approximately 70.[9] This average dropped substantially to about 62 by 1900, even more sharply to about 40 by 1960, and still continues a small downward trend at the present (see Figure 1–1).

Organized pressure for shorter hours shifted from the ten-hour work day to the eight-hour day by the turn of the century. With a major expansion in national union membership during the years of 1914 and '15, there was simultaneous pressure for the eight-hour day. World War I created an extremely heavy demand for labor. On the basis of this demand, unions were able to successfully bargain for, and gain acceptance of, the eight-hour day.

The 1920s and '30s were the decades in which the five-day week began its serious introduction into U.S. industry. The Great Depression focused national attention on shortening the work week as a means of giving more people employment opportunities. By mid-1930 the 5/40 (5 day, 40-hour work week) no longer appeared revolutionary. A Bureau of Labor Standards survey in 1932 showed that 25 percent of the firms in seventy-seven different industries had permanently adopted the five-day week.

Legislatively, the National Industrial Recovery Act of 1933 led to the inclusion of a forty-hour work-week provision in a large number of industry codes. The Public Contracts Act of 1936 and the Fair Labor Standards Act of 1938 were laws that required the payment of time-and-a-half for work over forty hours per week. As a consequence, these laws were instrumental in establishing the 5/40 work week as the standard in the United States.

**Figure 1–1.   Approximate Average Weekly Hours of Work
(1850–Present)**

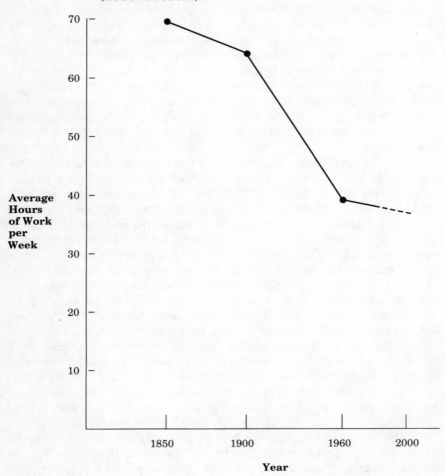

Rationale for Shorter Hours

Throughout the early twentieth century, a number of arguments were employed by workers and unions in order to secure a reduction of the work week. The following five themes stand out:

1. Shorter hours are essential to good citizenship. Through an increase in leisure time workers have an opportunity to educate themselves and to become active participants in local politics.

2. Shorter working hours are necessary in order to protect the health of the working population. Such humanitarian motives apparently characterized the initial legislative thrust to regulate the hours of work.[10] This regulation was influenced by the belief that some workers needed to be protected from themselves. It was argued that in the desire to profit financially from their labor some workers would subject themselves to physical and nervous strain, which would impair their health in the long run.

3. An increase in leisure time stimulates demand for the products created by society's industries. This increased demand would necessarily bring additional growth and increase the workers' standard of living.

4. Shorter working hours increase the efficiency of labor and organizational productivity. Physiological and economic considerations converged as a further inducement for legislation. Physical fatigue and mental strain were seen as leading to reduced output, lower quality work, increased sickness costs, and unnecessary absenteeism.

5. Shorter working hours create more jobs and therefore contribute to expanded consumption and product demand, and additional organizational profits and growth.

Although the union movement was in the vanguard for the reduction of the work week, the role of the general public's opinion should not be overlooked. For example, what we now cherish as leisure was once condemned as idleness. Shorter hours were once argued against as contributors to temptation and social decay. Now, however, shorter working hours are often identified as a vehicle that will contribute to a better society, a healthier worker, and a growth-oriented economy.

Since the end of World War II, there has been no major coordinated attempt by employers, individual employees, or unions to redefine the standard 5/40 employee work week. Of course, on occasion the issue of a shorter week has still surfaced. For example, the Air Traffic Controllers' strike of 1981 centered, in part, on the demand for a shorter week. Also, some members of Congress during the early 1980s occasionally mentioned creating legislation to shorten the work week as a cure for stubbornly high levels of unemployment.

A national survey of 47,000 households in the early 1970s found that the five-day week dominated, with only 16 percent working five-and-a-half to seven days a week, and just 2 percent working three to four-and-a-half days per week. In addition, the forty-hour week, even for those working less than a five-day week, was the most common.[11]

The primary trend apparent in this brief historical review has been the dramatic shortening of the work week. Within this trend, two dynamics are significant: first, there has been a reduction in the *number of days worked* (i.e., a movement from the seven-day week to six, to five-and-a-half, and finally to a five-day work week); and second, there has been a reduction in the *number of hours worked* on a weekly and a daily basis (i.e., a movement from as much as a sixteen-hour day down to an eight-hour work day). Today, for most nonprofessional and nonmanagerial workers in the United States, the standard work week is defined as eight hours per day for five days per week—5/40.

Recent Work-Scheduling Trends

From the 1930s until the late 1960s, *patterns* of work time remained remarkably stable in the United States. The following comment is indicative:

> There are few facets to the Western way of work which are more depressing and unimaginative than the way in which work time is arranged for us. Our jobs generally demand 40 hours of service in five consecutive eight-hour clips, during which we obediently come and go at rush hours appointed by others. Except for layoffs or prolonged periods of illness, a work life is laid out in front of a person: five day, 40-hour pieces stretch out like a seemingly endless passing train terminating abruptly at age 65 at a Chicken à la King banquet where a gold watch is presented and the boss picks up the tab for the drinks.[12]

Since then, as if to counter this depressing portrait, new interest has emerged in alternative ways to schedule work. Why did this interest in work scheduling appear? A number of social and economic factors contributed to a strong wave of experimentation (see Figure 1–2).[13] The following forces played an instrumental role in this development:

1. An increase in the number of women participating in the work force
2. Interest in and adoption of new lifestyles
3. An increase in the number of single-parent and two-paycheck households

Figure 1–2.   Social and Economic Forces Contributing to the Emergence of Alternative Work Schedules

1. Women in the work force
2. New lifestyles
3. Single-parent and dual-career households
4. Work–Education relationships
5. Aging of the work force
6. Service economy
7. High unemployment/inflation
8. Work–leisure time perceptions

4. New relationships between work and education
5. The aging of the work force
6. The growth of the service sector of the economy
7. The pressures of unemployment and inflation
8. A change in the way people perceive both work and leisure time.

As an outgrowth of these forces, four distinctive types of alternative approaches to work scheduling have become institutionalized in the United States: compressed work weeks, flexible hours, part-time employment, and shift work. Each of these is previewed here and then discussed in detail in Chapters Two through Five.

Compressed Work Week

Efforts to continue the historical trend of shortening the work week have continued since World War II. For example, the past-President of the CIO, Walter Reuther, unsuccessfully bargained for a 32-hour, 4-day work week in the 1950s. Yet the current interest in shortening or compressing the work week is quite recent in origin. The most common form of this compression is captured by the 4-day, 40-hour work week (4/40), in which employees typically work 4 (often consecutive) 10-hour days but still work a full (i.e., 40-hour) work week.

The first documented use of the 4/40 work week came with its 1940 adoption by Mobil and Gulf Oil for their truck drivers. However, it was not until two decades later (1960) that another company adopted the 4/40 system.[14] Aside from a few other experiments with the schedule during the mid-1960s, accelerated interest in the 4/40 did not arise until the 1970s. By 1972, however, approximately 100,000 employees in over 700 organizations in North America were working on a four-day schedule.[15] At that time it was reported that "the present rate of conversion is estimated between 60 and 70 companies per month. This rate has steadily gained momentum during the past 12 to 18 months, and is likely to continue in the immediate future."[16]

Other forms of work-day compression have appeared, for example, as 37½-hour weeks, 35-hour weeks, and 32-hour weeks *while still continuing the 5-day work schedule*. Another shortening format has been characterized by a simultaneous shortening of the number of days and the number of hours worked per week. This has produced the 3/35 and 4/35 work schedules. In sum, three major forms of shortened work weeks have emerged, resulting in: (1) a change in days only (e.g., 4/40), (2) a change in days and hours (e.g., 4/32), and (3) a change only in the number of hours worked (e.g., 5/35).

All of these systems by definition hold one factor constant—the total weekly pay earned by an employee. By comparison, in 1976 a plan called the *voluntary reduced work time system* was introduced by the Santa Clara (Cal.) County Service Employees' International Union, Local 715. This is a work-scheduling plan by which employees can request a reduction in hours *and income* (e.g., a 2.5, 5, 10, or 20 percent reduction). The voluntary reduced work-time system is a version of work for less than full compensation, and therefore a form of part-time employment.

Chapter Three provides a comprehensive discussion of the shortened or compressed work-week schedule.

Flexible Forms of Work Scheduling

A second method of modifying the work week is characterized by the various forms of discretionary-time systems that have been created during the past two decades. Two types, variable systems and flexible hours, are introduced here. Each provides employees with increased autonomy in deciding when to work.

A European precursor of a discretionary-time system was carried out as an experiment in 1955 in Metz, France.[17] Growing out of a desire to make better use of the existing public transportation system, schools and employers adopted a citywide *staggered start* system. Schools started and closed fifteen minutes earlier than before, while shop, factory, and office workers adjusted their schedule to fifteen minutes later than before. With the Metz experiment the concept of staggered starts emerged in Europe and was soon adopted in a number of European cities. During the 1960s firms in western Europe took the staggered-start concept and applied it at the departmental level as a way of managing traffic problems around their plants.

The staggered-start system is not compressed, for it neither decreases the total number of hours nor the number of days worked per week. Under this system the organization as a whole (or a group of employees such as a department, or the individual employee) chooses, from a number of management-defined options, when they wish to start their fixed-length working day. Some organizations employing the group-choice or individual-choice staggered-start system permit occasional changes in the chosen starting time (e.g., once every three months), thus providing a small measure of employee discretion. The success of these staggered systems at solving local problems stimulated new thought on the merits of totally standardized work days (especially start–stop times), and opened the door for variable and flexitime systems.

Growing out of early German experimentation with work scheduling was the *variable* system. Some German firms, for example, created a system where employees had complete freedom to choose when they wanted to work.[18] Under the variable system an employee contracted for a specified amount of time in a time accounting period (e.g., on a daily, weekly, or monthly basis). During the contracted period the employee was free to choose when the work would be carried out as long as the total hours were worked.

Christel Kammerer, a West German political economist and management consultant, is credited with the invention of this concept, called *gliding time.*

Messerschmitt-Bolkow-Blohm (MBB), a German aerospace firm, was experiencing major problems with employee tardiness and absenteeism. Management assessed the problem as the result of an inadequate network of roads leading to its research and development center near Munich. The firm sought a solution that was a compromise between the variable and staggered-hour systems that were already in use in numerous German firms.

The firm hired Kammerer with the hope that she would be able to apply her work-scheduling concept (gliding time) to alleviate the tardiness and absenteeism problems. In 1967 MBB introduced gliding time to its 2000 Ottobrunn employees. The employees could arrive at work any time between 7 and 8 A.M. and leave between 4 and 6 P.M. The system also included a time-banking component; that is, all employees were required to work their monthly contracted hours, plus or minus ten hours. The balance (gliding time) had to be carried forward and netted or balanced out during the following month.

MBB claimed that gliding time led to the reduction of the firm's traffic problem, which was accompanied by three results: absenteeism declined by 40 percent, tardiness disappeared, and employee morale rose appreciably.

The gliding-time concept spread rapidly in western Europe. By 1978 30 percent of the total labor force in West Germany, 40 percent in Switzerland, and 20 percent in France were under gliding time.[19] The idea of providing flexibility in work scheduling was also adopted rapidly in the Scandinavian countries. But the concept found neither acceptance nor ease of adoption in the United States.

Numerous federal and state laws (along with existing union contracts) slowed the experimentation with, and adoption of, various flexible work-schedule systems in the United States. At the federal level the Walsh-Healey Act of 1936, the Fair Labor Standards Act of 1938, and the Contract Work Hours and Safety Standards Act of 1962 slowed adoption through their emphasis on hours of work and associated compensation requirements.

Therefore, it was not until 1972 that the first major discretionary-time system was adopted in the United States by Control Data Corporation. By the mid- to late-1970s there were at least 400,000 employees working under some form of flexible working hours in the United States. The number of firms employing some form of flexitime was estimated to be around 100 in 1973 but it had grown to over 3000 by 1977.[20]

In its pure form, *flexitime* is a system under which every employee exercises a daily decision with regard to the time of day he or she will come to work. Management creates a band of time within which the employee exercises this starting-time decision. A set of core hours (i.e., hours that management requires all employees to be at work) also exist in the flexible work-schedule systems. The greater restrictions inherent in most U.S. flexitime systems are in contrast to the variable working-hour systems where there is no core-time component. Under variable-hour arrangements, employees "contract" with management for a specified amount of time to be worked on a daily, weekly, or monthly basis. The employee is then totally free to define when those hours will be worked.

Chapter Two is devoted to a review of the flexible work-schedule literature.

Permanent Part-Time Employment and Job Sharing or Splitting

Innovations in part-time employment represent the third contemporary movement to restructure the amount and timing of work. Two variations of the whole-day, part-time employment arrangement can be found. Under *job-sharing* programs a single job is divided and shared by two or more employees. Each employee engages in the complete set of tasks as defined by the job description. *Job splitting* is represented by the division of tasks that define a single job description and the assignment of subsets of these tasks to two or more employees. In either case the affected employees work fewer than forty hours, but may perform the required tasks in any proportion in whole or partial days as long as the sum of all contributing efforts equals one whole job.

Chapter Four discusses permanent part-time employment programs.

Shift Work

There has been a tendency toward the adoption of shift work by an increasing number of organizations,[21] which has begun to affect a number of both manual and nonmanual workers. Standard arrangements include: morning, afternoon, or night shifts, worked either on a fixed or rotating basis. Very little experimentation with forms of shift work has appeared in the work-scheduling literature. The few experiments conducted deal with forward–backward rotation and temporal duration between rotations (e.g., frequent rotation vs. infrequent).

Chapter Five reviews the shift-work literature.

Summary

The meaning of work from an ideological point of view has changed dramatically through the ages. Accompanying these attitudinal changes has been an evolutionary pattern in the hours that are worked and the ways in which the hours of work are scheduled. The highlights of these changes are presented in Figure 1–3.

Starting with early civilizations, work served as a means of survival. The hours and days that were worked were defined by the tasks that had to be executed. Sometimes seven consecutive days of labor from dawn to dusk were required; other times a mere twenty hours per week were necessary. Leisure time appears to have played an important, but varying, role in human existence.

Figure 1–3. Major Structural Changes in Work Schedules

Shorter weeks (number of days worked per week)
Shorter number of hours (number of hours worked per day or per week)
Compressed work weeks
Modified schedules
   Staggered start
   Variable
   Flexitime
Permanent part-time
   Job sharing
   Job splitting
Shift work
   Fixed
   Rotating
      Direction
      Frequency

With the domestication of animals, more and more of an individual's life was consumed by work with less time devoted to leisure. The development of highly organized societies seemed to expand the need for labor. Social strata also emerged, with an elite that relished leisure and sought freedom from labor.

The early Christian world brought attitudes encouraging labor and scorning idleness. Accompanying these religious beliefs were developments in technology and machine power, and a higher standard of living. People increasingly began to justify coupling work with rest and play and sought new ways to schedule work so as to enhance the quality of life.

Changing attitudes toward work have not only paralleled the trend to shorten the work week but have served as catalysts to some recent developments in the scheduling of work. A national survey in the late 1970s reported that the primary reason organizations implemented flexible working hours was to affect employee attitudes and the quality of their lives.[22] Similar reasons are frequently given for the implementation of various shortened- and compressed-time systems, as well as innovative forms of part-time employment. Whether or not the desired effects have materialized is discussed in the succeeding chapters.

Endnotes

1. R. B. Lee, "What Hunters Do for a Living, or How to Make Out on Scarce Resources," ed. R. B. Lee and I. DeVore, *Man the Hunter* (Chicago: Aldine Publishing, 1968), pp. 30–48.

2. R. Payne, *Why Work?* (Boston: Mendor Publishing Company, 1939) and G. Ritzer, *Man and His Work: Conflict and Change* (New York: Appleton-Century-Crofts).

3. S. de Grazia, *Of Time, Work, and Leisure* (New York: Anchor Books-Doubleday, 1962).

4. A. Tilgher, *Homo Labor: Work through the Ages* (Chicago: Henry Rogner, 1958).

5. Ibid.

6. Ibid.

7. Payne, op. cit., pp. 34–35.

8. Lee, op. cit.

9. W. Goldner, *Hours of Work* (Berkeley: University of California-Berkeley Institute of Industrial Relations, 1952).

10. A. A. Evans, *Hours of Work in Industrialized Countries* (Geneva: International Labor Office, 1975).

11. J. N. Hedges, "How Many Days Make a Work Week?," *Monthly Labor Review* (April 1975): 29–36.

12. P. Dickson, *The Future of the Workplace* (New York: Weybright and Talley, 1976), p. 209.

13. B. Olmsted, "Changing Times: The Use of Reduced Work-Time Options in the United States," *International Labour Review* 122 (1983): 479–492.

14. D. Hellriegel, "The Four-Day Work Week: A Review and Assessment," *MSU Business Topics* 20 (1972): 39–48.

15. Evans, op. cit., p. 91.

16. K. G. Wheeler, R. Gurman, and D. Tarnowieski, *The Four-Day Week: An AMA Research Report* (New York: American Management Association, 1972), p. 7.

17. D. Maric, *Adapting Working Hours to Modern Needs* (Geneva: International Labor Office, 1977).

18. M. Wade, *Flexible Working Hours in Practice* (Essex, Eng.: Gower Press, 1973).

19. J. C. Swart, *A Flexible Approach to Working Hours* (New York: American Management Association, 1978).

20. A. R. Cohen and H. Gadon, *Alternative Work Schedules: Integrating Individual and Organizational Needs* (Reading, Mass.: Addison-Wesley, 1978), p. 37.

21. M. Maurice, *Shift Work* (Geneva: International Labor Office, 1975).

22. S. D. Nollen and V. H. Martin, *Alternative Work Schedules, Parts 1, 2, and 3* (New York: American Management Association, 1978).

Part Two

Research and
Conceptual
Foundations

Chapter Two

Flexible Working Hours

▶ Flexible working hours provide employees with some degree of autonomy in the selection of the starting and ending times for their work day. At the beginning of the 1980s there were 7.6 million U.S. workers on flexible schedules. This constituted 11.9 percent of all nonfarm wage and salary personnel. If all professionals, managers, and salespeople were excluded from these statistics (since many of them have always set their own hours without calling it flexitime) the effective usage rate would still be 8.1 percent.[1] The *Monthly Labor Review* statistics for 1985 note that flexible hours were available to about 12 percent of all full-time wage and salary workers. Since the introduction of flexitime systems in the United States during the early 1970s there has been a steady growth in its rate of usage. Flexible work schedules are even more common in Europe, however. Estimates place the usage in Germany and Switzerland as encompassing more than one-third of their respective work forces.

The U.S. federal government, partially due to legislatively mandated experiments with new work schedules, is one of the major adopters of flexible systems. Flexitime is also used in all major industries in the private sector, with the greatest concentration in the finance and insurance fields.

Concurrent with two decades of use and many glowing reports in the popular press, flexible working hours were a popular topic in the academic management literature during the late 1970s and early 1980s. Since that time, research interest has apparently declined. Although most of the existing literature has not been based on a well-developed theoretical model, we review here some of the conceptual models that attempt to explain how and why flexible working hours influence employee attitudes and behaviors. Following this review of the theoretical literature, we summarize the state of knowledge pertaining to flexible working hours derived from empirical studies. This objective is accomplished by reviewing a representative sample of the literature that focuses on the impact of this form of work scheduling upon the organization and its employees.

Theoretical Foundations

There have been a number of different theoretical perspectives offered in order to provide (1) an intellectual justification for flexible working hours and (2) a conceptual explanation of how flexible hours should affect employee responses and work outcomes. This section outlines some of these theoretical underpinnings.

The models presented do not necessarily compete with one another. Instead they can be viewed as alternative ways of viewing the same phenomenon. Each provides a slightly different perspective, and when more than one is used simultaneously a richer understanding of the flexible hour–employee response relationship emerges.

Quality-of-Life Model

Two similar models have been provided in this area, encouraging consideration of the conditions under which an employee experiences *quality of life*. Employees need various kinds of fulfillment and therefore quality of life can be divided into two broad domains: work and nonwork. When an employee's needs are reasonably fulfilled in each domain, the products are both quality of work life and quality of nonwork life. According to Jamal and Mitchell[2] and Ronen[3], there is a relationship between the two domains, yet the level of satisfaction in one domain does not necessarily imply the same level of satisfaction in the other. The direction of causality between the two domains is not clearly understood either.

Three views of the relationship between the domains are postulated— the spillover, compensatory, and complementary effects. They are discussed in the contexts of need fulfillment, mental health, and quality of life. The *spillover effect* can be depicted by a case where, for example, an unhappy home life distracts the employee from successfully meeting the demands of the work domain. This predictably results in dissatisfaction (i.e., lack of need fulfillment) with the work domain. (See Figure 2–1, quadrant 3.) This spillover effect could also operate in the other direction, of course (quadrant 1). Employees experiencing the lack of need fulfillment in both domains (quadrant 2) predictably have the lowest levels of mental health.

Moderately high levels of mental health are presumably experienced by

Figure 2–1. **Alternative Views on Quality of Life and Quality of Work Life**

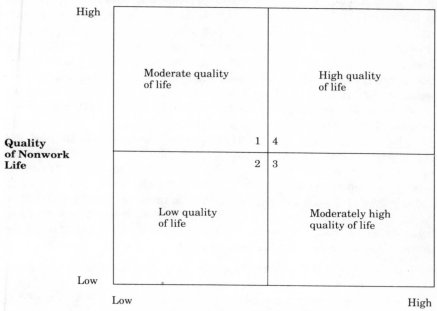

those employees who achieve need fulfillment in one domain but not in the other (quadrants 1 and 3). This *compensatory view* suggests that quality of life (need fulfillment) in one domain at least partially serves to compensate for a lack of need fulfillment in the other area. Jamal and Mitchell further suggest that mental health is higher for those who experience high work-domain need fulfillment and low nonwork-domain need fulfillment (quadrant 3) than it is for those who experience low work-domain need fulfillment and high nonwork-domain need fulfillment (quadrant 1). The rationale for this prediction revolves around the centrality of work. The theorists argue that the importance of paid work in modern society, coupled with the fact that adults spend most of their waking hours at work, provides the basis for this prediction. As a consequence, success or failure in the realm of work is likely to be extremely important to most individuals.

Finally, proponents of this model argue that the highest level of quality of life, need fulfillment, and mental health are achieved when the employee's needs in *both* domains are fulfilled. This state is referred to as the *complementary view* (quadrant 4).

What role do flexible working hours play in this quality-of-life model? Ronen employed an intrinsic–extrinsic job characteristics taxonomy as a vehicle to explain how flexible working hours influence employee motivation (see Figure 2–2). The two categories are considered to be two different kinds of rewards or sources of motivation for the individual. *Extrinsic* outcomes refer to incentives and rewards associated with the work setting (i.e., work environment or work context). Extrinsic rewards influence motivation primarily through the satisfaction of the lower order (physiological and security) needs. *Intrinsic* outcomes, on the other hand, represent those rewards and incentives that derive from the individual's investment of his or her physical and psychological energy in the job. These outcomes represent the feelings that stem directly from the work itself. Intrinsic rewards reinforce the individual's needs for growth, development, and self-actualization.[4]

Ronen argues that flexible working hours can satisfy needs that are associated with both the extrinsic and intrinsic categories and therefore influence quality of life by *both* routes. Here is how this happens. Flexible hours provide the employee with extrinsic rewards because basic work conditions are improved. For example, employees may be more comfortable commuting to and from work because of the ability to adjust their travel time so as to avoid rush-hour traffic. Some of the other extrinsic outcomes that can be derived from a flexible schedule are:

▶ Opportunity to work during quiet periods at the beginning and end of the day

▶ Reduced anxiety associated with tardiness (e.g., reduction of tardiness incidents might contribute to the improvement of superior–subordinate interpersonal relations)

▶ A shift in management's focus toward performance and away from attendance as a performance indicator.

According to Ronen, flexitime can also be seen as an intrinsic outcome for employees. More specifically, flexible hours predictably increase employee responsibility, independence, and potential for growth. These factors motivate the employee by satisfying higher order (esteem, autonomy, and self-actualization) needs.

In sum, Ronen argues that flexible working hours provide the employee

Figure 2–2.   Effects of Flexible-Hour Schedules in the Quality-of-Life Model

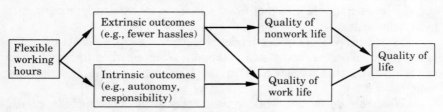

Source: Based on S. Ronen, *Flexible Working Hours: An Innovation in the Quality of Work Life* (New York: McGraw-Hill, 1981).

with greater opportunity for need fulfillment in the nonwork domain via the opportunity to respond to personal time demands through the flexibility provided for the scheduling of work. Flexible working hours also contribute to quality of working life through increased autonomy and responsibility. Provision of expanded autonomy and responsibility can in turn contribute to the satisfaction of the higher order needs of esteem, autonomy, and self-actualization.

Work Adjustment Model

Pierce and Newstrom[5] elaborate on the theory of work adjustment[6] to provide a conceptual explanation linking flexible working hours with employee attitudes and behaviors. The theory of work adjustment (see Figure 2–3) focuses on the individual's abilities and needs, on the one hand, and the work environment, or the role requirements for successful performance of the job and the reinforcers (intrinsic and extrinsic outcomes) available to the employee on the other. The theory defines *work adjustment* as the correspondence between (1) the abilities of the individual and the ability requirements of the job and (2) the needs of the individual and the satisfaction of those needs by the work environment. Thus work adjustment is high when individuals fulfill

Figure 2–3. Model of the Theory of Work Adjustment

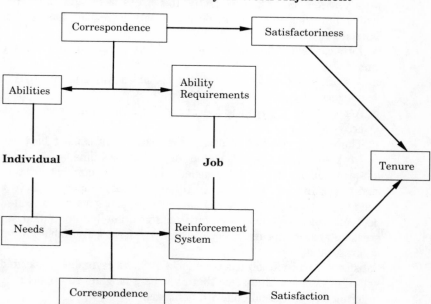

Source: Adapted from R. V. Dawis, G. W. England, and L. H. Lofquist, *A Theory of Work Adjustment* rev. ed., Minneapolis: University of Minnesota Studies in Vocational Rehabilitation XXIII, Bulletin 47 (April 1968): 12.

their role requirements and when the work environment simultaneously fulfills the needs that individuals bring to the job.

Pierce and Newstrom suggest that a flexible working-hour arrangement could provide the basis for a more efficient utilization of employees' circadian rhythms (the normal human twenty-four-hour physiological cycle) and could decrease the amount of stress, especially work arrival–related stress, experienced by some employees. Both of these results could contribute to work adjustment by permitting increased alignment between the employee's abilities and the ability requirements of the job, resulting in an increase in performance and organizationally encouraged tenure.

In addition, flexible working hours might reinforce the employee's needs for autonomy (independence), decision participation, and an appropriate balance between work and personal-time demands. Consequently, flexible working hours are seen as one dimension of the work environment capable of providing fulfillment of a particular group of employee needs. And under conditions where flexible work schedules reinforce specific employee needs, a contribution to satisfaction, job involvement, organizational commitment, and work attendance can be expected. In summary, application of the theory of work adjustment generates the following flexible working hour–employee response predictions:

1. Flexible work schedules help employees harmonize competing demands upon their time stemming from both their personal lives and work environments. Consequently, the stress associated with conflicting time demands should decrease with increasing amounts of discretionary time.

2. Performance might be favorably influenced by increased discretionary time if:
   a. A work schedule is selected that coincides with the employee's circadian rhythms
   b. A reduction in stress is associated with late or near-late work arrivals
   c. There is a reduction in stress associated with conflict between work and personal demands on the employee's time.

3. Job-provided opportunities for value, need, and expectation fulfillment lead to positive job attitudes. To the extent that employees have a need for autonomy/independence, a desire to participate in job-related decisions, or have a need for work–personal time harmonization, increasing amounts of discretionary time will have a favorable impact on job attitudes.

4. Satisfaction with off-job facets of life should be favorably associated with discretionary time since there will be a heightened opportunity to harmonize work and nonwork demands.

5. Flexible forms of work scheduling should strengthen organizational attachment from a number of perspectives. Flexible working hours

can be viewed as an employee benefit, resulting in appreciative feelings directed back toward the organization in the form of enhanced commitment toward it. Flexible working hours can also be perceived as a positive outcome obtainable through continued organizational membership, thereby influencing employee intentions vis-à-vis absenteeism and tenure.

6. Organizational attendance—that is, lower absenteeism—should increase along with an increase in the amount of discretionary time. The reasons might include:
   a. It is easier to get to work on time
   b. Employees can more easily respond to work–nonwork conflicts without organizational penalty
   c. The motivation to attend might be enhanced as a result of heightened organizational commitment and job satisfaction
   d. The employee may feel the need for a quid pro quo relationship with the organization (reciprocity).

In sum, the work-adjustment model helps to explain the dynamics of flexible working-hour systems. Multiple dimensions of flexible working-hour systems create the opportunity for employees to engage in work–nonwork time management. The more flexibility provided, the greater the amount of employee-perceived time autonomy, especially for those who use the flexibility fully. Enhanced perceived time autonomy is associated favorably with employee attitudes, motivation, and behaviors. Employee usage of the system through effective work-nonwork time management creates the occasion for stress reduction; and work- schedule alignment with the employee's circadian rhythms contributes to a greater correspondence between the employee's abilities and the ability requirements of the job. Usage of the system through work-nonwork time management should result in need fulfillment resulting in a greater correspondence between employee needs and need reinforcement. The final results of achieving a correspondence between these two dimensions of the work adjustment model include enhanced performance, organizational commitment, job involvement, satisfaction, and reduced stress and employee withdrawal behaviors.

The Commitment Model

Cohen and Gadon suggest that flexible working hours permit a closer alignment between work schedules and the timing and amount of an employee's desire for work versus leisure.[7] One expected consequence of this alignment-harmonization process is to strengthen employee commitment. This section presents a brief overview of commitment and involvement as the theoretical underpinnings for the flexible working hour–employee response relationship.

There appear to be two processes that can explain the development of organizational commitment (see Table 2–1).[8] The exchange approach views

Table 2–1.   Two Views of the Commitment Model

Exchange	*Psychological Attachment*
1. Management allows flexible working hours.	1. Employees have self-esteem, autonomy, and responsibility needs.
2. Opportunity for discretion represents an inducement to employees.	2. Flexible working hours satisfy these needs.
3. Employees contribute their commitment to the organization.	3. Employees perceive a bridge between their needs and the system's satisfaction of these needs.
	4. Employees become psychologically attached to the organization.

commitment as an outcome of the inducements–contributions transactions, between the organization and its employees. In essence, employees give their psychological attachment to the organization in exchange for the benefits received. This argument suggests that the greater the favorability of the exchange between the organization and the employee (from the employee's perspective), the greater will be the employee's commitment to the organization.

Organizational commitment has also been approached from the psychological-attachment perspective. Here commitment is viewed as an attitude or orientation toward the organization that links the employee's identity to it. Three components of this orientation have been identified:

1.   Identification with the goals and values of the organization
2.   High involvement in work activities
3.   Loyal attachment to the organization.[9]

Organizational commitment can be defined as internalization of, and psychological identification with, the organization's values; a strong desire to maintain membership in the organization; and a willingness to direct strong effort toward helping the organization achieve its goals.[10]

With this explanation of organizational commitment, a significant question remains unanswered: What are the antecedents and consequences of organizational commitment? With regard to antecedents, numerous studies have shown that organizational commitment stems from a wide set of employee experiences. Especially potent are those that produce satisfaction, create a sense of responsibility for work outcomes, and generate a sense of meaningfulness or purpose to one's role within the organization.[11]

Numerous organizationally relevant consequences have been associated with the employee's level of organizational commitment. For example, strong commitment should manifest itself in employee retention.[12] In addition, employees who are highly committed to the organization should display a relatively high level of motivation, which should be reflected in both performance and attendance behavior.

The exchange and psychological-attachment approaches to commitment provide a vehicle by which flexible working hours can be linked with employee responses. Employment of the inducements/contribution (or exchange) framework provides the following rationale for the flexible working hour–employee response relationship. Management's decision to give employees the opportunity to exercise discretion in defining their hours of work and nonwork time represents an inducement to those employees who value flexible hours and who see the offering gesture itself as substantive. From a reciprocity perspective the employee will predictably give back a stronger attachment to the organization and the consequences that flow from this commitment. An exchange process has unfolded through organizational inducements followed by employee contributions.

It can also be suggested that organizational commitment represents a psychological attachment and identification with the organization. This argument builds upon the need for self-esteem and its fulfillment. The more an environment provides for the fulfillment of an employee's needs, the more that individual will be attached to it. Since flexible working hours purportedly enable people to be more responsible for their work and the timing of their work, this method of scheduling helps satisfy needs for autonomy and responsibility. As these central needs get nurtured, employees begin to see that their self-esteem is linked to the environment that provides for this need fulfillment. The more their esteem needs get met by a flexibly scheduled work environment, the more they become psychologically attached to that organization.

At this time, none of the theoretical models discussed here has been fully tested. Each of them—quality of life, work adjustment, and commitment—has a relatively high degree of intuitive appeal. None appears to compete with the others, and therefore they are at least compatible, if not complementary.

Early Research

Through the years there have been a large number of attempts to observe and experiment with a variety of flexible working-hour schedules in order to identify their organizational consequences. At the same time there have been several attempts to develop conceptual (theoretical) models to detail the process through which flexible hours affect employee attitudes, motivation, and work-related behaviors. Very few of the studies that we have reviewed in preparation for this chapter have been designed to test a previously developed theoretical model. In fact, most of the existing literature has not been driven by a well-developed theoretical paradigm. Therefore you will see very few clear and direct connections between the studies reviewed and the theoretical models introduced above.

A comprehensive review of the early flexible working-hour literature was published in 1978.[13] That report is summarized here, focusing on the empirical quality of the literature through that time, the variables studied, the conclusions reached, and the issues raised. Following that, the recent literature is systematically reviewed.

The early literature was devoid of an explication of issues pertaining to the process or dynamics explaining how and why flexible work schedules influence organizational behavior. Those who wrote about flexible schedules, as well as those who designed and implemented such systems, failed to provide a systematic theoretical framework detailing the dynamics of the relationship between flexible working-hour arrangements and employee attitudinal and behavioral responses to those schedules. One exception to this viewed flexible working hours as one of many types of participative management systems that can influence employee satisfaction and performance.[14]

A technical review of the adequacy of the early research reports of flexible work schedule experiments, which included widely varied sample groups, can be characterized along three dimensions. First, the studies were generally deficient on technical grounds—that is, there was a general failure to use comparison groups, there was insufficient use of longitudinal perspectives, and most of the studies used only posttest designs. Second, given the small sample sizes and the limited number of occupational groups included (e.g., white collar and clerical), the generalizability of the findings was limited. Third, the organizations in which the flexible schedules were implemented were typically those in which there already existed a more participative climate than in many others. As a consequence it is difficult to generalize the outcomes to organizations with more autocratic cultures.

Five behavioral variables (i.e., sick leave or absenteeism, tardiness, turnover, overtime, and trends in costs) were identified in the review. With only an occasional exception in the data from the fourteen studies reviewed, *the introduction of flexible work schedules did not seem to induce negative or undesirable behavioral consequences.*

Regardless of the technical limitations associated with the earlier studies, the consistent thrust of the observations cannot be overlooked. *There was generally a profound and positive shift in employee attitudes following the introduction of flexible work schedules.* One conclusion was fairly typical: "Employees on flexible working hours overwhelmingly report increased personal satisfaction. . . . About 90 percent of the respondents wish to keep or extend the system."[15]

A major concern with flexible work schedules in the early studies revolved around the role of the first-line supervisor. Traditional arguments against flexible hours focused on communication problems and increased control problems for this group of managers. However, these issues have been studied in a number of organizations, and the available literature tends to dispel these concerns. "The weight of the available data clearly supports the view that direct supervisors, at worst, report only modest negative effects [due to flexitime arrangements]."[16] Coupled with occasional reports of increased scheduling and communication problems, there is an overwhelming recommendation coming from the same supervisors urging the continuation of the flexible schedule. Supervisors also subjectively report increases in employee morale and productivity.

Recent Reports

During the past decade, much has been written about the alleged merits of flexible work schedules, yet our understanding of employee responses to them still remains in a relatively embryonic state. The conceptual statements, observations, and research that comprise the current literature have not been based on a well-grounded theoretical model defining variables, relationships, and processes. Most flexible work schedules have consequently been designed on an ad-hoc basis. Although the literature continues to support flexible working-hour arrangements, methodological and analytical problems are still prevalent. The literature is strongly characterized by: (1) anecdotal reports of flexible working-hour systems, (2) the use of nonstandardized research scales, (3) failure to include statistical treatment of the reported data, and (4) the absence of other systematic data-collection strategies. On the positive side, most of the current literature has focused on the employee as the unit of analysis, as contrasted with the family, work group, organization, or community, as in many earlier reports.

A current review of the conceptually based flexible working-hour literature suggests that a number of factors, specifically organizational attachment, attendance, performance, stress, off-job satisfaction, and job attitudes, are associated with the flexible system. This review enables us to identify a set of potential advantages to the implementation of a flexible working-hour arrangement. For example, as was suggested earlier, employees might become increasingly psychologically attached to the organization as a result of the flexibility provided by a flexible working-hour arrangement. One author's work emphasized the process by which quality of life in the nonwork domain (i.e., satisfaction with off-job factors) would be impacted. Another approach drew upon the theory of work adjustment to highlight the conceptual relationship between flexible working hours and employee performance, job attitudes, work attendance, and stress.

Following the ideas proposed in those conceptual approaches, this review of the recent flexible working-hour literature is structured around several different dimensions of organizational behavior:

- ▶ employee performance
- ▶ attitudes
- ▶ organizational attachment
- ▶ attendance

Potential Advantages to Flexible
Working Hours

Performance. A dozen studies that report on the effect of flexible working hours on employee performance are reviewed here. The studies vary from those reporting no effect to observations of positive consequences. Two studies reported on field experiments involving experimental and comparison groups. In both studies there were negligible performance effects attributable to the flexible work schedules.[17]

Monthly measures on productivity were assessed for one year immediately before and after the implementation of a flexitime program for a group (*n* = 39) of claims personnel in an insurance company.[18] The results revealed a significant increase in an annualized production index following the introduction of the flexitime program. Another study provided both objective and subjective data on productivity from twenty-five public agencies that have experimented with flexitime.[19] The authors' classification and interpretation of data reflecting multiple dimensions of organizational effectiveness led them to conclude that there was a positive performance effect stemming from flexible working hours. The power of their conclusion is enhanced by the fact that across the twenty-five agencies there were *no* reports of performance decrements. Similar performance increases were reported in other studies.[20]

A comprehensive survey of 196 long- and short-term users of flexible working-hour schedules found an overwhelming number indicating that performance in their organizations either remained the same or increased subsequent to the introduction of flexible working hours.[21] The percentages for performance remaining the same versus increasing in the short and long term were nearly the same; that is, among short-term users 52 percent reported no change versus 45 percent reporting an increase; and among long-term users 44 percent reported no change versus 51 percent reporting an increase.

Another summary of eleven flexitime experiments found that nine of them provided productivity data.[22] One organization reported a decline in efficiency while the other eight reports indicated no change or a favorable change. Attitudinal reports on productivity changes were generally positive.

One experimental study provides a good representation of the literature reporting on the flexible working hour–employee performance relationship.[23] The researchers investigated changes in productivity (the dependent variable) associated with the introduction of flexible working hours for a sample of 246 clerical-level employees employed in five different production units of a large financial company. During the four-month flexible working-hour experiment, employees were permitted to define their starting time between the hours of 7:30 and 10 A.M. All employees were required to be present during the core hours of 10 A.M. to 3:15 P.M.

Groups 1 and 2 (clerical employees from the records section) were compared with the performance of a group of workers who did not experience the flexible work schedule (the control group). There were no significant differences in the productivity level for those in the experimental program relative to those on the straight work schedule. However, group 3 (clerical employees from a form-processing unit) did show a significantly higher level of production when compared to their performance during the same time period the previous year. Group 4 (a group of clerical employees from the finance unit) also had a significant increase when compared to their productivity level during the eight weeks immediately prior to the experiment. Finally, Group 5 (clerical employees from another form-processing unit) did not display any significant changes in their productivity across each of the four-month experimental periods.

In sum, the results from this study were somewhat mixed. Two groups had significantly higher performance than they previously displayed. Two groups did not display any performance differences compared to employees performing the same task on straight work schedules. The fifth group maintained a constant performance level for each month of the four-month experimental period. In spite of this variability, flexible working hours at least did not have an *adverse* impact on employee performance. The authors of the article conclude that flexible working hours can be introduced at little cost to the organization; could be perceived by the employees as an important organizational benefit; and might have a neutral, if not positive, impact on employee productivity.

A recent experimental study has shed new light on the reasons for the mixed performance effects of flexitime.[24] Studying employee-performance responses to flexitime over a two-year time period in a governmental agency, the researchers found that programmers' productivity jumped by 41 percent over two years, compared with a 5 percent increase for the control group. No significant change occurred in a second group of data-entry workers.

The researchers conclude that the key variable differentiating between the two groups was the need to use a shared physical resource (access to the computer) versus having a keyboard available for every operator. Apparently the introduction of flexible hours made it possible for programmers to find more open access time for computer uses, and as a result they received their output more quickly. In effect, flexitime sharply reduced a major barrier to performance.

Job Attitudes. Numerous employee attitudes have been measured (e.g., overall job satisfaction, satisfaction with work, satisfaction with supervision) in the various studies of flexible working hours. The results across the experimental and nonexperimental studies comparing flexible and nonflexible work-schedule groups are quite consistent: *there is a generally favorable attitudinal effect.*

One field experiment revealed that flexitime had a significant effect on employee satisfaction.[25] Another compared employee attitudes across three work-schedule groups—fixed, staggered start, and flexitime—in an experimental framework. The researchers observed a significant increase in satisfaction with both work and supervision in the flexitime group, but no significant changes for those given some flexibility through the staggered-start system.[26]

Survey reports quite consistently suggest that employee job satisfaction is enhanced following the introduction of flexible work schedules.[27] One exception compared work satisfaction for groups of fixed-hour versus flexible-hour employees and reported that there were no significant attitudinal differences.[28] Attitudes toward flexible work schedules themselves are also strongly favorable in a number of studies.[29] It is rare to find employees who are willing to return to fixed working hours once they have been a part of flexible arrangements.

A unique comparative study looked for systematic and significant differences in employee attitudes across four work schedules.[30] The four schedules, fixed, staggered, limited flexitime, and extended flexitime, were arrayed based on the amount of discretionary time available to the employees for the scheduling of their working day. The authors observed significantly higher job involvement in the flexitime groups and decreasing degrees of job involvement accompanying a decrease in discretionary time. They also reported that the fixed-hour employees were significantly less satisfied with both job and hours of work than the employees working under some form of discretionary schedule.

Off-Job Attitudes.   In the area of nonwork attitudes as a response to flexible work schedules, more time for leisure and better opportunity to attend to personal affairs are two opinions that have been frequently expressed by employees.[31] Another study comparing employee attitudes across a flexible and fixed work schedule, however, reported that there were no significant differences in terms of employee reports of leisure satisfaction.[32]

Two researchers examined the relationship between flexitime and its effect on twenty nonwork activities such as resting and relaxing, time with family, reading, religious observance, and outdoor recreation.[33] They found that flexible hours had a significant effect on nonwork activities in their sample of seventy-nine clerical employees. They concluded that flexible working hours are associated with an overall change in the level of participation in a number of nonwork activities. They also examined the moderating role of "regular versus nonregular flex-day users" (i.e., whether or not an employee made regular use of the flexibility provided by the flexible working-hour arrangement) on the flexitime–nonwork activity relationship. Regular users showed a significant change in nonwork activity participation, while those who were not regular flexitime users showed no significant change.

Five months after the introduction of a flexitime program for 232 clerical employees in an insurance company, their work and leisure attitudes were compared with a similar group of workers on a fixed-hour system.[34] Although day lifestyle changed very little, satisfaction with leisure was significantly greater for those on the flexitime systems. Following the lead of the two studies just reported, a later one measured a number of attitudes toward off-job factors (e.g., satisfaction with family, friends, recreation, volunteer work, cultural opportunities, religious observance, personal development, and overall life and leisure time satisfaction).[35] In this study, four different work-scheduling arrangements, differentiated from one another by the amount of flexibility provided to the employee, were employed to see if there were significant and systematic increases in positive worker attitudes accompanying the increase in work-scheduling flexibility. The results from this study run contrary to the results of the previous ones. The data suggest that there were no significant differences across the four groups of employees. Levels of satisfaction with leisure or other aspects of the nonwork domain were not different when comparing fixed-hour with flexible-hour employees. Life, recreation, and leisure-time satisfaction were, however, significantly correlated with employee perceptions of time autonomy (work-scheduling flexibility).

However, another study concluded that flexitime has a favorable impact on the employee's life outside the job. The nonjob areas observed in this case were child care, time available for family, leisure time, and control over work and personal life.[36] Favorable nonwork attitudes may also stem from increased ability to attend to personal business.[37]

Stress. Several studies have examined the impact of flexible hours on stress. One focused on interrole conflict and found that flexitime groups expressed less conflict than those employees working fixed hours.[38] Another reported that a reduction in morning tension is associated with the flexible working-hour arrangement.[39] A third one concluded that flexitime systems reduce the stress resulting from concern over child-care activities.[40] Although the comparative study referred to earlier did not observe a significant difference in symptoms of stress across the four different work-schedule groups, it did suggest a possible decline in experienced symptoms of physical and psychological stress in conjunction with flexible work schedules.[41] These researchers also found a significant negative association between employee perceptions of time autonomy and psychological and physical symptoms of stress.

Organizational Attachment. A significant difference in organizational attachment was found across the four work schedules (fixed, staggered start, limited and extended flexitime) included in one investigation.[42] The fixed-hour group of employees had weaker organizational attachment than did the flexitime groups. The group with the most discretionary time had the strongest attachment.

Three variables were used to assess organizational attachment. Inspection of the mean values for each variable across the four work schedules suggested that organizational commitment increased, and the expressed intention to quit or to be absent decreased, with an increase in work-schedule flexibility. The authors concluded that organizational attachment appeared to increase as employees experienced varying degrees of work-scheduling flexibility.

One other study looked at the same behavioral-intention variable representing organizational attachment.[43] The authors reported that approximately 90 percent of those included in their study indicated their intention to stay with the organization increased as a result of the implementation of the flexible working-hour arrangement.

Organizational Attendance. Three behavioral expressions of employee attendance behavior—tardiness, absenteeism, and turnover—have been investigated. One study comparing one fixed and three flexible work-scheduling groups found that the fixed-hour group had the weakest attendance behavior, while there were no significant differences among the three forms of flexible work schedules.[44] A recent study comparing absenteeism for a staggered-start group of employees (with quarterly change options) with a group experiencing a daily flex-schedule found lower absenteeism rates for the staggered group.[45]

Two other experimental studies tracked absenteeism. One reported that although their data did not provide for a thorough examination, it appeared as though absenteeism declined subsequent to the introduction of both staggered-start and flexitime systems.[46] Similar results were reported in a second study: the flexitime group exhibited a 35 percent decrease in short-term unpaid absences and a 45 percent decrease in long-term unpaid absences. However, the differences between the fixed and flexitime groups for a long-term paid absences were not significantly different.[47]

A pre–post investigation compared the level of absenteeism for a one-year period prior to the introduction of a flexitime program with the following one-year period.[48] The authors reported a significant decline in the level of absenteeism. The employees involved in the study attributed the decline to the elimination of the major reason for it; they now had more flexible time to attend to personal business. Similarly, a study of thirty-five agencies in the government sector reported a decrease in absenteeism and tardiness following the introduction of a flexitime program.[49] This decline in short-term leaves and sick-leave usage arose because flexitime allowed employees the opportunity to attend to personal business when there was a conflict between personal time demands and regularly scheduled hours of work. Another study reported there was a significant reduction in tardiness, with only minor changes (not worsened) in absenteeism.[50] Research in various departments of the Kentucky Personnel Division revealed situations where there were no changes in absenteeism and other cases where there was a reduction in absenteeism.[51]

A recent uncontrolled study of a federal government agency reported that two different alternative work schedules appeared to produce significant declines in leave-time usage.[52] Annual leave decreased 12 percent while sick leave dropped off by 25 percent.

One empirical report compared employee absenteeism, tardiness, and personal-leave days taken for a period of time prior to the implementation of a flexitime system, with a two-month postimplementation period.[53] It was reported that absenteeism dropped 50 percent, lateness was essentially eliminated altogether, and the number of personal days taken was significantly reduced.

Monthly absenteeism data for a two-year period of time, one year before and one year after the introduction of a flexible working-hour arrangement, were examined by two other researchers. They found a significant difference between the two years, reflecting a decline in the level of absenteeism following the introduction of flexible working hours.[54] Elsewhere, dramatic reductions in both absenteeism and tardiness were experienced by the ninety-two organizations that were surveyed in a national study of alternative work-schedule usage.[55]

In the area of turnover, two studies reported that it appeared to have stayed at the preflexitime level, with one suggesting that turnover decisions are unlikely to hinge upon a single factor like the presence or absence of flexitime.[56] To shed further light on this factor, another survey showed that for thirty-one organizations classified as short-term (i.e., less than one year) users 61 percent reported no change in turnover while 39 percent reported a reduction. Among the sixty-one organizations classified as long-term (three years or more) users 64 percent reported a reduction in turnover following the introduction of a flexitime program while 36 percent reported no change.

Management Effects.   Most of the research on flexible working hours has concentrated on employee attitudes and behaviors. Very little systematic research has focused on supervisory reactions to these systems. One major exception to this is the work of Schein and her colleagues.[57] They examined the reactions of sixty-three supervisory personnel to the introduction of flexitime in twelve work units of an insurance organization. Supervisors' perceptions of productivity, employee honesty, unit administration, employee time management, and work habits across a four-month experimental period were assessed. The results (self-reported data) suggest that these supervisors had a very favorable perception of the effects of flexible working hours on employee productivity, time handling, honesty, and work habits. From an administrative perspective the flexible working-hour arrangement was not seen as adversely interfering with the scheduling of meetings, reducing telephone coverage, or disrupting work. Less favorable attitudes did surface, however, in two areas. Sixteen percent of the supervisors perceived a negative effect on their own jobs, presumably because their overtime hours increased. This was barely offset by the 22 percent who reported positive effects in that area. Yet a phenomenal 97 percent recommended the permanent introduction of the flexible working hours.

The reactions of thirty supervisors who were managing work units included in another study were overwhelmingly positive.[58] Most of the supervisors included in this study claimed that there were only minor managerial problems associated with the presence of a flexible work schedule in their organizational units. Specifically the study found that 81 percent experienced little difficulty in keeping track of the time their employees were working or not working; 64 percent reported little problem with employees trying to take unfair advantage of the system (30 percent reported a moderate level of difficulty); 83 percent experienced little conflict with other supervisors in the scheduling of work; 68 percent experienced little conflict with their subordinates in the scheduling of work; 74 percent experienced little difficulty in obtaining needed work information from their subordinates; 86 percent perceived little difficulty in communicating with their subordinates; and 67 percent found little trouble in scheduling meetings (only 32 percent reported a moderate level of difficulty). When queried about how employee productivity was disrupted at the beginning and end of the work day as a result of employees staggering the time of their entries and exits, the majority indicated little problem in this area. Finally, 68 percent of the managers stated that the number of hours and the pattern of hours they had to work as a result of flexible hours for employees interfered little with their own job performance.

Another study reported on the results of a three-year pilot of a number of flexible work schedules.[59] The results indicated that most of the managerial sample ($n = 100$) indicated either a positive effect or no detrimental impact. Supervisors reported the following: driving time decreased; there was no impact on sick-leave utilization; decreased tardiness; increased productivity (only 3 percent noted a decrease); no impact on absenteeism; supervisor–subordinate relations unaffected; and employees' leisure time increased.

Six managerial issues (coverage of work situations, employee scheduling, work scheduling, difficulty of the managerial job, and internal and external communications) were examined in an organization-level survey of ninety-two firms.[60] The percentage of firms reporting better versus no change versus worse was approximately equal for coverage of work situation, employee scheduling, and work scheduling. Difficulty of the managerial job and internal communications were seen as either not changing or worse, while there was basically no change for external communications.

Several studies focused on the supervisor's job in order to see what effects were attributable to the introduction of flexible working-hour schedules. Flexitime significantly affected the supervisor's job, with short-range planning being the managerial activity most strongly affected.[61] An impact was also reported for the organizing, staffing, directing, and controlling activities. The introduction of flexitime was seen as the cause of first-line supervisors becoming more forward looking; and other studies reinforce this reported relationship between flexible hours and the supervisor time horizon.[62]

A change in style of management also appears to accompany the introduction of flexitime. Supervisors become more participative in their management approach and the new participative style helps create a climate where employees exercise greater self-control.[63]

However, supervisory attitudes in some studies are less positive about the impact of flexitime than are those within the rank and file.[64] Yet a number of studies suggest that supervisory attitudes with regard to the impact of flexitime on employee productivity and absenteeism, specifically, are quite positive.[65] Supervisors generally report improvements in both areas.

Other Observations. Flexible working hours have also been associated with a number of other effects. For example, there have been attempts to link flexible working hours to job-design characteristics, travel to and from work, and union attitudes.

The data from the studies suggest that there were only minor effects stemming from the implementation of flexible working-hour programs upon employee perceptions of the design of their jobs.[66] In both studies, however, an increase in perceived job variety and responsibility were noted. These observations are consistent with the conceptual arguments as to how and why flexible hours may affect employee motivation, attitudes, and behaviors discussed earlier.

Effects on commuting have also been identified in a number of investigations.[67] In each case the observations are positive and similar: employees report that travel to and from work has been favorably affected. There are reports of less traffic congestion, greater ease of parking, a reduction in commuting time to and from work, and less stress associated with the commuting activity.

Union attitudes toward flexitime systems have also been examined. Few labor leaders have praised the flexitime concept, almost none have actually urged its adoption, and a principal opponent of governmental experimentation with flexitime for federal employees was the president of the American Federation of Governmental Employees.

A number of major union objections have been identified.[68] First, unions are aware that under some circumstances flexitime effectively increases the amount of time given to the organization by the employee for the same weekly wage. In effect, the organization (management) gains from a reduction in tardiness or part-day absences because workers are more likely to make up lost time. Second, the system may reduce the employees' monthly earnings (by necessitating attendance only when there is work to be done) while increasing the intensity of their work. Third, the system may encourage longer hours of work. Fourth, increases in organizational profits may result from a more effective and frequently a more intense use of labor without a concurrent increase in the wage rates. Finally, reductions in total employee earnings are likely to accrue through less overtime.

To reduce this opposition a number of approaches to achieving closer relations between management and union have been suggested. First, they could jointly discuss and design any prospective flexible system so as to overcome many of the anticipated problems. Second, modification of some labor laws would permit employees to carry forward the time debits and credits they create, while management could still pay extra compensation for management-requested overtime work. Third, only under extreme and limited circumstances do flexitime systems bring benefits to the organization without employees' acceptance and use of them. Thus it is in management's interest *not* to use the system as a manipulative tool. Finally, some form of gain-sharing system could be worked out through which legitimate gains in productivity as a result of flexitime are shared with the employees.

Some union members are discontented with their representatives, of course. Many in the rank and file feel that not enough of their leaders' attention has been given to the newer quality-of-working-life (QWL) issues. This interest may provide an opportunity for the introduction of other flexible working-hour systems.

In summary of the empirical findings (see Figure 2–4), almost no substantial negative effects have been reported as a result of flexible working hours. The emerging empirical literature, though often weak in quality of design and unsystematic in its focus on dependent variables, has generally produced

Figure 2–4. Summary of Research Studies on Flexible Working-Hour Systems

Performance
- ► Limited experimentation
- ► No performance decrements
- ► Some increases reported

Job Attitudes
- ► Many variables studied (job, work, supervision, leisure time)
- ► Consistently favorable effects

Off-Job Attitudes
- ► No negative effects
- ► Positive impact on numerous nonwork activities

Stress
- ► Generally favorable impact perceived—stress reduced

Organizational Attachment
- ► Limited studies
- ► Positive impact noted

Organizational Attendance
- ► Frequent dramatic drops in absenteeism and tardiness
- ► No change or some reported declines in turnover

Management
- ► Generally favorable reactions

Unions
- ► Slow acceptance—wait and see how employees benefit

an overwhelming endorsement of flexible systems. Why this phenomenon is so is explored in the next section.

Central Features of a Flexible Work Schedule

To a large extent researchers have seen flexible working hours as a generic phenomenon with only minor variations on a basic theme. Very few investigators have attempted to look at flexible working-hour systems as multidimensional in nature. Through the accumulation of knowledge about flexible systems and as a result of their varied effects we have now come to the point where we need to look more closely at each system and its particular design features independently.

In this final section of the chapter we identify some of the critical design features of flexible working hours and detail one process through which this system impacts the employee.

Variations

Although the concept of flexible working hours has been a part of the literature for more than a decade, relatively little is still known about the concept itself. Practitioners and researchers have sought to identify the advantages and disadvantages of flexible hours, the relationship between flexible hours and numerous employee attitudes and behaviors, trends in its application, and legal issues associated with the system. A review of the literature reveals a large number of variations in the flexible systems designed and implemented. This variety is so great that a veritable semantic jungle has emerged, and there is a substantial risk that practitioner confusion will follow it. This jungle stems, apparently, from a desire to label or categorize system differences. For example, one author talked about flexitime, flexible work hours (flexitime for short), flexitours, gliding time, variable day, maxiflex, staggered hours, flextime, and flex-hours.[69] Another considered other alternatives such as group versus individual flexitime, flexible-settlement period, and weekend-redefined systems[70]; recent writers have added the concept of flexshift[71]; the flexiyear systems of annually flexible hours[72]; and modified flexitour or MFT.[73] The possibilities appear almost endless, with the differences between them sometimes trivial. Some of the variations seem almost impractical across a variety of situations.

Key Dimensions, Conceptually Based

Flexible working hours, under some circumstances and for some dimensions (e.g., employee job satisfaction), can make a difference. However, we do not know what dimension(s) of these multidimensional phenomena makes the difference. More specifically, we need to ask, What are the *salient* dimensions of a flexible working-hour system?

Two approaches, conceptual and empirical, have already been used in this chapter to answer this question. First, the three conceptual models reviewed earlier (commitment, quality of life, and work adjustment) attempt to explain the flexible working hour–employee response relationship. At the conceptual level, the three frameworks provide a theoretical perspective and initial insight into a structural definition of a flexible working-hour arrangement. Each model has implicitly or explicitly identified the same phenomenon as a critical design variable.

The key element defining flexible working hours in the commitment framework appears to be the degree of flexibility or autonomy available to employees to harmonize work and nonwork demands upon their time.

The quality-of-life model focused on the conditions under which employees experience a favorable quality of life. This approach implicitly suggests that the degree of flexibility and autonomy present to define hours of work and nonwork time represents the major work-schedule feature contributing to experienced quality of life.

The theory of work adjustment provides a third conceptual explanation linking flexible working hours and employee attitudes and behaviors. Flexible working hours, by taking advantage of circadian rhythms and reducing stress, may contribute to work adjustment by permitting an increased alignment between the employee's abilities and the ability requirements of the job, which can result in an increase in performance and organizationally encouraged tenure. In addition, flexible working hours can satisfy the employee's need for autonomy and decision participation, and help provide an appropriate balance between work and personal demands. Under conditions where flexible work schedules provide fulfillment of specific employee needs, a contribution to satisfaction, job involvement, organizational commitment, and work attendance can be made.

There are important similarities among the three frameworks reviewed here. The three conceptual formulations do not explicitly define the flexible working-hour construct, nor do they explain completely how its various features impact employee attitudes and behaviors. In each case the primary focus is on the flexible working hour–employee response relationship. All three conceptual frameworks implicitly suggest that it is the degree of flexibility (i.e., freedom, independence, or autonomy) provided for scheduling work and nonwork time that is the key element accounting for variance in employee attitudes and behaviors. Thus *flexibility is cast as the salient feature of a flexible working-hour arrangement.*

Since flexibility is a psychological concept, flexibility per se is not an objective design feature of a flexible working-hour arrangement, but is something that people experience. Although flexibility is possibly a central and salient feature of flexible working-hour arrangements, it is still important to ascertain what *objective* design features provide and/or constrain flexibility.

The reasoning embedded in the three conceptual models suggests a process by which flexible working hours influence employee attitudes and behaviors; and narrows the search for salient design features by raising a significant question: What specific design features of flexible working hours provide flexibility (autonomy) for the scheduling of work and nonwork time? Then another question can legitimately follow: Which of these design features are most salient for affecting employee attitudes and behaviors?

The three conceptual models implicitly suggest a *process* by which flexible hours influences employee responses (see Figure 2–5). Flexible working-hour arrangements provide flexibility (an experienced psychological state), which in turn impacts employee attitudes and behaviors. This suggests that flexibility (i.e., the freedom and independence provided for the scheduling of work) mediates or intervenes in the flexible work schedule–employee response relationship. More specifically, the process unfolds as follows: As the work schedule provides employees with the opportunity to manage a portion of their work and nonwork time, they come to perceive work-schedule flexibility and autonomy. The more time autonomy that employees perceive they have for scheduling their own work and nonwork time, the more their work-related attitudes and behaviors are impacted. For example, without directly testing this process Stevens and Elsworth's[74] data showed a differential reaction to flexible hours between regular and nonregular users. Thus those who regularly managed their work and nonwork time experienced work-scheduling flexibility and emerged with a significantly different behavior pattern than did the nonregular users of

Figure 2–5.   The Flexible Hour–Employee Response Process

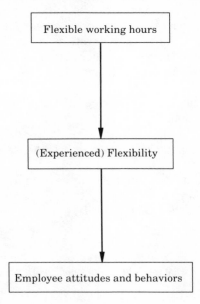

Flexible working hours

(Experienced) Flexibility

Employee attitudes and behaviors

the system. Unfortunately, none of the conceptual models explicates *which* objective design features provide flexibility and autonomy, and therefore which design features play a salient role in influencing employee behavior and shaping employee attitudes.

Key Dimensions, Empirically Based

The second approach to the identification of work-schedule dimensions has been taken in various reviews of the empirical flexible work-schedule literature. Golembiewski and Proehl identified seven work-schedule design features that appeared to characterize significant differences among the flexible working-hour arrangements included in their review of the literature.[75] The seven dimensions identified were:

1. Core hours: the total number of daily hours during which the employee must be at work
2. Band width: the total number of hours in the interval between the earliest starting time and the latest possible finishing time
3. Flexible hours: the total number of daily hours within which the employee can make choices about stopping and starting work
4. Length of work week: the length of the mandated work week; that is, the total number of hours that must be worked
5. Banking: the capacity to carry forward a surplus or deficit of hours worked from one time-accounting period (day, week, month) to another
6. Variability of employee's schedule: the freedom to vary hours from day to day and week to week without prior approval from supervisors
7. Supervisor's role: the degree of supervisory involvement in the determination of an employee's work schedule; for example, a hands-on role for the supervisor in negotiating all schedules versus giving prior approval for certain changes

More recently, another review suggested that flexitime schedules differ along three key dimensions[76]:

1. Daily versus periodic (weekly or monthly) choice of starting and quitting times
2. Variable versus constant length of working day (whether credit and debit hours are allowed)
3. Core time, or the hours of the day when all employees are required to be present.

The conceptual approaches converge with the empirical basis. As with each of the three conceptual models, the empirical literature also suggests that flexibility is a key variable. Each design feature contributes to the *amount of flexibility* available to employees for defining their work and nonwork time. Specifically, how do these factors operate to provide flexibility to employees? Shorter core hours, longer band widths, longer flexible hours, shorter work weeks, greater bankable hours, longer time-accounting periods, greater day-to-day and week-to-week schedule variability, and a less active supervisory role in work scheduling are expected to produce greatest flexibility in a flexible work-schedule program. At this point, then, a perspective on the *process* by which flexible working hours impacts upon employee attitudes and behaviors has been provided, and it offers insights into which design features influence flexibility.

The Process of Work-Schedule Influence

In an attempt to answer the question about what design features are most salient in terms of employee responses, a number of features, such as length of core hours and variability, and one psychological state, experienced flexibility/autonomy, have been identified. In this exploratory process another question emerged: What is the *process* through which flexible work-schedule features influence employee responses?

Pierce and Newstrom argued that six design features—core minutes, band width, bank length, schedule flexibility, schedule variability, and supervisory role—would influence the amount of employee flexibility experienced as a function of perceived scheduling autonomy.[77] They empirically investigated the relationship between six flexible work-schedule design features and a set of employee attitude and behavior variables. They also attempted to empirically identify the process by which flexible hours influence employee attitudes and behaviors by looking at whether experienced flexibility served as an intervening variable in the flexible working schedule–employee response relationship. The specific research questions studied were:

1. How much variance in employee attitudes and behaviors could be accounted for by this set of six flexible work-schedule features?
2. Which design features are most salient in accounting for variance in employee attitudes and behaviors?
3. Is the amount of time autonomy perceived by the employee an intervening variable in the flexible work schedule–employee response relationship?

In sharp contrast to almost all of the previous literature, one of the most startling observations emerging from this study was the *absence* of a significant and direct relationship between the flexible work-schedule variables and employee job satisfaction. With regard to the other employee attitudes, the data suggested that the flexible work-schedule variables may have a weak though direct association with the level of employee commitment to the employing organization. In addition, symptoms of psychological stress experienced may be fewer or lower under a flexible working-hour arrangement.

The weakest of the relationships observed between the flexible working-hour design features and the attitudinal variables can be explained by looking at the *process* through which this association occurs. Quite possibly, as work schedules become increasingly flexible, employees experience increased work-schedule flexibility (time autonomy). If and only if the employee *experiences* work-scheduling flexibility (autonomy) can the connection between flexible working hours and employee attitudes be realized. The authors further reasoned that as employees experience increasing amounts of time autonomy, they become increasingly satisfied with the job, committed to the organization and have fewer symptoms of psychological stress. Thus it was postulated that perceived time autonomy acts as an intervening variable in the flexible work schedule–employee response relationship.

In the process of testing the intervening variable relationship it was observed that the flexibility of the work schedule (especially flexibility stemming from schedule variability, schedule flexibility, freedom to schedule work time without supervisory approval, and a small set of core hours) was positively associated with employee perceptions of time autonomy. Time autonomy was also significantly associated with job satisfaction, organizational commitment, and experienced symptoms of psychological stress but not related to either behavioral variable. Testing the full intervening-variable model provided consistent and strong evidence that time autonomy mediates the flexible work schedule–employee *attitude* relationship. In other words, employees who experienced increased time autonomy were increasingly job satisfied, organizationally committed, and experienced fewer symptoms of psychological stress.

Results from this study suggested that perceived time autonomy does not mediate the flexible work system–employee *behavior* relationship. It was noted that there is a significant and direct relationship between schedule flexibility and employee absenteeism and performance. Both of the behavioral variables have a positive association with the work-schedule variables, suggesting increases in performance (and absenteeism!) with increasingly flexible working-hour arrangements. (A detailed explanation of the relationship between flexibility and performance is unavailable at this time. Concerning absenteeism, it is feasible that greater opportunities to be absent from work will result in a greater number of absences exhibited. For the organizations in the study absenteeism may not be a problem, though, since there was a positive association between absenteeism and performance.)

Conclusions

The results of the research to date have important implications for the design or modification of flexible working-hour systems. These implications center around the multidimensionality of flexible-hour systems, the critical design features to be included, and the necessity of ensuring employee perceptions of time autonomy. Three major conclusions are offered here under the assumption that prevailing organizational conditions permit their implementation.

1. The designer must be aware that flexible working-hour arrangements are multidimensional systems. As a consequence, the designer must consider not only the signals being sent to the employee from the system as a whole but the independent messages being transmitted from each of its component parts. That is, are *consistent* messages being transmitted to the employee, or are some features contributing to perceptions of autonomy while others restrict it?

2. Four design features appear to be particularly salient for favorable employee attitudes (job satisfaction, organizational commitment, and experienced symptoms of psychological stress) and behaviors (performance and absenteeism). The results suggest that the flexible work schedule should be designed with
   a. A relatively narrow set of core hours
   b. Multiple bands of flexible time
   c. The option to change frequently the pattern of hours worked
   d. No requirement to obtain prior supervisory approval.

3. The flexible working-hour system should be designed and implemented in such a way that employees *understand* its component parts (and their totality), *identify* the degree of autonomy that the system provides, and *experience* the inherent flexibility. These results may be better achieved by involving employees in the design of a

Table 2–2.   Summary of Flexible Working-Hour Effects

Criteria	Range of Reported Results		Predicted Consequences
Performance	No change	Positive change	No significant change
Job attitudes	No change	Positive effect	Positive impact
Leisure-time satisfaction	No change	Positive effect	Positive impact
Stress symptoms		Decrease	Slight decrease
Organizational attachment		Strengthen	Strengthen
Intention to quit		Weaken	Weaken
Intention to be absent		Weaken	Weaken
Attendance	No change	Improved	Slight improvement
Turnover	No change	Reduction	No change
Managerial effects	Very minor problems	Generally very favorable	Support change to flexible hours
Union reaction	Slow acceptance		————

work schedule that is conducive to the coordination of work while simultaneously in harmony with the employees' personal rhythms (social, personal, and circadian).

4. It is important to allow employees a voice in the design and implementation of a flexitime system. This necessity was sharply demonstrated following a failure to do so in a study at a California air force base.[78] For general guidance on avoiding the potentially dysfunctional consequences of flexible working hours, there are numerous useful guides to practitioners.[79]

Based upon existing theory and observation of flexible working-hour arrangements in operation, a number of positive organizational effects can be realized if systems are appropriately designed and managed. Table 2–2 summarizes our observations and makes predictions about what *ought* to happen following the design and appropriate implementation of a flexible working-hour system.

Endnotes

1. S. D. Nollen, *New Work Schedules in Practice: Managing Time in a Changing Society* (New York: Von Nostrand Reinhold, 1982), P. O. Flairs, "Work Schedules of Americans: An Overview of New Findings," *Monthly Labor Review* 109 (1986): 3–6.

2. J. Jamal and V. Mitchell, "Work, Nonwork, and Mental Health: A Model and a Test," *Industrial Relations* 19 (1980): 88–93.

3. S. Ronen, *Flexible Working Hours: An Innovation in the Quality of Work Life* (New York: McGraw-Hill, 1981).

4. C. P. Alderfer, *Existence, Relatedness, and Growth: Human Needs in Organizational Settings* (New York: Free Press, 1972).

5. J. L. Pierce and J. W. Newstrom, "Toward a Conceptual Clarification of Employee Responses to Flexible Working Hours: A Work Adjustment Approach," *Journal of Management* 6 (1980): 117–134.

6. R. V. Dawis, G. W. England, and L. H. Lofquist, *A Theory of Work Adjustment* rev. University of Minnesota Studies in Vocational Rehabilitation XXIII, Bulletin 47 (April 1968).

7. A. R. Cohen and H. Gadon, *Alternative Work Schedules: Integrating Individual and Organizational Needs* (Reading, Mass.: Addison-Wesley, 1978).

8. J. H. Morris and J. D. Sherman, "Generalizability of an Organizational Commitment Model," *Academy of Management Journal* 24 (1981): 512–526.

9. B. Buchanan, "Building Organizational Commitment: The Socialization of Managers and Work Organization," *Administrative Science Quarterly* 9 (1974): 533–546.

10. L. W. Porter, R. M. Steers, R. T. Mowday, and P. V. Boulain, "Organizational Commitment, Job Satisfaction, and Turnover among Psychiatric Technicians," *Journal of Applied Psychology* 59 (1974): 603–609.

11. J. L. Pierce and R. B. Dunham, "Organizational Commitment: Preemploy-

ment Propensity and Initial Work Experiences," *Journal of Management* 13 (January 1987): 163–178; R. T. Mowday, L. W. Porter, and R. M. Steers, *Employee Organization Linkages: The Psychology of Commitment, Absenteeism, and Turnover* (New York: Academic Press, 1982).

12. R. M. Steers, "Antecedents and Outcomes of Organizational Commitment," *Administrative Science Quarterly* 22 (1977): 46–56.

13. R. T. Golembiewski and C. W. Proehl, Jr., "A Survey of the Empirical Literature on Flexible Work Hours: Character and Consequences of a 'Major Innovation'," *Academy of Management Review* 3 (1978): 837–853.

14. A. O. Elbing, H. Gadon, and J. R. M. Gordon, "Flexible Working Hours: The Missing Link," *California Management Review* 13 (1975): 50–57.

15. Ibid., p. 52.

16. Jamal and Mitchell, p. 850.

17. Jamal and Mitchell, op. cit.; C. Orpin, "Effect of Flexible Working Hours on Employee Satisfaction and Performance: A Field Experiment," *Journal of Applied Psychology* 66 (1981): 113–115; J. S. Kim and A. F. Campagna, "Effects of Flexitime on Employee Attendance and Performance: A Field Experiment," *Academy of Management Journal* 24 (1981): 729–741.

18. J. L. Welch and D. Gordon, "Assessing the Impact of Flexitime on Productivity," *Business Horizons* 23 (1980): 61–65.

19. S. Ronen and S. B. Primps, "The Impact of Flexitime on Performance and Attitudes in Twenty-Five Public Agencies," *Public Personnel Management* 9 (1980): 201–207.

20. S. Craddock, T. Lewis, and J. Rose, "Flexitime: The Kentucky Experiments," *Public Personnel Management* (October 1985): 36–38; R. T. Golembiewski and R. J. Hilles, "Drug Company Workers Like New Schedules," *Monthly Labor Review* 100 (1977): 65–69; L. R. Gomez-Mejia, M. S. Hopp, and C. R Sommerstand, "Implementation and Evaluation of Flexible Work Hours: A Case Study," *The Personnel Administrator* 23 (1978): 39–41; F. T. Morgan, "Your (Flex)time May Come," *Personnel Journal* 56 (1977): 82–85.

21. S. D. Nollen and V. H. Martin, *Alternative Work Schedules, Part I: Flex-Time* (New York: Survey Report, American Management Association, 1978); In G. Salvendy, ed., 2 "Work Schedules," *Handbook of Industrial Engineering* (New York: Wiley Interscience, 1982) pp. 11.8.1–11.8.27.

22. D. J. Peterson, "Flexitime in the United States: The Lessons of Experiences," *Personnel* 57 (1980): 21–31.

23. V. E. Schein, E. H. Mauner, and J. F. Novak, "Impact of Flexible Working Hours on Productivity," *Journal of Applied Psychology* 62 (1977): 463–465.

24. D. A. Ralston, W. P. Anthony, and D. J. Gustafson, "Employees May Love Flextime, but What Does It Do to the Organization's Productivity?" *Journal of Applied Psychology* 70 (1985): 272–279.

25. Orpin, op. cit.

26. B. H. Harvey and F. Luthans, "Flexitime: An Empirical Analysis of its Real Meaning and Impact," *MSU Business Topics* 27 (1979): 31–36.

27. Kim and Campagna, op. cit.; Welch and Gordon, op. cit.; Ronen and Primps, op. cit.; Craddock et al., op. cit.; Gomez-Mejia et al., op. cit.; Morgan, op. cit.

28. W. D. Hicks and R. J. Klimoski, "The Impact of Flexitime on Employee Attitudes," *Academy of Management Journal* 24 (1981): 333–341.

29. Kim and Campagna, op. cit.; Ronen and Primps, op. cit.; Craddock et al., op. cit.

30. J. L. Pierce and J. W. Newstrom, "Employee Responses to Flexible Work Schedules: An Interorganization, Intersystem Comparison," *Journal of Management* 8 (1982): 9–25.

31. Kim and Campagna, op. cit.; Welch and Gordon, op. cit.; Golembiewski and Hilles, op. cit.

32. Hicks and Klimoski, op. cit.

33. E. D. Stevens and R. Elsworth, "Flexitime in the Australian Public Service: Its Effect on Nonwork Activities," *Public Personnel Management* 8 (1979): 196–205.

34. M. G. Evans, "Notes on the Impact of Flexitime in a Large Insurance Company: Reactions of Nonsupervisory Employees," *Occupational Psychology* 43 (1973): 237–240.

35. Pierce and Newstrom, op. cit.

36. Ronen and Primps, op. cit.

37. Golembiewski and Hilles, op. cit.

38. Hicks and Klimoski, op. cit.

39. Golembiewski and Hilles, op. cit.

40. R. A. Lee, "Flexitime and Conjugal Roles," *Journal of Occupational Behaviour*, 4 (1983): 297–315.

41. Pierce and Newstrom, op. cit.

42. Ibid.

43. Welch and Gordon, op. cit.

44. Pierce and Newstrom, op. cit.

45. J. B. McGuire and J. R. Liro, "Absenteeism and Flexible Work Schedules," *Public Personnel Management* 16 (1987): 47–59; S. D. Nollen, "Work Schedules," ed. G. Salvendy, *Handbook of Industrial Engineering* (New York: Wiley, 1982).

46. Harvey and Luthans, op. cit.

47. Kim and Campagna, op. cit.

48. Welch and Gordon, op. cit.

49. Ronen and Primps, op. cit.

50. Peterson, op. cit.

51. Craddock et al., op. cit.

52. E. J. Harrick, G. R. Vanek, and J. F. Michlitsch, "Alternate Work Schedules, Productivity, Leave Usage, and Employee Attitudes: A Field Study," *Public Personnel Management*, Summer, 1986, 15:2, pp. 159–169.

53. Morgan, op. cit.

54. Welch and Gordon, op. cit.

55. Nollen and Martin, op. cit.

56. Harvey and Luthans, op. cit.; Peterson, op. cit.

57. Schein et al., op. cit.

58. J. L. Pierce and J. W. Newstrom, *Supervisory Reactions to Employee Flexible Work Schedules* (Duluth: University of Minnesota Technical Report, 1983).

59. Gomez-Mejia et al., op. cit.

60. Nollen and Martin, op. cit.

61. L. A. Graf, "The Impact of Flexitime on the First-Line Supervisor's Job: A

Preliminary Investigation," Academy of Management Annual Meeting, San Francisco, Cal., 1978.

62. R. T. Golembiewski, C. W. Proehl, Jr., and R. G. Fox, "Is Flexitime for Employees 'Hard Time' for Supervisors? Two Sources of Data Rejecting the Proposition," *Journal of Management* 5 (1979): 241–259.

63. Ibid.; Graf, op. cit.

64. Welch and Gordon, op. cit.

65. Craddock et al., op. cit.; Golembiewski et al., "Is Flexitime for Employees," op. cit.

66. Welch and Gordon, op. cit.; C. W. Millard, D. Lockwood, and A. Wissmiller, "The Longitudinal Effects of Flexitime on Job Characteristics and Satisfaction," a paper presented at the annual meeting of the Midwest Academy of Management Conference, April, 1980.

67. Kim and Campagna, op. cit.; Ronen and Primps, op. cit.; Golembiewski et al., "A Survey," op. cit.; Gomez-Mejia et al., op. cit.; Nollen and Martin, op. cit; Hicks and Klimoski, op. cit.

68. J. D. Owen, "Flex-time: Some Problems and Solutions," *Industrial and Labor Relations Review* 30 (1977): 152–160.

69. S. D. Nollen, *New Work Schedules in Practice: Managing Time in a Changing Society* (New York: Van Nostrand Reinhold, 1982).

70. Ronen, op. cit.

71. J. E. Bailey, "Personnel Scheduling with Flexshift: A Win/Win Scenario," *Personnel* (September 1986): 62–67.

72. P. Lynch, "Annual Hours," *Personnel Management* (November 1985): 46–50; S. Connock, "Work Force Flexibility: Juggling Time and Task," *Personnel Management* (October 1985): 36–38; B. Terriet, "Flexiyear Schedules—Only a Matter of Time?," *Monthly Labor Review* (December 1977).

73. Morris and Sherman, op. cit.

74. Stevens and Ellsworth, op. cit.

75. Golembiewski and Proehl, op. cit.

76. Nollen, op. cit.

77. Pierce and Newstrom, op. cit.; J. L. Pierce and J. W. Newstrom, "The Design of Flexible Work Schedules and Employee Responses: Relationships and Process," *Journal of Occupational Behaviour* 4 (1983): 247–262.

78. R. A. Wheat, "The Federal Flexitime System: Comparison and Implementation," *Public Personnel Management* (Spring 1982): 22–30.

79. G. W. Rainey and L. Wolf, "The Organizationally Dysfunctional Consequences of Flexible Work Hours: A General Overview," *Public Personnel Management* 11 (Summer, 1982): 165–175.

Chapter Three

The Compressed

Work Week

► The compressed work week reallocates employee work time by condensing the total hours in the traditional work week into fewer days. The length of the total hours required is held constant (or sometimes reduced slightly) when a compressed schedule is introduced; but at the same time, employees work more hours in each day. (Other efforts to shorten the work week through a reduction in hours alone, such as a move from the 5/40 schedule to the 5/35, are not addressed here.)

The compressed work week is an anomaly in light of one of the trends noted in Chapter One. That is, it runs counter to the historical movement to shorten the number of hours worked per day. It is also a substantial departure from the relatively standardized work week of five days per week. Consequently, despite an initial rush of excitement over its development followed by some early experimentation, it has not achieved the levels of popularity some had predicted for it.

This chapter provides an overview of compressed work weeks by first identifying the two major structural forms: a change in the number of days only versus a change in both number of days and hours worked. Then the questions of why and how the compressed work week should influence employees are addressed. Two direct behavioral issues are explored: congruence with circadian rhythms and performance decrements due to physical or mental fatigue. In addition, two explanations for the possible effects on participants' attitudes are introduced: the impact of an employee's time frame of reference and the spillover effects from a less stressful and more satisfying nonwork environment.

A major part of the chapter is devoted to a comprehensive review of the research-based literature on the compressed work week. This review focuses on the relationship between the compressed work week and a number of attitudinal and behavioral dimensions such as those introduced in Chapter Two. Performance, fatigue, stress, turnover, attendance, and job attitudes are among those explored. The chapter concludes by noting several of the apparent advantages and disadvantages of compressed work weeks.

Major Forms of Compressed Schedules

Along with continued efforts to shorten the work week, two major work-scheduling themes characterize the compressed approach (see Table 3–1). First, there are several approaches that produce a *change in days* (Type A). These approaches hold constant the total (average) number of hours worked per week while reducing the number of days worked within the same accounting period. The primary examples of compressed work-week schedules in the published literature are (1) the 4/40 (four-day, forty-hour) work week; (2) the floating 4/40 work week; (3) the 4½/40 work week; and (4) the 5/45–4/36 plan, which with minor modifications generates averages of 40 hours and 4½ days per week.[1] Although a number of creatively different plans have been devised and implemented, the 4/40 system is the most visible and widely adopted compressed plan in the United States. European countries use a wide diversity of compressed systems.[2]

Table 3–1. Types of Compressed Work Weeks

Type A (Total hours constant, longer work days)	
Label	*Description*
1. 4/40	Four consecutive 10-hour days, 3 days off (usually on weekends)
2. Floating 4/40	Four 10-hour days worked, 4 days off in a repeating cycle (also known as the 8-day week)
3. 4½/40	Four 9-hour days plus one 4-hour day, 2½ days off
4. 5/45–4/36	9-hour days in alternating 5-day & 4-day weeks
Type B (Decreased hours, fewer work days)	
1. 4/36	Four 9-hour days
2. 4/32	Four 8-hour days
3. 3/38	Three 12½-hour days

Second, there have also been attempts to compress the work week through a change in both days and hours (Type B, Table 3–1). Systems that incorporate both a change in days and hours worked are more complex. The distinguishing feature, however, is a decrease in the weekly configuration of both days and hours worked. Some of the more popular models in this category are the 4/36 arrangement and the 4/32 system.

Conceptual Foundations

Behavioral Effects

Although several explanations for some of the specific effects of the compressed work week on employee behaviors have been offered, a well-grounded conceptual framework that both guides empirical research and integrates the findings to date has not yet been developed. The explanations available to connect compressed schedules with attitudinal or behavioral variables are often interesting but somewhat simplistic and therefore limited in their overall explanatory power. Nevertheless they may provide clues that can aid our understanding. This section examines a number of these arguments, focusing first on the models purporting to explain behavioral effects and then those focusing on explanations of attitudinal effects.

Circadian Rhythms.   A large body of literature links work output to some basic circadian rhythms such as body temperature, blood pressure, and muscle tone. This literature shows that performance varies with variations in physiological indicators. A close examination of body temperature curves, for example, reveals a limited number of hours in each day where the highest body temperature, the best performance, and the lowest propensity to become fatigued are reached. At other times during the individual's wakeful period these curves are either moving toward their peaks or troughs.

Our knowledge of circadian rhythms suggests, then, that employees are not equally productive throughout the working day because of the relationship between mental and physical efficiency and the employee's metabolic activities. Recognizing this, Pierce and Newstrom argued that the effects of the compressed work week on employee performance could be understood better through considering employee circadian rhythms.[3]

The prime structural characteristic of the 4/40—a longer working day— suggests the likelihood of an accompanying performance decrement. As the number of hours of work per day expands, the probability of including additional hours where body temperature is lower than the average obviously increases. Consequently the employee's capacity to apply skills and abilities effectively to the role requirements of the job decreases, and so does the individual's probable level of performance.

Fatigue. A similar argument, though conceptually distinct from the circadian-rhythm perspective, centers on fatigue. Theoretical models dealing with various aspects of human behavior (e.g., Selye's discussion of adaptation to stress[4]) have established that people have a relatively fixed supply of energy to utilize within a particular period of time. Expending effort at work draws upon this reservoir of energy. Any expansion of the work requirements that demands additional energy, such as the number of hours worked in a single day, predictably results in increased fatigue. As fatigue increases, the employee is neither as psychologically nor physically efficient as when the reservoir is full. The essence of this argument is that additional demands placed upon the individual's reservoir of energy are soon met with performance decrements because of the decline in available energy. In short, the 4/40 work schedule predictably increases the employee's fatigue over the course of a work day, possibly producing dysfunctional side effects.

Attitudinal Effects

Time Frame of Reference. Mahoney and his associates focused their attention on explaining attitudes that employees have toward the 4/40 work week.[5] They used economic models to provide a perspective on the work–leisure choices made by employees and their work-schedule attitudes. From the perspective of these economic models, work–leisure choices can be measured by two yardsticks.

The *wages earned/foregone* yardstick measures the dollars earned for one's organizational contributions in a given time period. Holding total performance constant, employee attitudes toward the 4/40 work week may be affected differentially as a function of their time frame of reference. Those who use a daily frame of reference recognize an increase of eight to ten hours worked and experience an increase of about 25 percent in daily economic rewards earned. Thus we would predict a favorable attitude to the 4/40 systems by day-oriented people. On the other hand, for those employees with a weekly frame of reference, the 4/40 produces no net change in economic rewards for the time frame important to them. Under this set of conditions, any attitudes toward the 4/40 would be a function of other forces.

If the individual focuses not upon wages but instead upon work and leisure time, another perspective (with a contrasting outcome) is postulated. If the employee thinks of work and leisure in terms of days, the 4/40 provides more leisure days and fewer work days. If, on the other hand, work and leisure are experienced in terms of hours per day, the 4/40 reduces daily leisure hours and increases the hours per day at work. This dichotomy is capable of producing two different reactions to the 4/40 as a function of the employee's time frame of reference. Those employees who see work–leisure choices in terms of days per week should favor the 4/40, while those who perceive the choice from an hours-per-day perspective would probably dislike it.

Mahoney et al. also suggest that work attitudes, especially job satisfaction, can be affected by the compressed working-hour arrangement. For example, dissatisfied workers who have an hours-per-day frame of reference are likely to experience the 4/40 in terms of increased exposure to a noxious stimulus (work). This predictably contributes to further dissatisfaction for them. Dissatisfied workers with a days-per-week frame of reference, on the other hand, are likely to view the 4/40 as an escape from the job. The escape would only be a neutral force, however, as the employee's direct job dissatisfaction is unlikely to increase or decrease. That is, job satisfaction should not increase since the new work schedule does not change the basic job conditions that initially produced the job dissatisfaction. The only exception to this prediction would stem from a condition where job dissatisfaction was a function of hours of work and where the 4/40 met the nature of these concerns.

In sum, time frame of reference could play a critical role in shaping employee attitudes toward compressed work systems. These frames of reference are shaped more by the individual's leisure time and interests, and are more dependent upon personal characteristics, than upon those elements of the job per se.

Spillover Effects. The spillover effect (presented in Chapter Two) suggests that the events unfolding in two domains simultaneously define the overall quality of life experienced by an individual. Employees are concerned about both work and nonwork domains and for each they carry a set of expectations and experience a set of events. Jamal and Mitchell[5] and Ronen[6] argue that there is a critical interface between these domains.

Ronen defines this interface and the operation of the spillover effect with a simple and straightforward example. He says that "many have witnessed the employee with an unhappy home life whose effectiveness at work is diminished by the spillover effects from . . . life outside work."[7]

Application of the spillover model to the effects of the compressed work schedule on employee effectiveness and satisfaction is also straightforward. The four-day work schedule should give people larger blocks of time away from work to attend to personal business and to engage in leisure-time activities. Thus the reduction of stress from the work–nonwork demands upon time and the increased life satisfaction in the nonwork domain should spill over into the work domain. An employee who becomes more satisfied with life in the nonwork domain carries a different mental state to the work environment than that held by a frustrated and dissatisfied individual.

Compressed Work-Week Literature

Similar to the flexible work-scheduling literature, the compressed work-week literature varies greatly in terms of its scientific quality. Unfortunately, very few of the studies systematically incorporated major characteristics of sound research design such as measurements both before and after the work-schedule change, experimental- and comparison-group designs, standardized research scales, and confidence intervals to decide upon level of statistically significant observations.

The compressed work week has not been studied as extensively as flexible work schedules. There have been even fewer attempts to explain the conceptual process through which this form of work scheduling impacts upon employee attitudes or behaviors. One observer's comments described the situation aptly when he noted,

> There is no scarcity of alleged advantages or disadvantages to the 4/40 plan. The writing on the subject has been highly impressionistic, emphasizing the perceptions of individuals, managers, union leaders, or journalists of what they see to be the present or future effects of conversion. While some hard data are available from a few firms on turnover, absenteeism, and productivity, systematic studies which readily can be used as guidelines for other firms have not been conducted.[8]

A number of employee attitudes, experiences, and behaviors have been studied in relation to the compressed work week. The single most popular topic has been employee attitudes toward the 4/40 schedule. Do employees like the 4/40? Are there certain demographic variables associated with groups of people who accept and/or like the 4/40? Who would prefer the 4/40 working-hour arrangement? Answers to these questions pervade the literature.

Ronen and Primps's review of the compressed work-week literature[9] concluded that employee attitudes toward it are generally favorable. The effect of the 4/40 on employee performance has produced mixed results, however. In some cases there appears to be no relationship, while in other cases performance increases have been reported. The most negative consequence of the compressed work week is the fatigue that is frequently associated with the longer work day.

The discussion that follows provides an elaboration of these initial conclusions. It is structured around the dependent variables of performance, fatigue, stress, turnover, organizational attendance, job attitudes, and other effects.

Performance

Seven investigations in which performance was examined in association with the compressed work-week schedule were reviewed. Four of the studies were longitudinal. Of the other three, one used case studies, another drew its conclusions from the attitudes of top managers in organizations after the introduction of the 4/40, and the third relied upon employee attitudinal data.

Four of the studies reported productivity increases. The first cited observations in three organizations, in one of which productivity was reported to be up 13 percent thirteen months after the introduction of the 4/40.[10] The second study examined top managements' attitudes toward the 4/40.[11] The authors reported a significant difference between the number of managers who claimed an increase in productivity versus those reporting no change. The managers who indicated that their organizations experienced productivity increases attributed the improvement to fewer start-up times, improved employee satisfaction, and a reduction in job redesign efforts. In the third study both supervisors and employees claimed that productivity (quantity and quality) improved.[12]

In the fourth study of productivity and the 4/40 work week, the researcher performed tests for a significant change and for a difference between experimental and control groups on five performance variables.[13] Performance measures were taken one month before the implementation of the 4/40, with similar measures taken after it had been in operation for twelve months. There was a significant increase in three of the five performance measures favoring those employees who converted to the 4/40 system. Level of production, effectiveness as team members, and overall performance had increased more for those experiencing the 4/40 than for their counterparts who continued to work on the 5/40 schedule.

On the other hand, no significant before–after productivity differences were found by Goodale and Aagaard.[14] They compared performance under a 5/40 work week with that after the shift to a compressed and shortened (4/38) work week. Likewise Calvasina and Boxx also observed the effects of a change from a 5/40 to a 4/38 schedule in two factories.[15] Weekly productivity data were collected for two time periods: one year before the introduction of the 4/38 schedule and one year after the shortened and compressed schedule went into operation. They reported that there were no significant changes in group productivity in either of the two factories. The only exception to this conclusion was related to age, where older workers were less productive than younger workers while on the four-day schedule. The researchers noted, however, that the jobs included in the study did not have significant start-up and shut-down characteristics—a commonly claimed source of time savings for compressed schedules.

In a followup to the fourth study mentioned above, a twenty-four–month observation of performance was made on the employees studied earlier.[16] The baseline data (i.e., the performance data collected one month before the introduction of the 4/40 schedule) were compared with data collected twenty-four months following introduction of the 4/40. The authors concluded that although there may be positive performance effects in the short run (one year) as a result of the 4/40 system, the long-run (two-year) data did not sustain these increases.

In summary, the effects on performance of the compressed work week are mixed. Short-term results may occur, but they could be simply the result of the attention surrounding the change, or the so-called *Hawthorne effect.* It also appears that some jobs may lend themselves to automatic improvement by reducing start-up and shut-down time 20 percent on the four-day schedule. Other clues suggest that some employees may not be able to endure the strain of the longer shifts required, as is discussed in the next section.

Fatigue and Other Physiological Reactions

Consistent messages emerge from investigations focusing upon fatigue and fatigue-related symptoms as dependent variables. Fourteen percent of employees in one survey cited fatigue as a major disadvantage of the compressed working-hour arrangement,[17] while 45 percent of those in another investigation reported fatigue as a disadvantage.[18] Similar reports highlighting fatigue as the principal disadvantage of the 4/40 system were reported in single firms[19] and in a study of twelve Midwest organizations employing the 4/40 schedule.[20]

To explore the fatigue issue further, 26 percent of the survey respondents in one 4/40 study indicated they experienced adjustment problems in response to the longer work day.[21] Older workers reported that longer hours per day and too little time per day to rest were major disadvantages of the 4/40 schedule for them. Similarly, 62 percent of those in one study indicated that they found work more tiring under the 4/40 schedule.[22] Another study assessed the results of the shift from a 5/40 to a 4/40 working-hour arrangement, observing that there were no actual weight changes among employees but people did report less sleep per night under the 4/40 arrangement.[23]

The proportion of participants reporting some type of negative physiological reaction to a 4/40 system is too large to ignore. Employees believe that they are more tired, sleep less, and do not adjust well to the new systems. It is not known whether such fatigue causes work (e.g., accidents) or nonwork (e.g., marital) problems. One recent report, however, indirectly assessed the effects of fatigue, noting that postimplementation error rates declined, possibly as a result of employee adjustment to the new 4/40 schedule.[24] It is possible, of course, that employees in the 4/40 programs, all of whom presumably had previously spent their work lives under a 5/40 system, simply *expected* to become more fatigued under the 4/40 and consequently confirmed their own expectations.

Stress

Two related empirical studies reported on the impact of compressed work weeks on the anxiety and stress experienced by workers. The original study examined anxiety and stress over three observation periods: one month before the introduction of the 4/40, and three and twelve months after it was introduced for both experimental and comparison groups. Examination of the mean level of the stress-anxiety index across the three observation periods revealed a continuous decrease (2.61, 2.42, 1.86) for those working under the 4/40 system. Across the thirteen-month period there was a significantly larger change in anxiety-stress for the experimental group than for the comparison group, reflecting a decrease in experienced anxiety-stress subsequent to the introduction of the 4/40 work schedule.

Twenty-four months after the introduction of the new schedule, a followup report noted that the favorable influence of the 4/40 on employee experiences of anxiety and stress had disappeared. While the mean level of stress for the experimental group at this time was still lower than its pre-4/40 level, it had crept up enough so that the difference was no longer large enough to be statistically significant. Also, the size of the residual change was not significantly more favorable for those employees on the 4/40 than it was for their 5/40 counterparts.

In summary, the stress effects of the 4/40 have not been extensively researched. Although early positive results (declines) may be experienced, they either do not endure by themselves or are later affected by other increasing pressures.

Turnover

Only two studies report on employee turnover following the introduction of a compressed work week. Both of these relied upon secondary (and impressionistic) data and their conclusions partially conflict.

Wheeler reported that turnover declined significantly in one of the four-day forty-hour work-week cases he reviewed.[25] (Changes in turnover were not mentioned in his other three case studies.) On the other hand, there were no significant changes in turnover claimed by the 139 top managers in organizations that had converted to a four-day week.[26] Apparently the 4/40 neither drives large numbers of employees away, nor is it by itself a strong incentive to remain.

Organizational Attendance

Partially mixed results, reflecting either a significant reduction or no significant changes in absenteeism, characterize the literature on organizational attendance. Several studies provided reports of reductions in absenteeism. Wheeler studied four different 4/40 experiments and in all four cases he found that absenteeism was reduced.[27] In two of the four cases specific figures were cited. In one organization, after thirteen months there was a dramatic drop in absenteeism from 7 percent to nearly zero, while an equally noteworthy 90 percent reduction was reported in the second organization. Another report, across a one-year period following a shift from a 5/40 to a 4/40 schedule, found that absenteeism decreased by a moderate 10 percent.[28] Two other studies found more substantial reductions. For a group of clerical and supervisory personnel in a multinational organization, Goodale and Aagaard noted that there was a 27 percent reduction in absenteeism,[29] while Latack and Foster cited a 40 percent reduction in personal leave time following the introduction of a 3/38 work schedule.[30]

The absenteeism rates in an organization that went from a 5/40 schedule to a 4/40 and then back again to the 5/40 working-hour arrangement were monitored in another study.[31] This reversal enabled the researchers to observe (1) changes associated with a 5/40 to 4/40 conversion, (2) changes associated with a 4/40 to 5/40 conversion, and (3) responses to a 5/40 schedule by employees who had not experienced a nontraditional working-hour arrangement. They observed a significant decrease in overall absenteeism following the conversion to the four-day week. When the 4/40 program was withdrawn, absenteeism rates in the "new" 5/40 system even exceeded the baseline rate of absenteeism established before the 4/40 program was first implemented.

By contrast to those seemingly incontrovertible reports, an analysis of top-management attitudes toward the 4/40 concluded that there was no significant reduction in absenteeism in their organizations.[32] These attitudinal data were reinforced with the observations made in the longitudinal studies mentioned earlier.[33] Analyses of absenteeism data twelve months and twenty-four months after the introduction of a 4/40 schedule, in comparison to a 5/40 group of employees, revealed no significant differences in unexcused absenteeism.

Only one investigation looked at tardiness as a second dimension of organizational attendance.[34] It reported an 11 percent increase in tardiness following the shift to a forward-rotating 4/38 working-hour arrangement. Presumably the employees had difficulty adapting to the earlier starting time on the days they worked.

In summary, the results of these studies quite strongly suggest that employee absenteeism can decline following conversion to a 4/40 system. The sizes of the reductions are not only statistically significant but pragmatically notable in many cases. It is not known whether top management was too far removed from studies of the 4/40 to report accurately on their effects, or were reluctant for other reasons to attribute observed changes to the compressed work week. Clearly, tardiness as an employee response requires more study.

Job Attitudes

This section reviews job attitudes associated with the introduction of compressed schedules. (A subsequent section reviews employee attitudes toward the compressed work-week schedule itself.) Given the strong interest in job attitudes in the management and organization literature and the frequency with which these variables are studied in reports on flexible schedules it is surprising that very few studies have focused on job attitudes such as satisfaction, involvement, and organizational commitment.

A nationwide survey reported that employees were substantially more satisfied with their jobs as a result of the conversion to a four-day week. Another investigation reported that a significant number of top managers claimed the job satisfaction of their employees had increased following the introduction of a four-day schedule in their organizations.[35]

Organizational commitment in thirteen firms with four-day schedules was researched in an early study. Of the 100 employees involved, 46 percent reported that they liked the organization more, 49 percent reported that they liked the company the same, and only 5 percent reported that they liked the company less under the 4/40 schedule. These results suggest a possibly favorable influence of the 4/40 on overall organizational satisfaction.

Changes in job satisfaction were also found by Ivancevich.[36] Twelve months after the introduction of a 4/40 schedule he observed a significant difference in four facets of job satisfaction, all favoring the 4/40 groups of employees. Small but significant increases in personal worth, social affiliation, security, and promotion opportunity were observed, while there were no significant differences for autonomy and self-actualization. However, after a twenty-four–month exposure to the 4/40 schedule only personal-worth satisfaction remained strong enough to discriminate between the 4/40 and 5/40 groups of workers.

Another field experiment with multiple data-collection periods reported that job satisfaction and internal motivation were significantly higher one month after the introduction of a 4/40 program than one month before.[37] Following the removal of the 4/40 program, satisfaction and motivation declined to the pre-4/40 levels.

Latack and Foster argued that the increase in job satisfaction often observed in 4/40 work groups may represent an *indirect,* not a direct, consequence of the altered schedule.[38] They suggested that under conditions where the implementation of the 4/40 leads to employee perceptions of job enlargement or enrichment, job satisfaction increases. The immediate and indirect force is the change to 4/40; the direct causal force is the change in job design. Consequently, if the 4/40 schedule impacts on employee job satisfaction it is through its influence upon job design and subsequent employee perceptions of this change. The researchers reported no significant job satisfaction differences in work, supervision, pay, or promotion satisfaction when they made a comparison of 5/40 and 3/38 groups of workers.

Only one study reported on a *decline* in job satisfaction following an introduction of the 4/40 work week.[39] The explanation provided for this surprising consequence was also based on the suggestion of an indirect relationship between the four-day week and employee job satisfaction.

Generally speaking, positive changes in the affective or attitudinal domain are associated with conversion to a compressed schedule. Top managers believe it happens to workers, employees report it, and it disappears (as expected) upon reversion to the 5/40 schedule. Whether the effects endure is open to question, as is the process by which attitudes do or do not change.

Job-Design Effects

Some evidence suggests that job-design changes may accompany the 4/40 intervention and explain its effects. Fottler reported that thirty-four of the forty-eight employees involved in a change to a 4/40 schedule perceived some type of change in their job functions.[40] Twenty of these individuals saw their jobs as enriched. In addition, those who perceived that their jobs had been upgraded the most were also those who were most favorably inclined to the 4/40. Those employees who saw the least impact upon the nature of their jobs were most opposed. Along similar lines, Latack and Foster claimed that subjects in their study saw their jobs significantly enriched as a result of the 3/38 intervention.[41]

Employees in another study indicated that their job knowledge was enhanced as a result of their compressed work week.[42] The rearranged work week required people to cover for one another more than required under a system where everyone worked the same schedule. Through this covering process employees become more familiar with the jobs of others and began to see their own jobs in a larger context. In summary, although compressed-work schedules were not created for the purpose of job enrichment or enhanced job knowledge, it appears possible that these are important side effects worth further exploration.

Leisure

This section on the 4/40's relationship to leisure is divided into two parts. Leisure has been viewed as both a predictor of employee attitudes toward a compressed work week and as a consequence of it. Leisure preferences as a predictor of 4/40 attitudes are reviewed first, followed by an assessment of the leisure activity consequences.

As an Antecedent. Mahoney, Newman, and Frost tested their argument that an individual's time frame of reference is a primary determinant of his or her orientation toward a 4/40 work week.[43] In their study, they predicted that those employees who perceived the 4/40 as a longer work day would dislike if not oppose it while those who perceived the 4/40 as a shorter work week would favor it. Their data supported these views: they found that employees who described the 4/40 as a shorter work week were indeed those who favored the system. Those employees who characterized the 4/40 as a longer work day opposed this working-hour arrangement.

Mahoney later expanded upon his original investigation of attitudes toward the 4/40 schedule.[44] Leisure orientation was found to be a significant factor influencing employee work-schedule preferences. Workers with a days-per-week leisure orientation were inclined to seek the 4/40 schedule, and those with an hours-per-day orientation were less likely to seek the 4/40 (versus a flexible working-hour arrangement).

However, it is critical to note that (traditionally) most organizations adopting a compressed schedule provide a system where a three-day weekend is available to the employee. Only one investigation examined the relevancy of this notion. State employees in Oregon favored the 4/40 system by a two to one margin if the day off was a Monday or Friday.[45] When the extra day off was a midweek day (thus not providing for a three-day weekend) 76 percent were opposed to this working-hour arrangement. Therefore, it is not just the total number of days per week available for leisure that is valued, but the blocks of three days (presumably including the traditional Saturday–Sunday weekend).

Other studies have found that people who had definite plans for how they would use their increased leisure time were more likely to favor a 4/40 system than were those who had no such plans.[46] Similarly, still another study found a significant difference between those favoring the 4/40 and those who were opposed, based on their perceptions of having enough leisure time.[47] Those who did not favor adopting the 4/40 claimed that they already had enough leisure time, while those seeking the 4/40 did not believe that they had enough.

Drawing upon our knowledge of leisure orientation as a predictor of employee attitudes, it is useful to characterize the 4/40 as a move toward a shorter work *week;* to emphasize the greater number of *days* available for leisure activities; to stress the importance of having *plans* for the use of the new leisure days; and to imply that many employees currently find they do not have *enough* free time under the 5/40.

As a Consequence.   A number of investigations have reported upon the leisure-time consequences associated with the implementation of a compressed work-week schedule. Hodge and Tellier conducted a nationwide study of the 4/40 schedule.[48] Based upon their sample of 223 employees from twenty-four different organizations they concluded that there were significant positive leisure effects from the 4/40 system. Specifically, the compressed schedule provided more time for travel and personal hobbies. There was a significant response indicating more leisure time, time for personal business, and time for family provided by the 4/40 schedule. Another nationwide survey, however, reported less supportive results.[49] For those employees in favor versus those opposed to the 4/40, only three leisure activities out of thirty-five differentiated the two groups.

Goodale and Aagaard studied the results of a shift from a 5/40 schedule to a forward-rotating 4/38 schedule.[50] Sixty-five percent of the employees indicated that they felt they had more leisure time with the new system. They also felt that the 4/38 was beneficial to both their marriage and social activities. Likewise, Poor and Steele reported that increases in perceived leisure time accompanied a 4/40 schedule.[51] Seventy percent of their respondents indicated that they spent more time resting; 75 percent indicated that more time was spent with the family; and there was a reported 121 percent increase in time spent visiting relatives. This evidence suggests that workers choose unorganized, relaxing activities over organized and disciplined ones. The researchers further noted that one-third of their sample indicated new spending patterns along with increases in the amount of money spent on leisure activities. Millard, Lockwood, and Luthans found that in a 4/40 system the actual use of leisure time exceeded its anticipated use. They found that more time was spent with the employee's family on recreational activities and more time was allocated to work around the home than had been planned.

One of the by-products of the compressed work week is without question a different pattern of time available for use away from work. Most employees seem to feel that this time and its use have positive effects on their recreational pursuits, personal needs, families, and general level of relaxation. Whether employees view their increased cash outlays under a 4/40 as positive or negative is unknown, however.

It is clear that employees tend to favor the adoption of compressed work schedules, and once they experience these schedules they generally prefer to stay with them in spite of some disadvantages. Numerous studies have provided statistics on the proportion of employees favoring the 4/40 schedule. These percentages range from a low of 43 percent[52] to a high of 89 percent.[53] The primary reasons employees cite for favoring the 4/40 arrangement are oriented to leisure time and longer weekends. Fatigue, longer work days, and conflicts with evening, family, and child-related activities are the primary reasons cited for opposing the compressed work-week system.

Group Reactions to the 4/40

An important question emerges, however. Exactly who favors the 4/40? There have been a large number of attempts to construct a profile of those employees who favor the compressed work week. Both demographic (e.g., age, sex, marital status) and individual-difference (e.g., intelligence, self-assurance) variables have been studied.

The sex of the employee appears to make no difference in attitudes toward the 4/40 system.[54] Younger employees tend to favor it while older employees (fifty-five years and older) oppose it.[55] Those favoring the 4/40 system also tend to have low income,[56] low job levels,[57] and be in craft occupations.[58] Age of children, number of dependents, and marital status appear to make no difference in influencing employee attitudes toward the compressed work week.[59]

We might hypothesize that personality characteristics could predict who would favor the 4/40 schedule. One study measured seven personality variables with the Ghiselli Personality Characteristics Inventory and correlated the scale scores with employee preferences for the 4/40.[60] The result was that personality type was not related to employee preferences.

Dunham and Hawk, in their predictive model of attitudes toward the 4/40, included measures on a set of organization (e.g., tenure, location, job level) and work-environment (e.g., organization climate, work-group climate, leadership) characteristics. Organization characteristics and work-environment factors accounted for statistically significant but small amounts (3 percent and 1 percent respectively) of the criterion variance in attitudes toward the 4/40.

A number of other studies have also looked at satisfaction with the 4/40 arrangement in terms of demographic variables. Satisfaction with the 4/40 has been related to low income, young age,[61] male,[62] and strong growth-need strength.[63] No differences in satisfaction were found for the following variables: sex,[64] age,[65] number of children, or marital status.[66]

Comparisons of employees on a compressed-work schedule with their 5/40 counterparts basically shows that there are no significant job satisfaction differences, but there are significant exceptions that should be noted. Research evidence suggests that favorable 4/40 attitudes may be explained by an *escape principle;* that is, if we dislike something, we will attempt to distance ourselves from it. Gannon and Reece's data suggest that as job satisfaction decreases, employee preference for the 4/40 increases.[67] Dunham and Hawk's profile of the employee who prefers the 4/40 is one who has low job satisfaction on measures of general job satisfaction, satisfaction with pay, kind of work, and company policy and practice; and who sees the organization climate in negative terms.[68] Both sets of authors hypothesize that preference for the 4/40 may stem from one additional day per week employees do not have to encounter (may escape from) the organization and their jobs. Mahoney's data, however, did not support the hypothesis that dissatisfied workers differentially favor the 4/40 schedule.[69]

Other Effects

Two studies investigated the relationships between the 4/40 schedule and organizational management. Poor and Steele noted that one major managerial problem was educating the public as to the organizational resources available.[70] It is clear that under most 4/40 arrangements the organization is going to be understaffed on Monday or Friday, which will have some impact upon outsiders who attempt to interact with the organization. The same study also mentioned the positive impact on recruiting. Employees involved in their study claimed that the 4/40 schedule was a major factor influencing their job-choice decisions—both to join and to remain.

Goodale and Aagaard's study of work-related effects showed that approximately 50 percent of the managers in their study reported coordination difficulties.[71] Specifically, scheduling problems and interpersonal contact problems were mentioned. In the same study 53 percent of the supervisors felt that the 4/40 had a detrimental effect upon their work. Clearly, managers bear much of the burden involved in maintaining the organization's productivity and sustaining positive external relations.

Moonlighting was mentioned in a number of studies. One found an increase from 4 to 17 percent of the labor force engaged in moonlighting after the shift from a 5/40 to 4/40 work week.[72] Another reported a very minor increase (1.7 percent) in moonlighting activity in their study of a shift to a 4/38.[73] Increased moonlighting opportunities were also identified by Hodge and Tellier.[74]

With regard to overtime costs, Latack and Foster reported that overtime was reduced by 33 percent following the shift from a 5/40 week to a 3/38 schedule.[75] Goodale and Aagaard noted a 10 percent reduction in overtime, but also an increasing tendency for employees to refuse overtime opportunities.[76] A reduction in overtime was also mentioned by Hodge and Tellier.[77]

Conclusion

A large number of attitudes and behaviors have been examined in association with efforts to compress the work week. Many of the studies center around the work–nonwork distinction. The major attitudes and behaviors associated with this form of alternative work schedule are associated with the nonwork domain. The potential advantages and disadvantages of compressed schedules are presented in Table 3–2 and summarized here. All of the following observations necessarily represent tentative statements as to the consequences of a compressed work schedule.

From a practical perspective, the conceptual arguments that attempt to explain the operation and effects of compressed work weeks offer only limited guidance. The circadian-rhythm model discourages the use of compressed

Table 3–2.   Potential Advantages and Disadvantages of Compressed Work-Week Schedules

Potential Advantages	*Potential Disadvantages*
Larger blocks of leisure time	Increased employee fatigue
Fewer weekly commutes to work	Greater cost of absenteeism to
Fewer conflicts with personal needs during the work day	employee
Less nonwork stress to spill over into work	Increased moonlighting
Enriched jobs (learning, autonomy, and responsibility)	
Favorable employee attitudes	
Decreased absenteeism	

schedules. The time-frame-of-reference models suggest that employers assess their employees' *individual* preferences and adopt *two* systems—a traditional one for those with a weekly or hours-per-day perspective and a compressed one for those with a daily time perspective. This would be extremely difficult in many circumstances but worth considering. Finally, the spillover model would imply that employers should periodically remind employees on compressed schedules about the advantages of taking care of personal responsibilities on the extra day off. Employers can also suggest that this presumably results in less conflict between nonwork and work domains, thereby creating positive expectations in the minds of employees.

In reviewing the research-based pros and cons of compressed work weeks, one of each stands out above the rest—leisure time and fatigue. The advantages are summarized first and then the disadvantages.

The primary reason offered in support for a 4/40 work week is that it provides employees with large blocks of leisure time to enjoy their recreational pursuits. This is highly consistent with societal trends and emphases in the past few decades and therefore could be a way to demonstrate organizational sensitivity to the needs of employees.

The research attempting to identify the work-related attitudinal and behavioral consequences of a compressed schedule is quite equivocal. Results are mixed for studies focusing on attendance (absenteeism, tardiness), turnover, and performance. Research and theoretical reflections have so far ignored the issue of organizational attachment. It is not known whether organizational commitment is associated with compressed schedules, and if so, in what manner.

Although the consequences of a compressed work week on employee performance are mixed, it is doubtful that there would be performance increases in the long run. Due to novelty effects, however, short-run performance increases may be obtained. Performance decrements may even emerge indirectly in numerous organizational settings. The critical variable here may well be the effects of fatigue. Increased fatigue quite consistently shows up as an outcome of the longer work day. Further, there are no inherent reasons or features of the compressed schedule that should lead to performance increases, while there are inherent reasons for performance decrements as well as potential increases in end-of-day accident rates.

Two potential forces operate to increase organizational attendance even though the empirical observations have produced mixed results. The economic consequences to the nonhourly employee of a lost day of work under the 4/40 system is 25 percent greater than under the traditional work schedule. In addition, the four-day week provides the individual with a week day to attend to personal demands upon his or her time. This flexible day should reduce the need to take an assigned day of work to attend to personal affairs.

In general, the results suggest that job satisfaction is favorably associated with the 4/40 schedule. The reason for this positive association remains unclear. There is some evidence that the results may be indirect; stemming, for example, from the perceived impact of the 4/40 upon the employee's job or activities outside of the organization. Negative effects have also been reported, but once again they are indirect and arise from fatigue.

There have been a few reported observations of the 4/40 having job-design effects. However, at the conceptual level there is nothing inherent in the 4/40 system per se that changes the design of an employee's job. Nevertheless, increased learning, increased autonomy, and increased responsibility have been observed. It is possible that these enriching experiences are a result of the way that the 4/40 system has been managed and not a function of the system itself. That is, new managerial styles may be used to manage the new work system and these new styles may lead to the reported employee experiences.

Finally, it is clear that most surveyed employees are favorably inclined to adopt a 4/40 system. Their predispositions, however, vary by employee orientation to time and leisure. Since most employees wish to retain a compressed schedule once they have it, employers should implement such a system only after careful diagnosis of its feasibility and possible consequences.

Endnotes

1. J. L. Pierce and J. W. Newstrom, "Alternative Work Schedules: The State of the Art," *The Personnel Administrator* (October 1979): 15–23; S. Ronen, *Flexible Working Hours: An Innovation in the Quality of Work Life* (New York: McGraw-Hill, 1981).

2. S. Ronen, *Alternative Work Schedules: Selecting, Implementing, and Evaluating* (Homewood, Ill.: Dow Jones-Irwin, 1984), ch. 3.

3. J. L. Pierce and J. W. Newstrom, "Toward a Conceptual Clarification of Employee Responses to Flexible Working Hours: A Work Adjustment Approach," *Journal of Management* 6 (1980): 117–134.

4. H. Selye, *The Stress of Life* (New York: McGraw-Hill, 1956).

5. M. Jamal and V. Mitchell, "Work, Nonwork, and Mental Health: A Model and a Test," *Industrial Relations* 19 (1980): 88–93.

6. Ronen, op. cit.

7. Ibid., p. 8.

8. D. Hellriegel, "The Four-Day Work Week: A Review and Assessment," *MSU Business Topics* 20 (1972): 39–48.

9. S. Ronen and S. B. Primps, "The Compressed Work Week as Organizational Change: Behavioral and Attitudinal Outcomes," *Academy of Management Review* 6 (1981): 61–74.

10. K. Wheeler, "Small Business Eyes the Four-Day Week," *Harvard Business Review* 48 (1970): 142–147.

11. R. I. Hartman and K. M. Weaver, "Four Factors Influencing Conversion to a Four-Day Work Week," *Human Resource Management* 16 (January 1977): 24–27.

12. J. C. Latack and L. W. Foster, "Implementation of Compressed Work Schedules: Participation and Job Redesign as Critical Factors for Employee Acceptance," *Personnel Psychology* 38 1, pp. 75–82.

13. J. M. Ivancevich, "Effects of the Shorter Work Week on Selected Satisfaction and Performance Measures," *Journal of Applied Psychology* 59 (1974): 717–721.

14. J. G. Goodale and A. K. Aagaard, "Factors Relating to Varying Reactions to the Four-Day Work Week," *Journal of Applied Psychology* 60 (1975): 33–35.

15. E. Calvasina and R. Boxx, "Efficiency of Workers on the Four-Day Work Week," *Academy of Management Journal* 18 (March 1975): 604–610.

16. J. M. Ivancevich and H. L. Lyon, "The Shortened Work Week: A Field Experiment," *Journal of Applied Psychology* 62 (1977): 34–37.

17. R. Poor and J. L. Steele, "Work and Leisure: The Reactions of People at Four-Day Firms," *4 Days, 40 Hours* (New York: Mentor, 1973).

18. Ivancevich, op. cit.

19. J. H. Hedges, "A Look at the Four-Day Work Week," *Monthly Labor Review* 96 (1971): 3–8; B. J. Hodge and R. D. Tellier, "Employee Reactions to the Four-Day Week," *California Management Review* 18 (January 1975): 25–30.

20. D. M. Maklan, *The Four-Day Work Week* (New York: Praeger, 1977).

21. Poor and Steele, op. cit.

22. Goodale and Aagaard, op. cit.

23. W. R. Nord and R. Costigan, "Worker Adjustment to the Four-Day Week: A Longitudinal Study," *Journal of Applied Psychology* 58 (1973): 60–66.

24. Latack and Foster, op. cit.

25. Wheeler, op. cit.

26. Hartman and Weaver, op. cit.

27. Wheeler, op. cit.

28. Nord and Costigan, op. cit.

29. Goodale and Aagaard, op. cit.

30. Latack and Foster, op. cit.

31. C. W. Millard, D. L. Lockwood, and F. Luthans, "The Impact of a Four-Day Work Week on Employees," *MSU Business Topics* 8 (February 1980): 31–37.

32. Hartman and Weaver, op. cit.

33. Ivancevich, op. cit.; Ivancevich and Lyon, op. cit.

34. Goodale and Aagaard, op. cit.

35. Hartman and Weaver, op. cit.

36. Ivancevich, op. cit.

37. Millard et al., op. cit.

38. Latack and Foster, op. cit.

39. Maklan, op. cit.

40. M. D. Fottler, "Employee Acceptance of a Four-Day Work Week," *Academy of Management Journal* 20 (1977): 656–688.

41. Latack and Foster, op. cit.

42. Goodale and Aagaard, op. cit.

43. Mahoney et al., op. cit.

44. Mahoney, op. cit.

45. M. T. Kenny, "Public Employee Attitudes toward the Four-Day Week," *Public Personnel Management* 3 (1974): 159–161.

46. Nord and Costigan, op. cit.

47. R. E. Allen and D. K. Hawes, "Attitudes toward Work, Leisure, and the Four-Day Work Week," *Human Resource Management* 18 (January 1979): 5–10.

48. Hodge and Tellier, op. cit.

49. Allen and Hawes, op. cit.

50. Goodale and Aagaard, op. cit.

51. Poor and Steele, op. cit.

52. T. L. Dickson and J. P. Wijting, "An Analysis of Workers' Attitudes toward the Four-day, Forty-hour Work Week," *Psychological Reports* 37 (1975): 383–390.

53. Poor and Steele, op. cit.

54. Kenny, op. cit.; R. B. Dunham and D. L. Hawk, "The Four- Day/Forty-Hour Week: Who Wants It?," *Academy of Management Journal* 20 (1977): 644–655.

55. Dunham and Hawk, op. cit.; Goodale and Aagaard, op. cit.; Kenny, op. cit.; Allen and Hawes, op. cit.

56. Dunham and Hawk, op. cit.

57. Ibid.; Allen and Hawes, op. cit.

58. Allen and Hawes, op. cit.

59. Kenny, op. cit.

60. Dunham and Hawk, op. cit.

61. Goodale and Aagaard, op. cit.

62. Poor and Steele, op. cit.

63. Latack and Foster, op. cit.

64. Goodale and Aagaard, op. cit.; Hodge and Tellier, op. cit.; Nord and Costigan, op. cit.; ibid.

65. Hodge and Tellier, op. cit.; Nord and Costigan, op. cit.

66. Latack and Foster, op. cit.; Nord and Costigan, op. cit.

67. M. Gannon and K. Reece, "Personality Characteristics, Job Satisfaction, and the Four-Day Week," *Proceedings of the Industrial Relations Research Association* 24 (1971): 116–120.

68. Dunham and Hawk, op. cit.

69. Mahoney, op. cit.

70. Poor and Steele, op. cit.

71. Goodale and Aagaard, op. cit.

72. Poor and Steele, op. cit.

73. Goodale and Aagaard, op. cit.

74. Hodge and Tellier, op. cit.

75. Latack and Foster, op. cit.

76. Goodale and Aagaard, op. cit.

77. Hodge and Tellier, op. cit.

Chapter Four

Permanent Part-Time Employment

 ▶ In recent decades there has been a significant increase in interest in part-time employment. Between the early 1950s and the late 1970s, the voluntary part-time work force grew at a rate more than double the rate of increase for full-time employment.[1]

Unlike some of the other work schedules discussed in this book, part-time work in and of itself is not a new concept. Relatively large numbers of workers are currently on part-time schedules. According to the Bureau of Labor Statistics, 14 percent of the total U.S. labor force was working part-time or seeking part-time work in the mid-1980s. Over one-fifth of the female work force and almost one-half of all working teenagers were working part-time. Substantial numbers of part-time workers are found in each of the major occupational groups: 27 percent of the white-collar work force (including technical and sales workers), 8.5 percent of blue-collar workers, and 29.5 percent of service workers are part-time employees.[2]

However, some of the recent thinking on part-time work is innovative in that it extends the notions of how, where, and why part-time employment should be used. Traditionally, part-time jobs were concentrated in low-level retail, service, and clerical jobs.[3] The choice to provide part-time work was typically driven by pragmatic concerns such as the need to staff organizations (e.g., restaurants and retail stores) more than eight hours but less than two full shifts per day; and the economic benefits of increasing staffs during peak business periods (such as lunch periods) even if those periods lasted for less than a full day.[4]

Current writing on part-time work focuses on broader potential benefits of this form of work schedule and recommends that part-time opportunities be extended into more sectors of the economy and in particular into higher-level jobs. Organization-level variables, such as those discussed in earlier chapters, have been considered and studied in relation to part-time work to a limited extent. Further, to a greater degree than is true for other alternative schedules, a great deal of discussion has centered on the benefits that could accrue to society as a whole if part-time work opportunities were expanded.

In this chapter, we review definitions of part-time employment. Reasons for its recent growth, and for the broad support it has received in some quarters, are discussed. Finally, the advantages and disadvantages of this particular work schedule from an organizational standpoint are reviewed.

Part-Time Employment Defined

There is little agreement in the literature as to how part-time employment should be defined. The extent to which a work schedule is considered full-time or part-time can vary along several dimensions: number of hours worked per day, number of days worked per week, number of weeks worked per year. As used in this chapter, part-time work is regular, steady work of less than thirty-five hours per week. This is the definition employed by the Current Population Survey; and it is also referred to as *permanent part-time employment*. Our main focus, then, is on schedules involving less than eight hours of work in a day or less than five days of work in a week. This review is limited to *voluntary* part-time work, disregarding involuntary part-time employment as the organizational and individual issues involved in a forced part-time situation may be quite different from those where the part-time schedule is chosen voluntarily.

Two new concepts in part-time work that have received considerable attention are job sharing and temporary employment. *Job sharing* is generally defined as a situation in which two qualified part-time employees divide the hours, responsibilities, and possibly the benefits of a full-time job. *Temporary employment* refers to the situation in which an individual works on an as-needed basis, usually through a temporary-help agency. Although they may not fit the definition above exactly, each of these concepts has some unique costs and benefits, which are reviewed and summarized in this chapter. Seasonal employment, where employees work for an organization full-time but only during certain times of the year, is another important form of scheduling that could be considered part-time. However, it is not discussed separately because the issues involved in seasonal work overlap with those discussed under the other types of part-time work.

The Increasing Support for Part-Time Work

A number of factors can be identified as having contributed to the growth of part-time employment. First are the demographic and structural factors. The composition of the labor force now includes more women and teenagers, both of whom have traditionally sought part-time work opportunities. In addition, there has been a substantial growth in the service sector of the U.S. economy and it is this sector that makes major use of part-time employees. A number of public policies (e.g., student assistance work–study programs and social security provisions) allow students and pensioners to work part-time without a substantial reduction in their benefits, and this also has encouraged its growth.[5]

Another factor which may have contributed to the growth of part-time employment is the active support received from a variety of public and private groups. Many states and the federal government passed legislation in the mid-1970s to increase the number of part-time jobs available in the civil service.[6] Various interest groups, such as New Ways to Work (San Francisco), Catalyst (New York), and the National Council on Alternative Work Patterns (Washington, D.C.) have actively encouraged the expansion of part-time opportunities and have provided information and assistance to organizations that want to use part-time workers and job sharers. Recently a national association of part-time professionals was formed, in part to promote part-time employment in upper-level jobs.[7]

Why has there been so much support for part-time employment? To the extent that there is any central idea behind this support, it appears to stem from the quality of work life (and quality of life) movement. In 1973, a special task force of the Department of Health, Education, and Welfare (now Health and Human Services) published a report on the state of mind of the worker in the United States. The *Work in America* report suggested that large numbers of employees were discontented and frustrated with their work; problems such as dull work and lack of involvement in the job were cited. To many readers this report suggested an impending crisis in the work place, and a variety of programs such as job redesign and participative management were implemented in the 1970s and 1980s in an effort to improve employee attitudes.[8]

Some, however, saw an even larger issue and speculated that individual attitudes toward work itself—regardless of the exact nature of the work—had changed. According to these writers, an increasing percentage of our population is questioning the merits of full-time work and is instead more interested in leisure time and recreational activities.

It has been suggested that leisure time has become increasingly important as people search for self-fulfillment, a level of satisfaction not often provided by a single full-time work activity. Part-time work is thus viewed as a means of providing a more flexible lifestyle and a different balance between work and the rest of life.[9] The desire for a different work–nonwork balance is not limited to workers with dull, low-level jobs either; rather, it is pervasive across numerous sectors of the work force. A study of 3500 Ph.D.s found that 11 percent of the women and 8 percent of the men who were employed full-time would prefer to reduce their hours in order to take advantage of other interests.[10] A Harris poll reported that between 30 and 40 million workers would accept a 10 percent pay cut if their hours of work were cut proportionately.[11]

Economic conditions, social programs, higher income levels, and the growth in the number of dual-career families have created the situation where more and more people *can* choose a different ratio between work and leisure than that provided by full-time work. The proponents of part-time work would like to see them have that option.

Organizations and individuals who promote part-time work, then, claim that part-time employment as well as other forms of alternative work schedules enhance the quality of work life and, indeed, the quality of life. In addition to claims of quality of work life, there are social benefits as an outcome of part-time employment. It has frequently been touted as a means by which more jobs can be created so that more individuals can be brought into the labor force. An important issue here, of course, is whether full-time jobs would be lost to the creation of part-time jobs. Another argument frequently cited favoring part-time employment is that it can significantly reduce the cost of unemployment insurance and welfare. The notion here is that many welfare recipients are single parents who cannot both work full-time and take care of their families. They might, however, be available for part-time work. There is some evidence that this could occur. One experiment with part-time work shifts in a relatively depressed community led to estimated welfare savings of $600,000 over a seven-year period.[12]

Supporters of part-time employment also point out that specific groups within the labor force may benefit greatly from the expansion of good part-time opportunities. Although many employees would prefer to work fewer hours, there are a number of groups within the labor force who particularly need the flexibility provided by part-time arrangements. Some handicapped employees, for example, are physically unable to work a full (eight-hour) day. Workers in the process of changing careers may need time during regular office hours to conduct their job searches. Students often need gainful employment while still in school.

One group that may realize substantial benefits from part-time employment are older employees who wish to phase themselves into retirement. Two problem areas confronting this group of employees can be addressed in part by the part-time arrangement—economic needs and psychological adjustment. While there has been a tendency in recent years to encourage early retirement to downsize organizations' work forces, the effects of inflation on fixed incomes has made even regular retirement difficult to manage (and enjoy) financially. In addition, many retirees have psychological difficulties in adjusting to life without job demands, a daily routine, and the long-established social networks of the work place. Once they have retired and discovered these difficulties, it is extremely difficult for retirees to reenter the work force. However, part-time employment can be a means by which an individual can move into retirement at a gradual pace.[13]

A survey conducted by the National Council on Aging indicated that 75 percent of the work force over fifty-five years of age preferred some kind of paid part-time work to total retirement. This preference was stated by both high- and low-income workers, suggesting that psychological as well as economic needs are relevant.[14]

Women are often identified as a group that benefits greatly from part-time employment. In fact, a great deal of the research done on part-time work deals with its effect on women. This is appropriate since 70 percent of all part-time employees are female.[15] Much of the discussion in this literature focuses on the ways in which moving from full- to part-time employment can reduce role conflict for the working woman; conflict between the employment role and the roles of mother and/or homemaker. One study suggested that the psychological health of both the mother and child improves when the mother goes from no employment outside the home to part-time employment.[16]

Another way in which women may benefit from part-time work is that it may reduce the level of unemployment for women as a group. There is no evidence to suggest that part-time work increases the duration of women's unemployment. "On the contrary, the availability of part-time jobs seems to increase the chances of women entering or re-entering the labor force without experiencing unemployment. In addition, policies to promote part-week work as a means by which women can continue working even when nonmarket demands are greatest will reduce unemployment by reducing the frequency of labor force entry and re-entry."[17]

Part-time work may also have a positive impact on women's lifetime earnings. Overall the compensation of part-time workers is usually considered a *dis*advantage to employees since part-timers as a group are paid less per hour than full-time workers.[18] By contrast, in the case of some women part-time work may be the only alternative to total withdrawal from the labor force. The woman who interrupts her career to raise a family suffers not only a short-term loss of earnings but also experience and seniority, leading to lower wages when she returns to work and an overall loss in earning capacity. These losses can be partially ameliorated by part-time work during the child-rearing years.[19]

In summary, there are numerous reasons for society and the work force to press for the expansion of part-time employment. At this point, however, we have not addressed the impact of part-time work on the organizations that provide the job opportunities. It is to this important issue that we now turn.

Organizational Issues

A variety of organizational benefits, and some drawbacks, are discussed in the part-time work literature. Some are quite practical in nature, others more abstract. In general, the claims are not based on any particular theory of human behavior. Furthermore, research has not progressed much beyond the case-study level on many of the issues and evidence is mixed on others.

Advantages of Part-Time Employment

A number of positive organizational effects have been attributed to the implementation of part-time employment. These include increases in job satisfaction, improvements in organizational participation (e.g., attendance and length of service), and higher productivity. Each of these is reviewed briefly.

Job Satisfaction. The most consistent and widespread claim associated with part-time employment is that it leads to an increase in job satisfaction. At this point there is no clear theory as to why this would be the case. There have been a number of studies undertaken to test this claim. The results, however, are inconsistent.

One study using a sample of professional and paraprofessional employees in Wisconsin's civil service found that part-time workers were significantly more satisfied than full-time workers with comparable jobs.[20] When employee satisfaction with a specific set of job facets (i.e., pay, coworkers, kind and amount of work, career future, supervision, company identification, and physical working conditions) was examined, there were no significant differences between the full- and part-time employees. Conversely, a study of clerical employees in a retail organization found that full-time workers were significantly more satisfied with their jobs than were their part-time counterparts.[21]

In an early study comparing part-time and full-time female hospital employees, the authors found no mean differences between them in terms of their satisfaction with five job facets—supervision, work, pay, coworkers, and promotion.[22] Another study of hospital employees found that part-time employees reported higher levels of overall job satisfaction than did full-time employees.[23]

Two researchers surveyed women college graduates who were either employed full- or part-time. The results of their investigation showed that there was less career satisfaction and greater role conflict and overload for women employed part-time.[24]

In summary, the early evidence on job satisfaction does not provide strong support for the claim that part-time workers are more satisfied than other groups of workers. In two cases, part-time workers were more satisfied; in two cases, there were no differences; and in one case, full-time workers were more satisfied. There are a number of possible explanations for the inconsistency of the findings. Results may be sample-specific. Part-time workers may have a different psychology of work than their counterparts and thus respond differently to the work environment. Or there may be confounding factors that explain any observed differences in job satisfaction across full-time and part-time groups. For example, part-time jobs are likely to be characterized as routine and low-skill level in nature. If this observation is true, the job-design literature[25] would suggest that part-time employees are likely to be job *dis-satisfied*, at least in part as a function of the characteristics of their jobs.

A recent study was designed to avoid some of the problems of interpretation found in the earlier ones. In 1984 an analysis was conducted of demographic and attitudinal differences between full- and part-time workers, using national survey data collected by the National Opinion Research Center. It found that part-time employees were relatively less satisfied with their jobs than were full-time employees. However, this difference did not persist when factors such as education, income, and prestige of the job were controlled.[26]

This study is significant in that it used a broad sample and controls for some confounding variables. Further research on this level will help clear up the confusion regarding the relative satisfaction of part-time workers. In addition, research focusing on the effect of a *change* in schedules for a group of employees should be conducted. Also, research taking account of individual needs and preferences would be enlightening, since the characteristics of workers who *choose* part-time employment may be different from those interested in full-time work. In the meantime the common claim that part-time work results in higher job satisfaction is *not* strongly supported by the empirical evidence.

Organizational Participation.   It is argued, based on some preliminary evidence, that various forms of employee participation in an organization (attendance, length of service) are improved as a function of part-time employment. One experiment comparing part-time and full-time social workers found the turnover rate for part-time workers to be 14 percent versus 40 percent for their full-time counterparts.[27] The Giant Food Company, a retail chain that hires large numbers of part-time employees, found that on average its part-time workers lost only half as much time due to lateness as did the full-time workers.[28] Wisconsin's civil service found that job sharers used significantly less sick leave than did full-time employees.[29]

Reasons for the belief that part-time workers have lower turnover and absenteeism are not entirely clear. One possibility is that participation is better because job satisfaction is higher. Yet the evidence is not entirely convincing that the job satisfaction of part-time employees is in fact higher than that of their full-time counterparts. A more plausible explanation may be found outside of the job-satisfaction construct. Turnover, as an example, may be lower because the part-time worker perceives part-time jobs as being hard to find. Attendance may be better simply because the part-time employee is more able to attend to personal business outside of the regularly scheduled hours of work. Part-time workers may also recognize the tenuous nature of their employment and therefore not want to risk their employment security by tardiness and absenteeism.

An earlier review of the empirical literature linking part- and full-time employment with turnover concluded that very little is known about the differences between the two. This investigation attempted to predict turnover among a group of full-time and part-time employees. It concluded that among the full-time employees traditional psychological antecedents (e.g., dissatisfaction, thinking about quitting, intention to quit) predicted subsequent turnover. These attitudes and behavioral intentions, however, did not successfully predict turnover among the part-time workers. It was further noted that during the study period voluntary turnover among the full-time employees was 26 percent versus 40 percent for the part-time workers. The authors concluded that individuals employed on a part-time basis do not make withdrawal decisions on the same basis as their full-time counterparts.[30]

As mentioned earlier, numerous authors have suggested that part-time workers may have a different psychology of work than full-time employees. Part-time employees may feel closer to other social systems (e.g., home, family, another job) than to a job's social system. These individuals may be more sensitive to fulfilling the role requirements in their dominant nonjob social system than are those who are full-time employees in an organizational social system. This greater sensitivity to and investment in the nonjob role may result in different attitudes toward work among the part- versus full-time worker. That is, the part-time worker may be less sensitive to immediate job experiences than the full-timer and therefore turnover may be less well predicted from traditional job, organizational, or personal psychologically based predictors.[31]

A study of so-called *peripheral employees*—those with lower career orientation, less psychological commitment to the employer, and work schedules involving fewer hours per week—suggests that they are not motivated by job-related attitudes. As a result, standard relationships between work attitudes and behaviors may not apply to these employees.[32] To the extent that part-time workers are peripheral employees, this would help explain difficulties in predicting their withdrawal behaviors.

As was the case with job satisfaction, more research needs to be done before we draw conclusions about this potential advantage of part-time work. There is some case-study evidence to support it, but controlled research is still lacking.

Productivity. It has often been argued that the hiring of part-time employees increases the productivity of an organization's work force. Part-time employment is said to allow for more efficient work scheduling and to provide a large applicant pool permitting the employer to be more selective in hiring. Further, it is claimed that part-time workers are more productive than full-time workers. A review of each of these claims follows.

Part-time work is expected to increase the flexibility of work scheduling for the employer and therefore to increase the productivity of workers when they are on the job.[33] By using part-timers, employers can readily increase their staff during peak periods of the day, week, month, or season. Part-time work enables the organization to reduce overtime, improve the utilization of equipment, and extend hours of service. At the same time, the organization avoids the costs of idle employees during slow periods. Some organizations feel it is cost effective to pay part-time workers a wage premium for working irregular hours.[34] However, there is as yet no real evidence on whether, or to what extent, part-time employment increases productivity through flexibility in scheduling.

The second contribution that part-time employment is expected to make to productivity is that it offers the employer a larger pool of potential employees. Students, unemployed spouses of primary wage-earners, and retirees are often available for part-time but not full-time work. The broader recruiting base that part-time opportunities appeal to should enable an employer to be more selective in hiring.[35] Part-time options may also alleviate worker shortages in specific job areas, such as routine jobs that may be perceived as terribly monotonous if worked full-time but acceptable on a part-time basis. An additional benefit is that part-time employment may also help an organization meet its affirmative-action goals by providing opportunities for members of protected groups who might otherwise be unable to work. In particular, it might become easier to attract talented women or disabled employees who for personal reasons may prefer part-time employment. In fact, a large number of organizations that have experimented with part-time work have attributed their successful affirmative-action hiring to their part-time programs.[36] But again, hard evidence of this benefit is not available.

A third and more controversial contention is that both the quantity and quality of the work of part-time employees are high relative to the work of full-time employees. A survey conducted by the American Society for Personnel Administration found that the majority of firms using part-time workers considered their part-time employees to be at least as productive as their full-time workers.[37] One mass-assembly department in a Southeast firm reported 7 percent higher output when it compared the production of part- and full-time workers.[38] The performance differential was in part attributed to less fatigue and the differential pace of work among the two groups.

There are a number of possible reasons for this alleged productivity advantage. One is that part-time workers (at least those working part-days) suffer less from physiological fatigue and therefore can sustain a faster pace for half a day than they can for a full day. Another argument is psychological in nature: It may be mentally easier for an individual to tolerate tedious work for part of a day without adverse effects on performance. Part-time employees may also use their time more efficiently, taking fewer rest or meal breaks and planning their time more carefully because they have fewer hours in which to complete their tasks.[39]

As was the case with both job satisfaction and absenteeism/turnover, there is little research focusing on the performance issue. The Wisconsin civil-service project studied the issue of productivity and found that *individuals* who reduced their hours were more productive on part-time schedules than they had been on full-time schedules, but no significant differences were found between part-timers and full-timers as groups.[40]

A study assessing part-time faculty members at a Midwest college found that students rated the part-time faculty higher than the full-time faculty in teaching effectiveness. The two groups were rated equally, however, when performance appraisals were conducted by the department chairpersons and other instructors in the academic units.[41]

The question of whether a half-time worker does more than one-half of the work of a full-time worker was addressed in a study of social workers reported by the Catalyst organization. Results indicated that the part-time employees carried an average caseload of forty-two families versus an average of seventy-eight for the full-time social workers. In addition, it was reported that part-time workers had 89 percent as many face-to-face contacts with their clients and 20 percent more phone contacts than the full-time group.[42]

Further research in this area is needed. The three studies cited focus on relatively high-level jobs. Since part-time jobs tend to be concentrated in lower-level jobs, and because it is suggested that the ability to tolerate tedious work may add to the relative productivity of the part-time workers, studies of relative productivity in routine, low-skilled jobs would be of great interest.

Other Benefits. There may be a number of other advantages to part-time arrangements. As the economy moves away from manufacturing and into the white-collar and service sectors, the needs of employers are also changing. While the hours of work and the ratio of full-time to part-time employees at a manufacturing plant are often determined by equipment utilization and mechanical processes, the work schedules and composition of the work force in service organizations are heavily influenced by the requirement of accessibility to the customer. With an increasing percentage of the population working during regular business hours, service organizations have to extend their hours in order to accommodate customer needs at other times. One consequence has been the increase in the number of part-time employees hired to cover these extended and nontraditional hours. Part-time employment is in effect "feeding on itself"; that is, as the expansion of part-time opportunities draws more people into the work force the need for extended service hours may increase, creating even more part-time jobs.[43]

There can also be financial advantages to hiring part-time workers. There is generally a fringe-benefit savings that accrues to the organization since many organizational benefits are not required for the part-timer. Further, many organizations that employ part-time employees have a no-work, no-pay rule, which means that absent part-time employees do not get paid. As a consequence, the costs of absenteeism are lower for part-time employees than for full-time employees, who often have a number of compensated personal and sick days to use. When part-time employees are laid off due to organizational cutbacks these employees do not normally increase the company's payroll tax.

Disadvantages of Part-Time Employment

Despite the many possible (and sometimes demonstrated) positive consequences of part-time work for both the employee and the organization, there are several disadvantages as well. We first discuss the direct disadvantages: increased administrative and training costs and increased fringe-benefit costs. We then consider some indirect factors that could become disadvantages to the organization through their impact on employee attitudes and behaviors: type of work activities, limited advancement opportunities, and lower compensation rates. Interestingly, however, these indirect factors may have just the opposite effect on employee satisfaction, participation, and productivity as that predicted.

Administrative and Training Costs.   One of the most frequently cited disadvantages of part-time employment is that the administrative and training costs are relatively high because they are not amortized as quickly. The differential in compensation noted above is in part a function of the organizational investment in employee training and expected return on it. Employers are reluctant to hire part-time employees for jobs requiring major training expense because it takes longer for them to recapture the training costs. In addition, whenever two (or more) part-timers are hired (versus one full-timer), this doubles the load on personnel departments' interviewing, testing, record keeping, and training. While these increases are apparent, there can be offsetting economies of scale that can be obtained once the basic personnel systems are created and put in place.

As discussed earlier, part-time employees may have a significantly lower turnover rate than full-time employees. The fact that employers have fewer hours per day in which to recapture their administrative and training costs may be offset by the fact that part-time workers remain with the organization longer.

Employee Benefits.   One of the greatest organizational concerns with regard to hiring part-time employees pertains to benefits. The costs of providing part-time workers with benefits comparable to those received by full-time workers can be substantial, although some benefits can be easily prorated. Between 50 and 75 percent of the employers who have part-time employment arrangements do provide prorated vacation and holiday benefits.[44] Pension plans, life insurance, and health-insurance benefits are more difficult to prorate. Medical insurance can be a particular problem because it is among the most expensive benefits offered by employers. Statutory benefits such as social security, unemployment insurance, and disability insurance present problems in that they must be provided and cannot be prorated.

Many employers have dealt with the problem of benefits for part-time workers by not providing them with any. This raises the question of how critical benefits really are to part-time employees. There is some evidence that many part-time workers are already enrolled in life- or health-insurance plans as someone else's dependent. Few, however, have benefits such as sick leave or retirement plans.[45] Thus there may be selective interest in employee benefits as a function of dependency and benefit type.

There is a question of equity involved in denying some benefits to such a large group of employees. There may also be a need to consider the worker's morale and sense of identification with the organization. An additional reason to consider providing benefits to part-time workers is the fact that more and more unions are demanding coverage.

The challenge then becomes one of designing a benefit package that is considered equitable by part-time employees while not being overly expensive for the organization. Fortunately there are some guidelines available. Catalyst, for example, has prepared a paper called "Constructing an Employee Benefit Package for Part-Time Workers."[46] Among its suggestions are a number of ways to offset the expensive costs of medical insurance. They propose that the employer not offer medical insurance to employees covered elsewhere; provide some components of medical coverage but not others; limit coverage to the individual instead of extending it to the individual's family; or decline to pay for the insurance but make a group plan available for employees not otherwise covered. It is clear that with some imagination a number of attractive packages can be designed.

Another approach to providing fringe benefits to part-time employees is the implementation of a flexible- or cafeteria-benefits program. Under such a program, individual employees select those benefits they want most, up to a certain dollar-value limit. Flexible benefits have been recommended as a means of increasing the perceived value of fringe benefits to all employees, full- and part-time, thus leading to greater pay satisfaction.[47] Although there are some administrative costs involved in such a program, they may be offset by the increase in the cost effectiveness of the various benefits. A flexible-benefits plan would be a fairly simple way to provide adequate benefits to part-time employees: the total allotment to each employee could be prorated based on proportion of time worked and individuals could tailor their package to those benefits they do not receive from other sources.

Type of Work Activities. Possibly the greatest disadvantage faced by individuals who choose to work part-time is the type of work currently available to them. Many part-time positions are in low-skilled, low-status jobs such as clerical work, retail sales, and food services. In addition, part-time workers may often be given the least pleasant tasks and the least convenient hours within their job category. For example, executives in a retail organization stated that "many unit managers viewed part-time employees as temporary help to be assigned the unfinished work of full-time employees and the less desirable tasks associated with the job classification."[48] Similarly, a study of part-time faculty showed they were assigned the most undesirable courses with respect to scheduling, levels, and class size.[49] There is, however, no evidence that indicates whether these assignments of low-level tasks to part-timers are commonplace or just isolated incidents.

As noted above, the literature on employee motivation indicates that factors intrinsic to a job (e.g., how challenging or prestigious it is) can have a positive effect on employee performance. If in fact part-time workers are given undesirable work their motivation to perform may suffer. This negative effect could counteract any of the potential productivity gains discussed earlier.

Advancement.   Some evidence suggests that part-time workers face the problem of slow or blocked advancement. Very few part-time workers hold managerial jobs, even within organizations with large numbers of part-time jobs. At Control Data's Selby plant, for example, all production workers are part-time employees while all the management staff works full-time.[50]

A more interesting question is why it appears that part-time employees advance more slowly than their full-time counterparts. It has been argued that managers perceive upper-level jobs as more responsible positions and therefore unsuitable for the part-timer. The primary factor may well be that there are special coordination and communication problems associated with highly responsible jobs and part-time employees are basically not available to handle these issues.[51] A more provocative explanation is that part-time employees are stereotyped as being uninterested in advancement and lacking commitment to their jobs.[52]

The underlying empirical question is, Do part-time employees in fact advance more slowly (if at all)? Answering this question will require research on the following questions: Are there advancement opportunities for part-timers? Do they desire advancement? Should the speed of advancement be measured by total time with the organization or total time actually worked? Only then can it be known whether an advancement issue actually exists.

However, to the extent that part-time workers do feel blocked at lower levels, organizations may again be missing an opportunity to motivate higher performance. In many organizations, advancement is to at least some extent contingent on performance, and employees who want to get ahead are motivated to perform. If part-timers believe they will not be promoted because of their work schedule regardless of performance level, then the motivation to perform may well suffer.

Compensation.   As noted earlier, part-time workers as a whole earn less on an hourly basis than do full-time workers. One study showed that male part-timers earn 30 percent less than male full-timers; and female part-timers earn 17 percent less than female full-timers.[53] These observations were made after the effects of race, education, and experience were held constant. Furthermore, in addition to hourly wage differentials, there is evidence suggesting that part-timers do not receive fringe benefits commensurate with those offered to full-time employees.[54] What we do not yet know, however, is how part-time workers are paid relative to full-time workers *within their organizations*. Fairness issues may arise if workers doing the same work for the same organization are paid differently simply because of their work schedules. If part-time workers do feel underpaid relative to their full-time counterparts, they may respond by slacking off or leaving the organization altogether.

Other Disadvantages. In the administrative arena, a potential burden is placed upon an organization's span of control as a result of part-time work.[55] For example, a manager with ten part-time employees versus five full-timers has a more difficult administrative responsibility. This problem is not usually insurmountable, however. An interesting solution, particularly in the case where part-time work is used to cover peak business periods, is to hire supervisors who also work on a part-time peak-hours schedule.

Another potential disadvantage of part-time employment is the possibility of labor union opposition. Trade unions perceive numerous drawbacks to the use of part-time workers. A major union objection is that part-time employment can be used to evade overtime payments to full-time employees.[56] Part-time employment also enables organizations to hold labor costs down at the expense of employee rights in areas such as fringe benefits, seniority, and pension plans. Unions are concerned about the possibility that part-time workers could take jobs away from full-time workers by increasing competition when jobs are scarce.[57] Another possible, if not frequently mentioned, reason for union displeasure with attempts to increase part-time opportunities is the low rate of unionization among part-time workers. Dues avoidance, lack of long-term job commitment, and lack of identification with other full-time union members are some of the reasons suggested for this low rate of union involvement demonstrated by part-time employees. Union leaders may be concerned that a growing part-time labor force might make their organizing efforts more difficult.

However, not all unions respond negatively to the issue of part-time employment. Several unions have recognized the value of including part-time employees. The Service Employees' International Union, for example, has become more supportive of part-time work now that 13 percent of its membership works part-time.[58] The Retail Clerks' International Union, with almost half of its members on part-time schedules, has been particularly active in organizing and negotiating for part-time workers.[59] From a management perspective, it might be wise to involve unions directly in any planning for expansion of part-time employment.

Other Forms of Part-Time Employment

Job Sharing

Job sharing, job pairing, and job splitting all belong to the family of part-time employment. Basically, job sharing refers to a situation in which two qualified part-time employees divide the hours, responsibilities, and possibly the benefits of a full-time job. Each participant in the job-sharing process is responsible for a set of duties and each sees particular projects through to completion. Along similar lines, job sharing has been viewed as an arrangement "whereby two (or more) employees hold a position together, whether they are as a team jointly responsible for the whole or separately for each half."[60]

We can also differentiate between vertical and horizontal job sharing as a way to distinguish it from job splitting and job pairing (see Table 4–1). Vertical job sharing results in job splitting, in which two people with complementary skills share one job, but the tasks performed and especially the level of responsibility differ for each employee. Horizontal job sharing, or job pairing, similarly requires that two workers share one job but with each taking equal responsibility for all parts of the total job.

Job sharing is significant in that it provides part-time work in positions that must be staffed full-time. Employers seem more willing to let responsible jobs be shared than to convert them to traditional part-time positions. Under job sharing they know that someone is always covering a particular job even if the person covering it varies from day to day. Many of the higher-level part-time positions reported in the literature (e.g., the Wisconsin civil service

Table 4–1. Task Roles for Two Employees under Job Sharing, Splitting, or Pairing

	Job Sharing		Job Splitting		Job Pairing	
	Person		Person		Person	
Task Assignments	A	B	A	B	A	B
1. Higher-level responsibilities						
A.	X		X		X	X
B.		X	X		X	X
C.		X	X		X	X
D.	X		X		X	X
2. Lower-level responsibilities						
E.		X		X	X	X
F.	X			X	X	X
G.		X		X	X	X
H.	X			X	X	X

project, many teaching positions) are in fact job-sharing arrangements. Another potential benefit of job sharing is the symbiotic relationship of the job sharers. Members of a job-sharing team may counterbalance each other's weaknesses with their strengths. In some organizations, experienced employees have shared jobs with new employees to facilitate the training process.[61]

Although a job-sharing relationship can be seen as a benefit it may also create problems, especially if the two parties involved are not compatible. A great deal of cooperation and communication between the partners, and with their supervisor, is required to ensure that the job is fairly divided and adequately covered. There is also a performance-appraisal problem potentially associated with job pairing when performance of one individual is indistinguishable from that of his or her partner.

Temporary Work

A work-scheduling technique that almost defies classification is the phenomenon of temporary work. Temporary workers may work sporadically or regularly, for a series of short jobs with various employers or for long assignments with a single employer. However, the vast majority of temporary workers work less than thirty-five hours per week and their issues are similar to those of part-time workers.[62] Therefore we consider this work schedule a form of part-time work.

The temporary-help industry has boomed in recent years. It is currently a $6 billion business that is growing at a rate of 20 percent per year, far outpacing the rest of the economy. While in the past most temporary-help agencies dealt primarily with clerical workers, now medical, industrial, and professional temporary workers are also in demand.[63]

Employers are interested in temporary workers because of the labor cost savings they can create. Employers pay for workers only when they need them to work and also avoid many of the costs of benefits and training.

Employees who choose to work as temporaries may do so because of the job variety and exposure to different environments that temporary work can provide. They may also prefer temporary work because it provides them with maximum flexibility in scheduling; temporary employees work only when they want to work. A 1984 survey of temporary health-care workers suggests that flexibility is the key reason they chose temporary work.[64]

Temporary work provides a few advantages that permanent part-time work often does not. The growth in the service industry has led to a shortage of temporary workers there. As a result temporary agencies are offering training and benefits to qualified workers.[65] Also, temporary work has been able to provide flexible-scheduling opportunities for a variety of upper-level jobs—such as accountants, engineers, lawyers, and doctors, where traditional part-time jobs have been scarce.[66]

Summary

Part-time work (regular, steady work of thirty-five hours a week or less) is already fairly common in certain industries and in certain types of jobs. To a great extent, part-time opportunities are concentrated in lower-level jobs, typically in the service industry. Proponents of part-time work as an alternative work schedule seek the expansion of opportunities into a broad variety of occupations and settings.

Some of the cited benefits are broad in scope. One argument, apparently stemming from the quality-of-work-life movement of the 1970s, is that individuals are seeking a better balance between work and nonwork. Leisure is seen as growing in importance and part-time work allows individuals more flexibility in determining how their time is allocated. It is also believed that part-time work can provide satisfying work opportunities for individuals who might not otherwise have meaningful employment; for example, some of the handicapped, the elderly, and mothers. In some cases, the availability of good part-time jobs might even reduce the need for public financial assistance for some of these individuals.

Other arguments focus on the organization that offers part-time work. Some of the benefits are pragmatic in nature—for example, the ability to increase staff during peak business times. Others focus on the expected effects that part-time work can have on employees and how employers might profit from those effects. It is hypothesized that

1. Job satisfaction will be high for part-timers relative to full-timers
2. Organizational participation (attendance, remaining with the organization) will be higher for part-time workers than for full-time workers
3. Productivity will be higher for part-timers.

None of these contentions, however, has been strongly supported by research (see Table 4–2). Furthermore there is little theoretical explanation for why these effects should be expected.

Table 4–2.   Effects of Part-Time Work on Organization Variables

		Research Findings		
	Expected Effect	*Positive Effect*	*No Effect*	*Negative Effect*
Job satisfaction	Positive	X	X	X
Organizational participation	Positive	X		X
Productivity	Positive	X	X	

There are also some potential disadvantages of part-time work. These include

1. Higher administrative and benefits costs for the organization
2. Possible reduction in employee motivation stemming from the routine nature of the work
3. Lack of promotion opportunities
4. The low pay that characterizes many part-time jobs.

There is currently no research available to either support these claims or to estimate the magnitude of their impact.

In short, most of the arguments for and against the expansion of part-time opportunities are based on anecdotal evidence at best. Research that is both internally and externally valid, and grounded in theory, is badly needed.

Endnotes

1. W. Deuterman, Jr., and S. Brown, "Voluntary Part-Time Workers: A Growing Part of the Labor Force," *Monthly Labor Review* 101 (June 1987).

2. Bureau of Labor Statistics, *Employment and Earnings* 31 (June 1984): Tables A9 and A31.

3. J. N. Hedges and S. J. Gallogly, "Full and Part-Time: A Review of the Definitions," *Monthly Labor Review* 100 (March 1977).

4. R. Graham, "In Permanent Part-Time Work, You Can't Beat the Hours," *Nation's Business* 67 (January 1979).

5. Deuterman and Brown, op. cit.

6. A. R. Cohen and H. Gadon. *Alternative Work Schedules: Integrating Individual and Organizational Needs* (Reading, Mass.: Addison-Wesley, 1978); P. Dickson, "When Two Halves Equal More Than One," *The Future of the Work Place: The Coming Revolution in Jobs* (New York: Iveybright and Talley, 1975).

7. "Free-Lance Execs," *Working Woman* (July 1982).

8. W. G. Scott, T. R. Mitchell, and P. H. Birnbaum, *Organization Theory: A Structural and Behavioral Analysis* (New York: Richard D. Irwin, 1981).

9. B. Most, "Job Sharers: Two Workers for the Price of One," *Kiwanis Magazine* (May 1981).

10. Cohen and Gadon, op. cit.

11. C. S. Granrose and E. Appelbaum, "The Efficiency of Temporary Help and Part-Time Employment," *Personnel Administrator* 31 (January 1986).

12. D. Robinson, "Control Data's Selby Plant Employs 100 Percent Part-Time Staff of Mothers and Students," *World of Work Report* 2 (September 1977).

13. B. Olmsted, "Job Sharing: A New Way to Work," *Personnel Journal* 56 (February 1977).

14. H. L. Sheppard, "NCOA Survey Shows Pronounced Preference for Part-Time Work," *Aging and Work* 4 (1981): 221–223.

15. Bureau of Labor Statistics, op. cit.

16. Cohen and Gadon, op. cit.

17. E. B. Jones and J. E. Long, "Part-Time Work and Human Capital Investment by Married Women," *Journal of Human Resources* 14 (1979): 563–578.

18. J. D. Owen, "Why Part-Time Workers Tend to Be in Low Wage Jobs," *Monthly Labor Review* 101 (June 1978).

19. Jones and Long, op. cit.

20. S. F. Meives, *Part-Time Work: A Multiperspective Analysis,* Doctoral dissertation (Madison: University of Wisconsin, 1979).

21. H. E. Miller and J. Terborg, "Job Attitudes of Part-Time and Full-Time Employees," *Journal of Applied Psychology* 64 (1979): 380–386.

22. N. Logan, C. A. Reilley, and K. H. Roberts, "Job Satisfaction among Part-Time and Full-Time Employees," *Journal of Vocational Behavior* 3 (1973): 33–41.

23. P. W. Hom, "Effects of Job Peripherality and Personal Characteristics on the Job Satisfaction of Part-Time Workers," *Academy of Management Journal* 22 (1979): 551–565.

24. D. T. Hall and F. E. Gordon, "Career Choices of Married Women: Effects on Conflict, Role Behavior, and Satisfaction," *Journal of Applied Psychology* 58 (1973): 42–48.

25. J. L. Pierce and R. B. Dunham, "Task Design: A Literature Review," *Academy of Management Review* 1 (April 1976): 83–87; R. W. Griffin, *Task Design: An Interpretive Approach* (Glenview, Ill.: Scott, Foresman, 1981); J. R. Hackman and G. R. Oldham, "Development of the Job Diagnostic Survey," *Journal of Applied Psychology* 80.

26. B. J. Eberhardt and A. B. Shani, "The Effects of Full-Time versus Part-Time Employment Status on Attitudes toward Specific Organizational Characteristics and Overall Job Satisfaction," *Academy of Management Journal* 27 (1984): 893–900.

27. Catalyst, *Part-Time Social Workers in Public Welfare* (New York, 1971).

28. J. Loblin, "Mutual Aid: Firms and Job Seekers Discover More Benefits of Part-Time Positions," *Wall Street Journal* (4 October 1978).

29. Meives, op. cit.

30. L. Peters, E. Jackofsky, and J. Salter, "Predicting Turnover: Comparing Part-Time and Full-Time Employees," *Journal of Occupational Behaviour* 2 (1981): 89–98.

31. R. P. Vecchio, "Demographic and Attitudinal Differences between Part-Time and Full-Time Employees," *Journal of Occupational Behaviour* 5 (1984): 213–218.

32. M. J. Gannon, "The Management of Peripheral Employees," *Personnel Journal* 54 (September 1975).

33. C. Greenwald and J. Liss, "Part-Time Work Can Bring High Productivity," *Harvard Business Review* 51 (September/October 1973).

34. S. J. Mahlin and J. Charles, "Peak-Time Pay for Part-Time Work," *Personnel Journal* 63 (November 1984).

35. Committee on Alternative Work Patterns and National Center for Productivity and Quality of Working Life, *Alternatives in the World of Work,* Washington, D.C., 1976.

36. Ibid.

37. Cohen and Gadon, op. cit.

38. Granrose and Appelbaum, op. cit.

39. Greenwald and Liss, op. cit.

40. Meives, op. cit.

41. E. J. LaPointe, "A Comparison of Full-Time and Part-Time Faculty Teaching Performances at an Indian Community College in South Dakota," *Dissertation Abstracts* 39 (March 1979).

42. Catalyst, op. cit.

43. "The Army of the Partly Employed," *Forbes* (1 March 1977).

44. Cohen and Gadon, op. cit.

45. "Part-Timers: Why Their Ranks Are Growing," *Savings and Loan News* 99 (April 1978).

46. Catalyst, *Constructing a Fringe-Benefits Package for Part-Time Employees* (New York, 1974).

47. J. S. Rosenbloom and G. V. Hallman, *Employee Benefit Planning* (New York: Prentice-Hall, 1981).

48. Miller and Terborg, op. cit.

49. R. Slocum, "Part-Time Faculty at an Urban University," *Dissertation Abstracts* 40 (January 1980).

50. Robinson, op. cit.

51. Owen, op. cit.

52. S. D. Nollen, "What Is Happening to Flexitime, Flexitour, Gliding Time, and the Variable Day? And Permanent Part-Time Employment? And the Four-Day Work Week?" *Across the Board* 17 (April 1980).

53. Owen, op. cit.

54. Granrose and Appelbaum, op. cit.

55. L. Rich, "Job Sharing: Another Way to Work," *Worklife* (May 1978).

56. Graham, op. cit.

57. Nollen, op. cit.

58. "Part-Timers: Why Their Ranks Are Growing," op. cit.

59. Graham, op. cit.

60. G. S. Meier, *Job Sharing: A New Pattern for Quality of Work and Life* (Kalamazoo, Mich.: Upjohn Institute for Employment Research, 1979).

61. Most, op. cit.

62. W. W. Macauley, "Developing Trends in the Temporary-Services Industry," *Personnel Administrator* 31 (January 1986).

63. M. L. Carey and K. I. Hazelbaken, "Employment Growth in the Temporary-Help Industry," *Monthly Labor Review* 109 (April 1986).

64. M. J. Gannon, "Preferences of Temporary Workers: Time, Variety, and Flexibility," *Monthly Labor Review* 107 (August 1984): 26–30.

65. Macauley, op. cit.

66. S. Rubinstein, "These Temps Don't Just Answer the Phone," *Business Week* (2 June 1986); S. Fenn, "Professional Temps Fill Top Positions," *Inc.* 8 (February 1986).

Chapter Five

Shift Work

The term *shift-work schedules* refers to a pattern of working-hour arrangements whereby employees work organizationally defined different blocks of time (e.g., 7 A.M.–3 P.M., 3–11 P.M., or 11 P.M.–7 A.M.) on a regular basis. Some workers stay on one shift permanently; others usually rotate across scheduling blocks on a weekly or monthly basis. Approximately one-fourth of the labor force in the United States works under some form of shift schedule, and this proportion has remained relatively constant in recent years.

The Impact of Shift Work

Most of the attention paid to alternative work schedules such as flexitime or compressed work weeks has been driven by a belief that an alternative schedule would be more attractive to workers. It has been hoped that a more attractive schedule would motivate more effective organizational behavior from employees and lead to greater satisfaction. Thus these schedules have been viewed as a tool for enhancing organizational effectiveness by satisfying the needs and desires of workers.

Shift work, however, is quite a different issue. The driving force behind shift work has been a desire to obtain more hours of productivity per day from physical rather than human resources. Shift work allows machines and buildings to be used for sixteen or twenty-four hours a day rather than eight. Thus the primary purpose underlying shift work has been financial rather than a consideration of employee needs and preferences. Although the employer reaps the greatest rewards, many employees also enjoy the benefits of shift work. As an incentive for working the presumably less-desirable shifts, employees are often given shift differentials in their hourly wages, ranging from a few cents per hour to substantial amounts. Other employees, especially those in two-career families with children, may desire shift work because it allows one or the other parent to be at home most of the time while still providing two incomes.

Despite these benefits most of the research conducted on shift work has focused on documenting the various types of problems experienced by the workers involved. These problems appear to be caused by the incompatibility of the nontraditional work hours with individual and community rhythms. Our discussion of the impact of shift work revolves around personal consequences (e.g., physical health, social activities, family effects, psychological reactions) and organizational consequences (e.g., employee performance, employee attitudes, turnover, attendance).

Physical Health

Several studies have focused on the physical-health consequences of shift work. These problems typically include sleeping, appetite and digestive, bodily elimination, and upper-gastrointestinal disturbances. Less-specific health problems have also been noted, as in a study of 350 Swedish shift workers who reported that they registered more medical complaints than those working regular day schedules.[1] Similarly, when a group of police officers switched from a shift schedule to a day schedule their cardiorespiratory fitness and blood pressure improved, and they were able to achieve higher work loads with less physiological strain. These results were attributed to the concurrent observation of improvements in sleep (i.e., duration, quality, and subsequent alertness) and greater regularity in their eating and recreational habits.[2]

Sleep.   A large number of studies have linked sleep problems to shift-work schedules. The problems identified typically include fewer total hours of sleep, shorter sleep periods, more interruptions to sleep, and more frequent noise disturbances. For example, traditional housing often does not successfully filter out noises that typically arise in a day-oriented world. As a result, the day sleep of shift workers has been found to be of significantly shorter duration (by about one and one-half hours), lower in quality (showing different rapid-eye-movement patterns), and characterized by a greater number of interruptions.[3] Further, social and community rhythms are generally geared to the more traditional daily-work schedule. Consequently they can compete with the sleep periods of the shift worker.

In one study work schedules were experimentally changed and the effects observed. As the number of shifts was reduced, there was an increase in the amount of sleep. With the change from a shift to a day schedule the amount of sleep required on employees' free days decreased, presumably due to the lower level of accumulated fatigue.[4] Another study of police officers changing from a shift to a day schedule reported that there were improvements in their sleep habits—they slept longer, had better-quality rest, and were more alert upon waking.

Even the specific shift worked has an effect on the employees. In a study of 885 food-processing industry employees exposed to four different work-scheduling arrangements (fixed days, afternoons, or nights; or rotating shifts) it was found that night-shift workers averaged the least amount of sleep and experienced the most interruptions. They, along with the rotating-shift workers, reported the most difficulty getting back to sleep once they awakened and both groups felt more tired and sleepy upon completion of their sleep period.[5]

The most frequent complaint of shift workers, however, concerns disrupted sleep. Research reports consistently conclude that shift work is associated with as much as four fewer hours of sleep per night, greater difficulty in getting to sleep, frequent awakenings during sleep (often disturbed by noise), and a general lack of feeling refreshed upon getting up.[6] In particular, workers on rotating shifts generally have a higher level of insomnia.[7]

Why do these sleep problems occur? One possibility is the lack of harmony between employees' circadian rhythms and their daily pattern of work. Specifically, circadian troughs (i.e., low periods in the twenty-four-hour cycle) are associated with lower levels of arousal and activation and therefore cause drowsiness while the worker is awake; circadian peaks (high periods in the cycle) produce high levels of arousal and therefore interfere with shift workers' attempts to sleep. Thus it may be that sleep problems are more a function of internal factors than external ones such as housing.[8]

Appetite and Digestion.   Shift work has also been associated with various types of disruptions of employee appetites and other digestive disturbances. Workers on the rotating shift in one study had poorer appetites than workers exposed to any of the three fixed shifts.[9] They also expressed dissatisfaction with their eating habits. In particular, their major concern was not being able to eat major meals with family members.

Elimination (bowel-movement) problems have been linked to employee difficulty in adapting to changing work schedules.[10] In addition, several investigators have claimed that shift work directly or indirectly causes various upper-gastrointestinal disorders as a function of workers' inability to obtain sufficient sleep.[11] Partial support for this observation stems from one study that reported the gastrointestinal functioning of employees improved following the change from a three- or four-shift schedule to a two-shift schedule.

Stress.   Apparently stress is produced by the nontraditional work schedule and its disharmony with family rhythms. Two specific stress symptoms observed have been migraine headaches and gastritis.[12] In addition, workers assigned to the "graveyard" (i.e., late night) shift have reported higher levels of tension than their day-shift counterparts.[13] In another study, a group of hospital workers on a fixed-shift schedule reported a lower level of psychological and physiological stress than their rotating-shift colleagues.[14] Possibly as a by-product of these stress levels, workers on rotating shifts have been found to consume more alcohol than employees working either fixed morning, afternoon, or night schedules.[15]

Fatigue.   Another health problem associated with shift-work schedules is fatigue. Hospital nurses in two settings reported that the "most serious health-related problem" they associated with shift work was the fatigue that accompanied the night and rotating schedules.[16] Other studies also confirm higher levels of fatigue among night-shift workers, apparently as a result of higher levels of sleeplessness following an interrupted and shorter sleeping period.[17]

Worker Injuries.   Surprisingly few studies have examined the accident rates or incidence of injuries of workers on shift schedules versus those on regular schedules. One partial examination of this phenomenon compared the injury rates for employees on the night and rotating shifts to the incident level for morning and afternoon shift-work employees and found the former group to have the higher rate.[18]

Only some shift workers experience physiological problems, of course, and it seems to be those who cannot adapt their own rhythmic functioning to the demands of the shift schedules. One interpretation is that some workers continue on shifts up to a breaking point—either biological or psychological—at which point their bodies become vulnerable to dysfunction.[19]

Social Activities

There is a limited amount of evidence about the impact of shift work on interaction with friends and family, participation in nonwork organizations, and leisure activities. In general, shift workers appear to reduce the frequency of contacts with friends but not with relatives. When they change from shift to more regular work, they report improvements in the social dimensions of their lives.[20]

Shift workers reduce the number of organizations they belong to and participate in away from work, presumably because of the irregularity with which they are able to attend functions.[21] Finally, with regard to employees' use of free time, a two-sample study of workers on rotating shifts found that they spent more leisure time alone than did their colleagues on fixed schedules.[22]

Family Effects

The balance of evidence seems to suggest that shift-work schedules are related to family and marital problems. In shift-work families, there are reports of general family disturbances, a higher incidence of sexual problems, higher divorce rates, and general role-fulfillment problems of the husband/father. These problems can apparently be attributed to the fact that the shift worker is out of phase with the family and its activity schedule, and this in turn causes the family to be at least partly out of phase with the surrounding community.[23]

Staines and Pleck investigated the family-life effects attributable to nonstandard work schedules. They note that working nonstandard days as well as nonstandard hours was associated with poorer quality family life.[24] When the work week included Saturdays and Sundays, fewer hours per week were spent with children and doing housework. Constantly changing schedules were associated with more family conflict. However, it is equally important to note that these negative effects of shift work on family life are apparently moderated by one critical variable: the employees' perceptions that they have flexibility to permanently change the pattern of days or hours worked.[25]

Taking another view, some studies have shown that shift work actually seems to hinder relations with nonfamily members more than it does with family.[26] Furthermore, a rotating shift seems to be more detrimental to family relations than a fixed-shift schedule.[27] There is, however, considerable variance in the level of work-schedule hindrance across studies, leading to the tentative conclusion that the level of interference may be more a function of family characteristics than of the schedule itself.

Finally, it should be noted that the effects of shift work on the family are not all negative. Some activities are apparently even facilitated by shift-work schedules, such as the amount of the shift workers' time spent on housework, shopping, maintenance of the house, and running errands. In sum, it appears that organized activities (those community functions with inflexible schedules) are typically hindered by shift work, whereas the more flexible activities (those functions within one's control) may even be facilitated, perhaps out of a desire to compensate for the loss of participation in the others.

Psychological Reactions

Popular belief might suggest that shift workers suffer from various minor psychological disorders, perhaps as a by-product of the physical dysfunctions they naturally experience. However, the evidence is somewhat incomplete, and certainly mixed, in this regard. Early studies found that factors like self-esteem, anxiety, and conflict-pressure were unrelated to shift work.[28] More recently, Akerstedt and Torsvall observed the change in psychological states that accompanied an experimental change in the number of shifts worked.[29] The employees' moods improved when the number of shifts decreased. On the other hand, no significant differences in mood states were found in another study of four different shift-work conditions.[30]

Two other studies did report specific psychological differences between shift and nonshift workers. Zedeck's investigation of power-company employees found that shift workers were more irascible late in their shift period than were day workers at similar stages in their daily schedule.[31] In addition, enthusiasm was reported to be lowest for the "graveyard" group of workers. In another study, psychological depression was found to be higher for those manufacturing employees working under a rotating shift, but this was not replicated in a hospital sample.[32] Consequently the observation of a linkage between psychological depression and rotating shifts may be a function of the technology or character of the job.

Employee Performance

Early reviews of the literature on the effects of shift work on employee productivity were somewhat confusing and inconclusive.[33] The balance of the evidence indicated that there might be a cumulative effect from extended shift work that would predictably cause productivity to decline. This was supported by two early studies providing evidence that night workers not only made more mistakes than day workers but also had lower overall productivity.[34]

A more recent review of six studies by Folkard and Monk revealed that shift workers' performance was both slower and less accurate than straight day-workers' performance, and this conclusion has been supported by other research reports.[35] Other studies have concluded that employee reaction time suffers as a result of night work; and it also appears that rotating shifts are more detrimental to employee performance than straight shift work.[36]

What accounts for the performance decrements of workers on shift schedules? One clue is found in the studies of Indian textile-mill workers conducted by Malaviya and Ganesh.[37] They found that some workers actually performed *better* when they were assigned to a night shift and concluded that "afternoon types" may adjust better to shift work. Other workers may find the late shifts largely incompatible with their circadian rhythms.[38] However, despite early declines in an employee's productivity and efficiency when work schedules are not attuned to the established waking cycle, it is reasonable to assume that some employees can adapt themselves to shift work. Some observers suggest that this adaptation is easiest when employees' shifts rotate clockwise—from day to evening to overnight.[39]

Employee Attitudes

Several studies have investigated employee attitudes toward shift work. Although the preponderance of evidence suggests employees dislike many aspects of it, the studies also reveal some positive elements. On the positive side, a study of nurses indicated that they liked the camaraderie they developed with their coworkers as well as the lower number of interruptions from their supervisors when working a shift-work schedule.[40]

In contrast to that isolated conclusion, other studies report negative attitudes, either directly or indirectly. For example, employees who changed from a three- or four-shift schedule to a two-shift schedule developed a more positive attitude toward the latter.[41] Shift workers had more negative attitudes toward their hours of work than those employees working a regular day shift. Seventy-five percent of workers rotating across three- or four-shift schedules reported wanting to change their schedules. Crosscultural confirmation of this dislike appeared in a study of British steelworkers on shift work.[42] The vast majority of respondents characterized the night shift as tiring, restricting their social life, and causing drowsiness. In general they were unhappy with the effects on their social life, the consequent irregular sleeping and eating times, and the overall idea of having to work at night.

There is little direct evidence available regarding preferences for various schedules (other than regular days). A single study compared the attitudes of 671 continuous-process employees on a midnight to noon schedule with those on a noon to midnight schedule. The results showed that the P.M. schedule was more strongly favored than the A.M. shift.[43] The abnormal length of shifts in this study makes the generalizability of the conclusions suspect and the results also run counter to a persuasive argument advanced by Dunham.[44] He suggested that most communities are oriented to some degree toward work schedules where people have a "window of freedom" between approximately 4 P.M. and 12 midnight. Afternoon-shift workers and night-shift workers find themselves at least partially in conflict with this pattern. Consequently, he predicted employee responses to the idea of working shift schedules will vary as a function of these community rhythms. If the social community has not adapted to the needs of shift workers a higher incidence of attitudinal and other problems can be expected.

A final cautionary note is in order regarding attitudes toward shift work. Peterson suggested that it would be useful to discover whether the frequently observed negative attitudes of shift workers are inevitably a product of the unique characteristics of a specific department or organization.[45] In his interviews with 272 nurses in thirty hospitals, he found no significant differences in attitudes across shifts; the shift on which a nurse was working explained a maximum of 2 percent of the variance. He concluded that intershift differences in attitudes may often be an illusion, unique to the specific department or job type.

Turnover

Four studies conducted among Swedish steelworkers explored the self-reported reasons why they terminated their employment.[46] A major cause frequently mentioned was dislike of shift work.

Likewise Herbert studied the behavioral intentions of shift workers, assessing their reported willingness to stay versus quit.[47] He concluded that employee dissatisfaction with shift work was a major contributor in intentions to leave. Clearly, those who actually quit reported they were dissatisfied with shift work and saw it as interfering with their leisure-time activities.

Attendance

As with turnover, very few studies of the relationship between shift schedules and employee absenteeism have been conducted. Of those reported here, one suggested a positive relationship, one a negative association, and the third addresses other variables.

A change in work schedules from shift work to straight-day arrangements was experimentally conducted in one study. The results showed that the workers subsequently reduced their number of sick-day absences.[48] By contrast, another study examined two years' worth of organizational records to see if there was a significant difference in absenteeism rates across different shifts.[49] No one main reason was found for shift differences.

There is some evidence, however, indicating that there are pronounced *individual* differences in the relationship between shift work and attendance behavior. Both employees' willingness and ability to go to work vary across times within the twenty-four-hour day.[50] When the shift cycle is rapid, fatigue and the inability to adapt may produce absenteeism. Furthermore, certain days of the week are more susceptible to shift workers' absenteeism.

Table 5–1 provides a summary of shift work–related problems for fixed, slowly rotating, and rapidly rotating schedules.

Table 5–1.   Shift Work–Related Problems

	Type of Shift Schedule		
Problem	*Fixed*[a]	*Slowly Rotating*	*Rapidly Rotating*
Sleep	−	∘	∘
Appetite or digestion	+	−	∘
Stress	+	−	∘
Fatigue	−	−	∘
Injuries	+	+	−
Social interactions	−	−	∘
Family interactions	−	−	∘
Psychological	−	−	−
Performance	−	−	∘
Attitudes	−	−	−
Turnover	−	−	−
Absenteeism	+	+	−

> [a]   For nonday-shift workers
> +   Few or no problems
> −   Some problems
> ∘   Frequent or severe problems

Adjustment

The vast bulk of the research literature has examined attitudes such as satisfaction and behaviors such as absenteeism as presumed products of shift schedules. As we have seen, results have indicated a variety of problems. This section examines alternative explanations for why such problems may emerge while noting simultaneously that there is no simple and direct relationship between shift work and employee responses.

Three dimensions appear in the various discussions of employee adjustment to shift-work schedules:

- ► The individual's circadian rhythms
- ► The rhythms in the social or community network
- ► Characteristics of the schedule itself.

Circadian Rhythms

A number of studies have shown that some employees on shift work suffer from what is called *shift maladaption syndrome*.[51] In essence, their bodily clocks cannot adapt easily to shift changes and thus their hours of work may not be synchronized with their natural circadian rhythms. Three dimensions have been shown to differentiate between those who adapt and those who do not:

- ► Flexibility or rigidity of sleeping habits
- ► Ability or inability to overcome drowsiness
- ► Morningness or eveningness.[52]

Evening types appear to have circadian rhythms that result in greater flexibility of sleep habits and seem to adjust more successfully to shift-work schedules.[53]

Schedule Characteristics

Numerous suggestions have emerged for bringing about a better fit between shift work and employees' personal needs, with the presumption that work can be better structured for the mutual benefit of both worker and employer.[54] The fact that many of these suggestions directly contradict one another illustrates the diversity of opinions about the basis and potential solutions to shift-work problems. Among some of the more substantial shift-work features identified are:

1. Rapid rotation every two-four days (as opposed to the more common weekly rotation) is expected to minimize the disturbance of the employee's biological rhythms and to avoid an accumulation of sleep deficits.[55]

2. Permanent assignment to a single shift allows even workers on stable night shifts to show a better adjustment of body-temperature rhythms than rotating-shift workers.[56]

3. If shifts must rotate, do so by incorporating delays between successive phases and making the intervals long enough for employees to adjust to each new schedule.[57]

4. Delay the start of the morning shift by an hour or so to reduce its impact upon normal sleep patterns.[58]

5. Avoid short intervals of time between any two shifts so as to minimize the extreme fatigue associated with back-to-back shifts.[59]

6. Rotate shifts clockwise, from mornings to afternoons to nights.[60]

7. Create a system of relatively predictable shift changes to permit employees to plan and schedule their leisure-time activities.[61]

8. Consider shortening the night shift somewhat, while slightly lengthening the morning and afternoon shifts, to make the night shift less noxious to participants.[62]

Community Rhythms

Numerous observers of shift work have argued that it is important to harmonize the individual's work and personal lives. Shipley and Cook noted that well-being is high when the worker's home and work rhythms are compatible.[63] Frost and Jamal introduced the notion of "closeness of fit" between the hours of work and the constraints or opportunities vis-à-vis leisure and voluntary activities.[64] They predicted that under conditions of a high level of fit, workers would report favorable attitudes and engage in more acceptable behaviors; and this was empirically verified. In a separate study Jamal suggested the importance to employees of "routine formation" in their lives.[65] Rotating shifts make it difficult for people to establish routines and they therefore experience a more disrupted life. As a result, they may have lower levels of job satisfaction, emotional and psychological well-being, and organizational commitment. They may also exhibit higher levels of behavioral withdrawal.

Support for the impact of shift work upon satisfaction, emotional and psychological well-being, and commitment is found in a comprehensive study that focused on the relationship between shift work schedules and employee health, adaptation, turnover intentions, and satisfaction.[66] Employees who were satisfied with their work schedule took fewer sick days, reported less trouble sleeping, used less medication, and adjusted more quickly to new meal times and sleep schedules. In particular, satisfaction with a work schedule was highest for those employees who lived in communities with rhythms that fit their work schedules. In other words, the majority of worker problems occur when the worker is out of phase with either established physiological or social rhythms. But when there is harmony between the hours of work and the employee's physical and social rhythms, the level of adjustment predictably increases and the negative consequences associated with shift work lessens.

Conclusion

The general conclusion that emerges from the literature on shift work is that there are a number of negative worker reactions and problems that stem either directly or indirectly from these schedules. Rotating shifts, as well as fixed afternoon and evening shifts, seem to be associated with greater levels of problems than fixed day-shift schedules. In particular, health problems, including alcohol-consumption levels, poorer appetites, lower levels of sleep quality, and higher levels of fatigue, have been documented by a number of investigators. Higher levels of stress and interrupted gastrointestinal functioning also may accompany nontraditional work schedules.

Although the evidence is not overwhelming, it appears that there are a greater number of accidents and a higher frequency of injuries on the night shift when compared to either the morning or afternoon schedules. An employee's social life is often impaired through assignment to shift schedules, with reductions in opportunities to participate in traditional social engagements and recreational activities. Consequently shift workers typically spend more time in solitary free-time activities.

With regard to work-related attitudes, employees are generally more favorably oriented toward the traditional day schedule than toward the night shift or rotating shifts. Workers on the latter schedules are more likely to be predisposed toward eventually terminating employment. With regard to performance, available evidence suggests that employees are more productive on fixed shifts rather than rotating ones.

Endnotes

1. L. Torsvall and T. Akerstedt, "Summary of a Longitudinal Study of Shift Work Effects on Well-Being," *Reports from the Laboratory for Clinical Stress Research* 926 (November 1978): 1–6.

2. B. Peacock, R. Glube, M. Miller, and P. Clure, "Police Officers' Response to Eight- and Twelve-Hour Shift Schedules," *Ergonomics* 26 (May 1983): 479–483.

3. A. J. Tilley, R. T. Wilkinson, P. S. G. Warren, B. Watson, and M. Drud, "The Sleep and Performance of Shift Workers," *Human Factors* 24 (June 1982): 629–641.

4. T. Akerstedt and L. Torsvall, "Experimental Changes in Shift Schedules— Their Effects on Well-Being," *Ergonomics* 21 (October 1978): 849–856.

5. M. J. Smith and M. J. Colligan, "Health and Safety Consequences of Shift Work in the Food-Processing Industry," *Ergonomics* 25 (1982): 133–144.

6. T. Akerstedt and L. Torsvall, "Shift Work: Shift Dependent Well-Being and Individual Differences," *Ergonomics* 24 (April 1981): 265–273; P. Knauth, E. Kies-

swatter, W. Ottman, M. J. Karvonen, and J. Rutenfranz, "Time–Budget Studies of Policemen in Weekly or Swiftly Rotating Shift Systems," *Applied Ergonomics* 14 (April 1983): 247–252.

7. C. A. Czeisler, M. C. Moore-Ede, and R. M. Coleman, "Rotating Shift Work Schedules that Disrupt Sleep Are Improved by Applying Circadian Principles," *Science* 217 (July 1982): 460–463.

8. T. Akerstedt and M. Gillberg, "Displacement of the Sleep Period and Sleep Deprivation: Implications for Shift Work," *Human Neurobiology* 1 (October 1982): 163–171.

9. Smith and Colligan, op. cit.

10. N. Kleitman, *Sleep and Wakefulness* (Chicago: University of Chicago Press, 1963); R. Duesberg and W. Weiss, "Reichsgesundheitsblatt," *Arbeitsschutz* 3 (August 1939); cited by P. E. Mott et al., *Shift Work* (Ann Arbor: University of Michigan Press, 1965).

11. B. Bjerner and A. Swenssen, "Shift Work and Rhythm," *ACTA Medica Scandinavica, Supp* 278 (1953): 102–107.

12. J. C. Hood and N. Milazzo, "Shift Work, Stress, and Well-Being," *Personnel Administrator* 29 (December 1984): 95–105.

13. S. Zedeck, S. E. Jackson, and E. Summers, "Shift Work Schedules and Their Relationship to Health, Adaptation, Satisfaction, and Turnover," *Academy of Management Journal* 26 (1983): 297–310.

14. M. Jamal and S. M. Jamal, "Work and Nonwork Experiences of Employees on Fixed and Rotating Shifts: An Empirical Assessment," *Journal of Vocational Behavior* 20 (1982): 282–293.

15. Smith and Colligan, op. cit.; Akerstedt and Gillberg, op. cit.

16. Zedeck et al., op. cit.

17. Smith and Colligan, op. cit.; Akerstedt and Gillberg, op. cit.

18. Smith and Colligan, op. cit.

19. M. Frese and K. Okonek, "Reasons to Leave Shift Work and Psychological and Psychosomatic Complaints of Former Shift Workers," *Journal of Applied Psychology* 69 (1984): 509–514.

20. Akerstedt and Torsvall, 1978, op. cit.

21. P. E. Mott, F. C. Mann, Q. McLoughlin, and D. P. Warwick, *Shift Work* (Ann Arbor: University of Michigan Press, 1965).

22. Jamal and Jamal, op. cit.

23. Mott et al., op. cit.

24. G. L. Staines and J. H. Pleck, "Nonstandard Work Schedules and Family Life," *Journal of Applied Psychology* 69 (1984): 515–523.

25. G. L. Staines and J. H. Pleck, "Work Schedule Flexibility and Family Life," *Journal of Occupational Behaviour* 7 (1986): 147–153.

26. A. Herbert, "The Influence of Shift Work on Leisure Activities: A Study with Repeated Measurement," *Ergonomics* 26 (June 1983): 565–574.

27. Jamal and Jamal, op. cit.

28. Mott et al., op. cit.

29. Akerstedt and Torsvall, 1978, op. cit.

30. Smith and Colligan, op. cit.

31. Zedeck et al., op. cit.

32. Jamal and Jamal, op. cit.

33. F. C. Mann and L. R. Hoffman, *Automation and the Worker* (New York: Henry Holt, 1960).

34. Bjerner and Swenssen, op. cit.; E. Ulich, "Zur Frage der Belastung des Arbeitenden Menschen Durch Nacht-Und Shicktarbeit," *Psychologische Rundschau* 8 (1957): 42–61; cited by P. E. Mott et al., op. cit.

35. S. Folkard and T. H. Monk, "Towards a Predictive Test of Adjustment to Shift Work," *Ergonomics* 22 (January 1979): 79–91; M. Glenville and R. T. Wilkinson, "Portable Devices for Measuring Performance in the Field: The Effects of Sleep Deprivation and Night Shift on the Performance of Computer Operators," *Ergonomics* 22 (August 1979): 927–933.

36. Tilley et al., op. cit.; Jamal and Jamal, op. cit.

37. P. Malaviya and K. Ganesh, "Shift Work and Individual Differences in the Productivity of Weavers in an Indian Textile Mill," *Journal of Applied Psychology* 61 (1976): 774–776; P. Malaviya and K. Ganesh, "Individual Differences in Productivity across Types of Work Shift," *Journal of Applied Psychology* 62 (1977): 527–528.

38. Kleitman, op. cit.

39. "Working Rotating Shifts Takes Toll on Health, Researchers Say," *Duluth News-Tribune and Herald* (1 June 1986): 12A.

40. Hood and Milazzo, op. cit.

41. Akerstedt and Torsvall, 1978, op. cit.

42. A. A. I. Wedderbaun, "Some Suggestions for Increasing the Usefulness of Psychological and Sociological Studies of Shift Work," *Ergonomics* 21 (October 1978): 827–833.

43. J. A. Breaugh, "The Twelve-Hour Work Day: Differing Employee Reactions," *Personnel Psychology* 36 (1983): 277–288.

44. R. B. Dunham, "Shift Work: A Review and Theoretical Analysis," *Academy of Management Review* 2 (1977): 624–634.

45. M. F. Peterson, "Attitudinal Differences among Work Shifts: What Do They Mean?," *Academy of Management Journal* 28 (1985): 723–732.

46. Torsvall and Akerstedt, op. cit.

47. Herbert, op. cit.

48. Torsvall and Akerstedt, op. cit.

49. S. E. Markham, F. Dansereau, Jr., and J. A. Alutto, "On the Use of Shift as an Independent Variable in Absenteeism Research," *Journal of Occupational Psychology* 55 (1982): 225–231.

50. N. Nicholson, P. Jackson, and G. Hawes, "Shift Work and Absence: An Analysis of Temporal Trends," *Journal of Occupational Psychology* 51 (1978): 137.

51. "Working Rotating Shifts Takes Toll on Health, Researchers Say," *Duluth News-Tribune and Herald* (1 June 1986): 12A. Also see S. Siwolop, "Helping Workers Stay Awake at the Switch," *Business Week* (8 December 1986): 108.

52. S. Folkard, T. H. Monk, and M. C. Lobban, "Towards a Predictive Test of Adjustment to Shift Work," *Ergonomics* 22 (January 1979): 79–91.

53. F. W. Finger, "Circadian Rhythms: Implications for Psychology," *New Zealand Psychologist* 11 (January 1982): 1–12.

54. S. Folkard and T. Monk, eds., *Hours of Work: Temporal Factors in Work Scheduling* (New York: John Wiley and Sons, 1985).

55. A. Reinberg, N. Vieus, P. Andlauer, and M. Smolensky, "Tolerance to Shift Work: A Chronobiological Approach," *Advanced Biological Psychiatry* 11 (1983): 35–

47; P. Knauth, J. Rutenfranz, M. J. Karvonen, K. Undeutsch, F. Klimmer, and W. Ottman, "Analysis of 120 Shift Systems of the Police in the Federal Republic of Germany," *Applied Ergonomics* 14 (June 1983): 133–137.

56. K. Dahlgren, "Adjustment of Circadian Rhythms and EEG Sleep Functions to Day and Night Sleep among Permanent Night Workers and Rotating-Shift Workers," *Psychophysiology* 18 (April 1981): 381–391.

57. Czeisler et al., op. cit.

58. Knauth et al., op. cit.

59. Ibid.

60. Folkard et al., op. cit.; Knauth et al., op. cit.

61. Knauth et al., op. cit.

62. Ibid.

63. P. Shipley and T. C. Cook, "Human Factors Studies of the Working Hours of U.K. Ships' Pilots, Part 2: A Survey of Work Scheduling Problems and Their Social Consequences," *Applied Ergonomics* 11 (March 1980): 151–159.

64. P. J. Frost and M. Jamal, "Shift Work, Attitudes, and Reported Behavior: Some Associations between Individual Characteristics and Hours of Work and Leisure," *Journal of Applied Psychology* 64 (1979): 77–81.

65. M. Jamal, "Shift Work Related to Job Attitudes, Social Participation, and Withdrawal Behavior: A Study of Nurses and Industrial Workers," *Personnel Psychology* 34 (February 1981): 535–547.

66. Zedeck et al., op. cit.

Part Three

Organizational Applications: How to Do It

Chapter Six

Exploring and Selecting

Work Schedules

▶   Part Two dealt with the experiences of a wide range of organizations that have used hundreds of different types of work schedules. As you read about the experiences of these organizations, you may have been intrigued by some of the alternative work schedules. You may also have found some things you liked and some things you disliked about the several types of schedules. And you may have wondered whether a particular schedule which worked quite well for one organization would work in yours. How would your employees feel about it? How would your customers or clients react to it? Would your organization benefit from it?

    Unfortunately it is not possible to provide a list to identify which alternative schedule would best fit your organization's needs. As the reviews of the literature in the preceding chapters made clear, each alternative schedule has both advantages and disadvantages. In one organization, for example, employees may think a four-day work week is wonderful because it gives them an extra day off each week. But employees at another organization may react quite negatively to the four-day schedule because it requires them to work two more hours each day. To anticipate the reactions to an alternative schedule you are likely to receive from employees you must develop an organizational diagnostic and evaluation process.

    How can you identify the strengths and weaknesses of your current schedule? What is a good way to determine the potential advantages and disadvantages of various other schedules that interest you? Is there a method you can use to compare your schedule to possible alternatives? The primary purpose of this section is to describe a systematic procedure you can use to

- ► Evaluate the merits of your current schedules
- ► Identify viable alternative schedules
- ► Determine whether one of these alternatives would be desirable for your organization.

Chapters Six and Seven are intended to help you design, implement, and evaluate the effectiveness of one or more alternative work schedules. Whether you want to implement a totally new schedule or simply refine your existing one to meet organizational and employee needs, the procedures described here can save you time, effort, and money. More important, a systematic procedure will reduce the uncertainties involved in implementing an alternate schedule. Most important, of course, these procedures can help identify a schedule that makes more effective use of your human resources.

Before you examine our process for evaluating work schedules, let us once again emphasize that these two chapters do not provide you with the one answer to the appropriate schedule for your organization. Rather, they present you with tools you can use to identify alternative schedules appropriate for your organization and to accurately predict their effects.

Overview of the Process

There are many ways to design, implement, and evaluate alternative work schedules. No matter which method you choose, the process should be done in a systematic, comprehensive fashion to maximize its success. This chapter offers a systematic approach that has proven successful for some organizations. The process is described one step at a time and includes a specific illustration of how it can be applied.

There are several distinct steps to the process outlined in these two chapters (see Figure 6–1). The first step involves specification of the objectives for an alternative schedule. In other words, what do you hope to accomplish by revising or replacing the existing work schedule? In Step 2 you identify a list of feasible alternative schedules to explore. The third step involves collecting information from employees, management, and perhaps from external constituents such as clients, customers, or suppliers. During Step 4 you evaluate the information collected. This evaluation includes determining whether there is in fact a viable and desired alternate schedule. Step 5 consists of planning the implementation of a change to a new schedule. The sixth step is the actual implementation. In Step 7 you evaluate the results, benefits and

Figure 6–1. Steps for Designing, Implementing, and Evaluating Alternative Work Schedules

1. Specify the objectives for an alternative schedule.
2. Make a list of potential alternative schedules.
3. Collect information.
4. Evaluate information.
5. Plan for implementation of a new schedule.
6. Implement alternative schedule.
7. Evaluate the results (advantages and limitations) of the new schedule.
8. Fine-tune the new schedule.

problems alike, of the new schedule. The eighth and final step involves fine-tuning the alternative schedule based on your evaluation of its effectiveness.

Step 1: Specifying Objectives

Unfortunately the majority of organizations that have explored or implemented alternative schedules have probably done so without giving adequate thought to the specific objectives they hoped to accomplish. Many organizations have adopted an alternative schedule in the naive belief that it would serve as a cure-all for a variety of organizational ailments. Other organizations have erred by focusing on a narrow and limited set of objectives. Still others have set inappropriate or unreasonably optimistic objectives.

The first step in designing an alternative schedule is to consider and specify the objectives you hope to attain through its use. After reading the earlier chapters in this book, you probably have thought of some potential advantages that alternative schedules could provide to your organization. Perhaps you have a problem you need to address, such as an unusually high turnover rate for certain types of employees or an inability to recruit skilled workers effectively. It may be that you already know your employees are dissatisfied with the current work schedule; or that you are concerned about organizational-effectiveness issues such as work-flow coordination or service provided to customers or clients. Alternatively, the objectives may have less to do with fixing current problems than with avoiding future ones or capitalizing on opportunities for improving the organization and its employees.

Figure 6–2 helps you to specify the objectives you could accomplish for your own organization. In addition to defining an array of possible objectives, many managers find it useful to rank-order the importance of the objectives before beginning their search for an alternative schedule. It is much easier to identify an appropriate alternative if you have first specified carefully what you want it to do for you.

Figure 6–2. List of Possible Objectives for an Alternative Schedule

My Opinion(s)

1. Fix problems
   A.
   B.
   C.
2. Avoid problems
   A.
   B.
   C.
3. Seize opportunities
   A.
   B.
   C.
   D.

Top Execs' Opinion(s)

1. Fix problems
   A.
   B.
   C.
2. Avoid problems
   A.
   B.
   C.
3. Seize opportunities
   A.
   B.
   C.
   D.

Key Managers' Opinion(s)

1. Fix problems
   A.
   B.
   C.
2. Avoid problems
   A.
   B.
   C.
3. Seize opportunities
   A.
   B.
   C.
   D.

Union Rep's Opinion(s)

1. Fix problems
   A.
   B.
   C.
2. Avoid problems
   A.
   B.
   C.
3. Seize opportunities
   A.
   B.
   C.
   D.

Other Important Opinion(s)

1. Fix problems
   A.
   B.
   C.
2. Avoid problems
   A.
   B.
   C.
3. Seize opportunities
   A.
   B.
   C.
   D.

Other Important Opinion(s)

1. Fix problems
   A.
   B.
   C.
2. Avoid problems
   A.
   B.
   C.
3. Seize opportunities
   A.
   B.
   C.
   D.

Rank-Order Importance of Objectives

1.
2.
3.
4.
5.

6.
7.
8.
9.
10.

When specifying objectives it is politically advisable to consult key internal and external constituents. These are people such as top executives, key managers from each functional area, operations managers, and union (employee) representatives who would be involved in either deciding whether to implement an alternative or evaluating the effectiveness of the implemented alternative. Upon completion of Step 1 you should have a written set of objectives such as that shown in Figure 6–3.

Before proceeding to Step 2, however, you should submit these written objectives to a reality test. Is it really reasonable (based on prior research) to expect that an alternative schedule will produce the effects specified in these objectives? Have other organizations successfully met objectives of this type through alternative schedules? Is there sufficient reason to believe that your organization could hope to do so? The best objectives are those that are difficult, specific, reachable, and accepted by those involved. It is unlikely that organizational members will work to achieve these objectives unless they are con-

Figure 6–3. Sample Organizational Objectives

Objective 1: Increase satisfaction level for at least 75 percent of all employees
1. Is this objective difficult?
2. Is this objective specific?
3. Is this objective reachable?
4. Will an alternative schedule help to attain this objective?
5. Comments:

Objective 2: Reduce turnover from 45 percent to 30 percent among employees who are young, single parents
1. Is this objective difficult?
2. Is this objective specific?
3. Is this objective reachable?
4. Will an alternative schedule help to attain this objective?
5. Comments:

Objective 3: Increase by 25 percent the number of qualified applicants for entry-level technical job openings
1. Is this objective difficult?
2. Is this objective specific?
3. Is this objective reachable?
4. Will an alternative schedule help to attain this objective?
5. Comments:

Objective 4: Increase by 25 percent the proportion of candidates who accept job offers from the organization
1. Is this objective difficult?
2. Is this objective specific?
3. Is this objective reachable?
4. Will an alternative schedule help to attain this objective?
5. Comments:

sistent with individual and organizational values and overall organizational objectives.

Step 2: Identifying Potential Alternative Schedules

As discussed in Part Two, there are numerous work-schedule variations. In Step 2 you need to identify a relatively small subset of these. Suggestions for viable alternatives can emerge from many different sources: some based on experience such as that previously encountered within your organization, some based on personal experiences you or others have had at other organizations, published reports about other organizations, and empirical research summaries such as those provided in this book. Creative ideas for alternative schedules can also be generated by individuals, both managerial and nonmanagerial, within the organization. Useful proposals may be sought from union representatives. Management typically decides which of these alternatives to consider seriously, but joint labor–management cooperation throughout the process is advisable.

It is most constructive to generate a comprehensive list of potential alternatives before evaluating their merits. Premature evaluation often results in overlooking other very useful possibilities. We suggest that you use input from all of the sources mentioned above to identify an extensive list of alternative schedules such as that shown in Figure 6–4. You should then inspect them on a schedule-by-schedule basis, removing only those alternatives that are clearly inappropriate. In other words, do not delete an alternative at this stage unless there is almost no chance that it could be implemented effectively. If you do find it necessary to eliminate a schedule, you may wish to keep a record stating why it is not—and cannot be made—feasible. Agreement on this should be obtained from the key constituents mentioned earlier.

After you have completed the preliminary weeding-out process, subject the remaining alternative schedules to their first detailed evaluation. During this assessment, examine each alternative from the perspective of how well it is expected to meet each of the objectives identified in Step 1. Figure 6–5 is a sample rating form to illustrate this process. Your evaluation should be based on information available in the literature and your knowledge of the specific organizational situation. From the results of this subjective evaluation, you should identify a key subset of one to five alternatives that you wish to consider in much greater depth.

Step 3: Systematic Collection of Data

In Step 2 you identified at least one alternative schedule you believe would help you accomplish the objectives specified in Step 1. In Step 4 you will

Figure 6–4.   Potential Alternative Schedules

Current Schedule
5/40 Fixed: Monday-Friday, 8 A.M.-4:30 P.M., 30-minute lunch break

Other 5/40 Fixed Schedules
1. Monday-Friday, 7:30 A.M.-4 P.M., 30-minute lunch break
2. Monday-Friday, 8:30 A.M.-5 P.M., 30-minute lunch break
3. Monday-Friday, 9 A.M.-5:30 P.M., 30-minute lunch break
4. Monday-Friday, 8 A.M.-5 P.M., 60-minute lunch break
5. Monday-Friday, 7:30 A.M.-4:30 P.M., 30-minute lunch break

Compressed Schedules
6. 4/40   Monday-Thursday for all employees
7. 4/40   Tuesday-Friday for all employees
8. 4/40   Monday-Thursday for half, Tuesday-Friday for rest of employees
9. 4.5/40 With Friday afternoon off
10. 4.5/40 With Monday morning off

Staggered Schedules
11. 7-3:30, 7:15-3:45, 7:30-4, 7:45-4:15, 8-4:30
12. 7-3:30, 7:30-4, 8-4:30, 8:30-5
13. 6-2:30, 7-3:30, 8-4:30, 9-5:30

Flexible Schedules
14. Flexitime, core hours 10-12 and 1-3
15. Flexitime, core hours 1-3
16. Flexitime, core hours 10-12
17. Flexitime, no core hours

evaluate the alternative(s) and compare it or them to your existing work schedule. Step 3 is the stage where you collect data by using a survey to gather a variety of information, which makes later evaluation possible. This information can aid your understanding of employee preferences and help you anticipate the effects alternative schedules might have on organizational effectiveness, interference with the activities of employees, attitudes toward the schedules, and a variety of other worker reactions.

To help you develop your own survey containing specific items you wish to include, we have provided a sample survey in Appendix C. The following sections explore issues related to its administration and scoring (using microcomputer-based surveys) and designing feedback reports to communicate the survey results to employees.

Survey Design

Before we discuss how you might actually design a survey, let us review the types of questions you should consider. The first section of the survey

Figure 6–5.   Objectives Rating Form

Directions: Each of the alternative schedules listed below could influence each of the four objectives listed on this page. For each schedule, circle the number that best corresponds to the degree to which you expect that schedule would have a positive or negative effect on attaining each objective. If you feel the schedule would neither aid nor hamper reaching the

Objective 1: Increase satisfaction for at least 75% of employees

Schedule	Very Negative Effect	Negative Effect	No Effect	Positive Effect	Very Positive Effect
1. 5/40 fixed, M–F, 7:30–4	1	2	3	4	5
2. 5/40 fixed, M–F, 8:30–5	1	2	3	4	5
3. 5/40 fixed, M–F, 9–5:30	1	2	3	4	5
4. 5/40 fixed, M–F, 8–5	1	2	3	4	5
5. 5/40 fixed, M–F, 7:30–4:30	1	2	3	4	5
6. 4/40 comp., M–Th for all employees	1	2	3	4	5
7. 4/40 comp., T–F for all employees	1	2	3	4	5
8. 4/40 comp., M–Th/half, T–F/rest	1	2	3	4	5
9. 4.5/40 comp., Fri. P.M. off	1	2	3	4	5
10. 4.5/40 comp., Mon. A.M. off	1	2	3	4	5
11. Staggered, 7–3:30, 7:15–3:45, etc.	1	2	3	4	5
12. Staggered, 7–3:30, 7:30–4, etc.	1	2	3	4	5
13. Staggered, 6–2:30, etc.	1	2	3	4	5
14. Flexible, core hours 10–12 and 1–3	1	2	3	4	5
15. Flexible, core hours 1–3	1	2	3	4	5
16. Flexible, core hours 10–12	1	2	3	4	5
17. Flexible, no core hours	1	2	3	4	5

format in Appendix C asks a series of questions about the demographic and organizational characteristics of respondents. This is followed by a brief scale measuring employees' resistance to, or support for, change. The third section presents a series of questions about the organization's current work schedule and each of the alternatives to be considered. The last portion contains items to measure general worker reactions. Each of these sections is discussed briefly below. (For specific examples refer to Appendix C.)

Section I: Demographic/Organizational Questions.   One of the things that will prove helpful when you later evaluate the existing and alternative schedules is to identify the characteristics of various subgroups of employees. *Subgroups of employees often react differently from one another to both their existing work schedules and alternative work schedules.* You can identify the

Figure 6–5. *Continued*

objective, circle *3* for "no effect." If you feel the schedule would interfere with meeting the objective, circle a *1* or a *2* to indicate how negative you believe its effect will be. If you feel the schedule would help meet the objective, circle a *4* or a *5* to indicate how positive an effect you expect.

Objective 2: Reduce turnover from 45 to 30% among employees who are young, single parents					Objective 3: Increase by 25% the number of qualified applicants for entry-level technical job openings					Objective 4: Increase by 25% the proportion of candidates who accept job offers				
Very Negative Effect	*Negative Effect*	*No Effect*	*Positive Effect*	*Very Positive Effect*	*Very Negative Effect*	*Negative Effect*	*No Effect*	*Positive Effect*	*Very Positive Effect*	*Very Negative Effect*	*Negative Effect*	*No Effect*	*Positive Effect*	*Very Positive Effect*
1	2	3	4	5	1	2	3	4	5	1	2	3	4	5
1	2	3	4	5	1	2	3	4	5	1	2	3	4	5
1	2	3	4	5	1	2	3	4	5	1	2	3	4	5
1	2	3	4	5	1	2	3	4	5	1	2	3	4	5
1	2	3	4	5	1	2	3	4	5	1	2	3	4	5
1	2	3	4	5	1	2	3	4	5	1	2	3	4	5
1	2	3	4	5	1	2	3	4	5	1	2	3	4	5
1	2	3	4	5	1	2	3	4	5	1	2	3	4	5
1	2	3	4	5	1	2	3	4	5	1	2	3	4	5
1	2	3	4	5	1	2	3	4	5	1	2	3	4	5
1	2	3	4	5	1	2	3	4	5	1	2	3	4	5
1	2	3	4	5	1	2	3	4	5	1	2	3	4	5
1	2	3	4	5	1	2	3	4	5	1	2	3	4	5
1	2	3	4	5	1	2	3	4	5	1	2	3	4	5
1	2	3	4	5	1	2	3	4	5	1	2	3	4	5

average responses of these employee subgroups and still guarantee anonymity to the respondents.[1]

The questions typically included in this section ask for information on factors such as age, education level, job level, and organizational tenure. In the survey questionnaire presented in Appendix C we have included the types of demographic and organizational questions that are typically most useful for identifying differences among employees in their reactions to work schedules. For your own purposes you may choose to ask somewhat different questions in order to isolate responses of important subgroups of employees.

Section II: Resistance to or Support for Change. Your employees' orientation toward change will be important to you in Step 5 when you begin planning the implementation of an alternative schedule. *Employees differ sub-*

stantially in their general orientation towards change. You can use a brief scale to identify whether your employees (or subgroups) tend to view organizational change positively or negatively. This information can prove extremely useful in deciding whether to proceed and how to address resistance.

Section III: Specific Work Schedules.   This section of the survey is the longest and will provide the information most directly relevant to evaluating the existing work schedule and identifying the potential strengths and weaknesses of any alternatives you are considering. So that you can make a direct comparison of employees' reactions to the various schedules, the same questions are presented for the current work schedule and all the alternatives.

These questions ask about the degree to which a particular schedule (present or potential) affects employees' personal activities involving family and friends; access to services, events, and consumables; and financial activities. There are also questions that assess workers' general attitudes toward the schedule, the impact of the schedule on service to external constituents, the impact on work coordination, effects on social and family life, effects on transportation and personal security, and perceptions of the uniqueness of the work schedule. Last, employees rank-order the schedules, both in terms of their personal preferences and their perceptions of the degree to which the schedules might influence organizational effectiveness.

Section IV: General Worker Reactions.   It is unusual for a work schedule by itself to exert a major influence on the general reactions of employees. The final section of the survey provides information about these general reactions and how they are influenced by a wide range of personal and organizational factors such as the nature of the work, compensation, and leadership. It can be quite useful to assess the general feelings and behavioral propensities of workers before implementing an alternative work schedule. The sample survey in Appendix C gathers data on several of these general reactions, including many facets of job satisfaction as well as behavioral intentions for tardiness, absenteeism, and turnover. You may wish to study some of these reactions and perhaps even measure other factors such as organizational commitment, job involvement, motivation, or stress.[2]

Appendix C contains all of the types of questions described above. Section I contains demographic and organizational questions. Section II is a brief orientation-towards-change scale. Section III presents questions specific to the strengths and weaknesses of work schedules. In our sample survey, these questions are presented once for reactions to an existing work schedule and again for reactions to an alternative schedule. In practice they would be repeated for each alternative to be explored in depth. Also scattered throughout Section III are several open-ended questions so that employees have the opportunity to expand upon their answers to the structured questions. Section IV contains short scales to measure satisfaction with amount of work, kind of work, physical work conditions, pay, supervision, coworkers, career future, and company policies and practices. Section IV also contains single-item measures of behavioral intentions concerning tardiness, absenteeism, and turnover.

Target-Group Identification

Before administering the survey, you of course need to identify your target group(s). In other words, who can provide you with the information you need? Normally a survey should be administered to all employees who are likely to work under, react to, or be influenced by an alternative schedule. This includes the workers whose own schedules would be changed as well as those supervisory and nonsupervisory coworkers who interact with these employees on a regular basis. It is important, for example, to know whether supervisors believe an alternative work schedule would facilitate or impede the coordination of work.

Whereas the main target group for your survey would usually be the employees described above, it is sometimes desirable to include information from other sources. If, for example, an organization has had a problem with turnover which is believed to be related to work scheduling, an abbreviated version of the survey designed for current employees might also be appropriately administered to former personnel. If there have been problems with recruiting, perhaps a shortened version of the survey could be administered to potential employees. In situations where contacts with external customers or clients are critical, it might also be useful to obtain information from those sources, either through informal discussions or through a brief survey of those groups.

Another issue to consider is whether groups to be surveyed should be sampled or canvassed. Although it is less expensive to sample (survey a representative portion of the target group) than to canvass (survey the entire target group), there are arguments in favor of canvassing. In deciding whether to sample or canvass, you should consider the fact that *employees frequently look forward to a survey.* Workers often see a survey as a means of expressing their feelings and preferences in hopes of influencing organizational decisions. Canvassing can also increase the chances that employees will approach the implementation of a new work schedule with the attitude that everyone expressed their opinions, a new schedule was chosen, and now they should support it.

The dangers inherent in sampling include the possibility that those employees asked to complete the survey may react negatively because they feel they have been singled out as being different for some reason. Furthermore the employees who are excluded from the sampling may feel that their opinions are not valued and may therefore be offended. If you choose to sample rather than to canvass you can obtain assistance in identifying appropriate sample sizes from almost any introductory statistics text.

Survey Administration

Many methods have been used for administering surveys to employees. Organizations have mailed them to employees at home, distributed them at work for employees to complete at their convenience (on or off the job), and administered them in formally scheduled sessions. Our preference is to schedule a formal time for employees so that they can complete the survey on job-release time during the normal work day. Usually this can be done most efficiently by scheduling employees in groups of five to fifty at a time.

Figure 6–6 contains a sample script of directions you could follow (or adapt) when administering your work-scheduling survey. This particular script

Figure 6–6.   Survey Administration Script

Hello, my name is Randi Huntsman. As some of you may know, I work in the corporate personnel office. As part of my job, I've been asked to administer surveys to employees to get your reactions to an important project that has recently been undertaken. You've been asked to attend this session today so that you can participate in this survey by filling out a questionnaire. Since it is important that everyone taking the questionnaire receive the same instructions, we are using this videotape.

What we would like you to tell us is how you feel about our current methods of scheduling work. The survey will also ask your feelings about several alternative work schedules. This survey is very important, and I hope you will give your full cooperation by being completely frank in your answers. You are not being asked to sign your name to this questionnaire so that you can be confident of total anonymity. Your answers to the survey questions will be analyzed based on groups of employees. Other than the few of us who are processing the surveys, no one will ever even see any of the individual questionnaires.

We have tried to design this survey so that the questions are fairly easy to answer. For most of the questions, all you need to do is circle a number to indicate your answer. We have also presented several open-ended questions so you can describe your feelings in your own words.

After all employees have completed the questionnaires they will be analyzed. A report will be prepared describing the results, and each of you will receive a summary of those results. The company will provide you with this feedback through a work-schedule newsletter, which we will distribute to all employees on March 1. Should any work-schedule changes come about as a result of this survey, rest assured that we will communicate with you before introducing those changes.

[Distribute surveys now.]

Please open the survey booklet to the first page and look at the directions for filling out the questionnaire. This questionnaire has four sections. The first section obtains information about some of your personal characteristics and work experiences so that we can determine if different groups of employees have different feelings about work schedules. Section II asks how you feel about organizational changes. Section III is the longest and asks specific questions related to work schedules. The final section explores some of your general reactions to your work experiences.

Again, let me assure you that your individual responses will be kept confidential so please do not put your name on the survey. When you are done, you may place your survey in the box at the front of the room and leave. Please answer each question carefully. There are no right or wrong answers. The only appropriate answer is one that presents your personal feelings and opinions. Your first reaction to a question is usually the most appropriate. Thank you very much for your help on this project. Go ahead and begin. If you have any questions as you work, raise your hand and I will come to your table.

is one we used recently when conducting a study on work schedules. In that study we prepared a videotape of the administrator giving these directions so that we could use a standardized approach for each survey group. Our survey administrator played the videotape at the beginning of each survey session. As shown in the figure, survey administrators introduce themselves and briefly explain the purpose of the survey. This explanation should

- ► Promise anonymity for all individual respondents,
- ► Describe the timetable for analyzing results,
- ► Specify when employees can expect to receive feedback on survey results, and
- ► Describe the form this feedback will take.

Surveys are then distributed to respondents. The survey administrator highlights the directions for completing the survey and tells the respondents to begin. Completed surveys should be deposited in a collection box at the front of the room. At the end of a survey session, the box should be sealed and taken directly to the location where the completed surveys are to be analyzed.

How a survey is administered is critical to its success. Survey administrators should carefully limit their comments. They should provide only the type of information just described, and in a standardized fashion to all survey groups. Deviation from the standardized approach, off-hand comments, and jokes can distort survey results. Also note that once surveys have been returned to the administrator they should be handled very carefully. An administrator should never remove a completed survey from the box and examine it in front of a survey group as this will only raise suspicions. If multiple survey-administration sessions are required, steps should be taken to hold these sessions as close to one another in time as possible. Otherwise employees tend to discuss the survey between sessions which in turn will affect later survey results.

Survey Analysis

Analysis of survey results can be approached from several different perspectives. It might be interesting, for example, to know how many people answered certain questions in each particular way (frequency distributions). It might also be useful to discover the overall response to a question (calculation of averages). More advanced analyses can identify whether different subgroups of employees (e.g., long-term versus short-term employees) answered a question differently.

For many of the items in our sample survey, there are two or more questions intended to measure a single underlying concept. Multiple items are used to improve the reliability and validity beyond what would be possible using only a single item. When multiple items are used it is necessary to combine the answers to the various (but related) questions. *The resulting scale score is the information you should focus upon rather than concentrating on answers to the individual questions that comprise the scale.* When developing a scale score, we recommend that you add the answers for each question and then divide by the number of questions.

An example of a three-item scale used to measure effects of a schedule on social and family life is shown in Figure 6–7. Inasmuch as each answer could range from 1–5 possible scale scores also range from 1–5. You will also notice that the first and third questions are worded negatively while the second question is framed in a positive direction. An answer of 4 to the first and third questions would be negative responses but a 4 on the second question would indicate a positive response. Before you can create a scale score that meaningfully combines the answers to these questions you must make the numbers have a consistent interpretation across the three questions.

To do this, you need to "reverse-score" the two negative items. Figure 6–8 shows the same questions with the numbers adjusted to make the answers consistent. Thus for the first and third questions, we have changed answers of 5 to 1, 4 to 2, 2 to 4, and 1 to 5. Now adding the answers for the three questions and dividing the sum by 3 will produce a scale score for each individual respondent. *Group* scale scores can then be computed directly. A high score on this particular scale reflects a favorable perception regarding the schedule's effects on social and family life. (Appendix D contains complete scoring instructions for the sample survey in Appendix C.)

Tabular Presentation of Results.   Tables can summarize survey results in a very efficient manner. Table 6–1 presents a sample that summarizes average (mean) reactions to 5/40 and 4/40 schedules. This table displays the

Figure 6–7.   Scale to Measure Effects of an Alternative Schedule on Social and Family Life

	Strongly Disagree	Disagree	Neutral	Agree	Strongly Agree
1. The _____ work schedule would have an unfavorable influence on my family life.	1	2	3	4	5
2. The _____ method of scheduling would make it easier for me to coordinate my schedule with the schedules of other family members.	1	2	3	4	5
3. The _____ work schedule would have an unfavorable influence on my social life.	1	2	3	4	5

Source: R. B. Dunham and J. L. Pierce, "Attitudes toward Work Schedules: Construct Definition, Instrument Development, and Validation," *Academy of Management Journal* 29 (January 1986): 170–182.

Figure 6–8. Obtaining an Overall Scale Score

	Strongly Disagree	Disagree	Neutral	Agree	Strongly Agree
1. The _____ work schedule would have an unfavorable influence on my family life.	5 / 1	④ / 2	3	2 / 4	1 / 5
2. The _____ method of scheduling would make it easier for me to coordinate my schedule with the schedules of other family members.	1	2	3	4	⑤
3. The _____ work schedule would have an unfavorable influence on my social life.	5 / 1	4 / 2	③	2 / 4	1 / 5

To obtain a scale score, add the values for the answers for items 1, 2, and 3 and divide by 3. A person who circled answers as shown above would have a scale score of:

$$\frac{4 + 5 + 3}{3} = 4$$

Table 6–1. Tabular Presentation of Results

	Employee Group		
	All	Hourly	Salaried
General Affect			
5/40	3.6	3.4	3.7
4/40	4.2	4.1	4.3
Client Service			
5/40	3.6	3.5	3.7
4/40	3.5	3.4	3.6
Work Coordination			
5/40	3.3	3.3	3.3
4/40	3.2	3.6	2.8
Social, Family Effects			
5/40	2.8	2.7	2.9
4/40	3.4	3.5	3.3
Uniqueness			
5/40	1.7	1.7	1.7
4/40	4.0	4.1	3.9
Transportation, Security			
5/40	3.2	3.0	3.4
4/40	2.8	2.6	3.0

Note: Higher scores indicate more favorable responses. For the Uniqueness scale, a high score indicates a high level of uniqueness. For the Transportation, Security scale, a high score indicates convenient transportation and good personal security.

survey results obtained for all employees and two key subgroups, hourly and salaried. It shows, for example, that all employees associate greater positive general affect with a 4/40 schedule than with a 5/40. It also shows that although the employee group as a whole sees little difference between 5/40 and 4/40 schedules in terms of work coordination, hourly employees view a 4/40 schedule as having relatively positive effects on work coordination while salaried employees perceive it to have somewhat negative work-coordination effects.

Appendix E includes a series of table formats you can use to summarize the results of the sample survey presented in Appendix C. If you choose to use our sample survey (or a similar one), these tables should prove quite useful. Regardless of the nature of the survey you use, these sample formats should help you prepare tabular reports of your own results.

Graphic Presentation of Results.   Many people prefer to examine results of a survey visually. Graphs have the advantage of making differences stand out more easily. In addition, many "number-shy" individuals who are reluctant to study tables of data are more comfortable with graphs and will spend time reviewing them. Figure 6–9 graphically presents some of the same results that were shown in Table 6–1. Notice how some of the key differences

Figure 6–9.   Graphic Presentation of Results (For all employees)

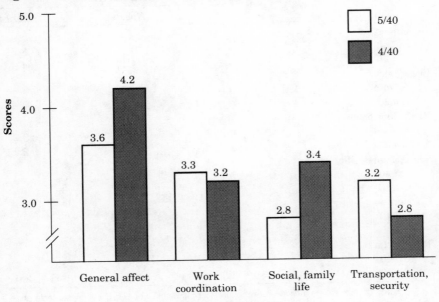

stand out dramatically in this figure. The advantages of graphs are somewhat offset, however, by the fact that they usually show less detailed information than can be presented in a table. Appendix E also contains graph formats you can use to summarize results from sample surveys like that in Appendix C.

Statistical Analyses of Results. Although tabular and graphic presentation of results are quite straightforward and easy to inspect visually, statistical analyses usually facilitate more in-depth understanding of your findings. Statistical evaluation can help you determine, for example, whether differences between two employee groups are large enough to merit further investigation or whether the employees' preference for an alternative schedule is strong enough to warrant its implementation. Often results of a survey produce a wide range of differences across employee subgroups or among alternative schedules. Statistical analyses can help you sort out the differences between those that are powerful and those that are weak or likely to have occurred due to chance variations.[3]

Table 6–2 illustrates how useful statistical tests can be. In this table the responses of supervisory and nonsupervisory employees are compared for a wide variety of survey responses. The right-hand column in this illustration shows which of these comparisons produced statistically significant results. This information helps you focus on the few supervisory–nonsupervisory differences large enough to merit attention.

Computer-Based Surveys

The preceding sections on survey administration and analysis assumed a traditional (paper-and-pencil) approach for administering and processing surveys. An alternative method is to integrate the structured questions from the survey presented in Appendix C into a computer program that runs on microcomputers. The program could be designed so that you tell the computer which alternative schedules interest you and which questions you wish to ask employees. You could also specify whether you want employees to receive feedback about their own responses immediately after they have completed the questionnaire.

To complete a computerized survey, employees sit down at a microcomputer, follow the complete instructions shown on the screen (contained in the program on their diskette), and answer the questions using the keyboard.[4]

The computer program can keep track of every answer to the survey questions until all respondents have completed it, at which time a simple analysis routine will score the surveys automatically. This approach can provide a summary of results that can be presented in both tabular and graphic formats. If you use the computerized approach you could easily request output for each employee group that interests you.

Table 6–2.   Sample of Results Showing Statistical Significance

In this table, comparisons of supervisory and nonsupervisory employees are shown for a wide variety of survey responses. The right-hand column shows which of these comparisons produced statistically significant results. This will help you focus on the few supervisory–nonsupervisory differences that are large enough to merit attention.

Organizational Effectiveness	*Schedule*	*Supervisory*	*Nonsupervisory*	*Statistical Significance*
Work coordination	5/40	4.5	4.1	
Work coordination	4/40	3.2	4.0	b
Client service	5/40	4.1	4.0	
Client service	4/40	3.7	4.2	a
Work-Schedule Attitudes				
General affect	5/40	3.8	3.7	
General affect	4/40	4.1	4.3	
Social, family effects	5/40	2.9	2.6	
Social, family effects	4/40	3.0	3.2	
General Reactions				
General job satisfaction	5/40	3.4	3.3	
General job satisfaction	4/40	3.6	4.0	a
Work-itself satisfaction	5/40	3.7	3.2	a
Work-itself satisfaction	4/40	3.7	3.4	
Organizational commitment	5/40	3.5	3.4	
Organizational commitment	4/40	3.9	4.1	
Physiological stress	5/40	3.1	3.6	a
Physiological stress	4/40	3.2	3.8	a
Psychological stress	5/40	3.6	3.4	
Psychological stress	4/40	3.7	3.5	

  [a] Significantly different at .05 level
  [b] Significantly different at .01 level

Survey Feedback

Employees who participate in a survey are typically very interested in its results. They are curious to know, for example, how their own preferences and opinions compared to others' answers. It has been our experience that a brief report, consisting of two or three pages of text and possibly a table and a graph or two, is usually adequate. This feedback report should be prepared and distributed promptly and include a description of major findings such as the following:

Of all employees surveyed, 85 percent stated that they would prefer a 4/40 work schedule over their current schedule. Seventy percent of the respondents felt the 4/40 schedule would improve service to clients, 20 percent believed the 4/40 schedule would have no effect on service to clients, and 10 percent felt service would decline under a 4/40 schedule.

It is also crucial to share information on what the organization intends to *do* with the survey results:

> Based in part on favorable employee reaction, a committee was appointed on September 3 to explore the potential implementation of a 4/40 work schedule. This committee consists of Joan Walker (vice president of operations), Del Smith (a supervisor in the supply department), Sandi Baker and Paul Jones (from accounting), and Chuck Boyer (from human resources). The committee will be chaired by Juan Rodriguez, Director of Sales. The committee has been asked to make a final recommendation by November 1, which will include a cost–benefit projection for the 4/40 schedule.

It should be noted that managers using a computerized-survey approach have the option of providing one additional piece of feedback to respondents. Although individualized feedback is typically not possible if anonymity is to be preserved, a visual or printed summary of a respondent's own answers to the survey questions can be provided immediately upon completion of the survey by the computer program if you desire.

Step 4: Evaluation of Results

Upon completion of Step 3 you will have a set of tables and graphs that provide information about your current schedule and the alternatives you have explored. Now it is time to evaluate the strengths and weaknesses of all the possible schedules. To do this, you must compare your current schedule to each of the alternatives and also compare the alternatives to one another. The choice of a new work schedule is made at this step; and you can use the results from the survey to assist you in the decision-making process.

One approach to evaluating work schedules is to examine the current schedule first and to identify its apparent strengths and weaknesses. Next you can look at the first alternative being considered, identify its strengths and weaknesses, and then follow a similar process for each alternative. This type of approach allows you to organize survey results in the manner shown in Figure 6–10.

A different approach is to look at the first scale (e.g., general affect toward schedule) and compare how each schedule fared on this single scale.

Figure 6–10. Comparison of Three Schedules, Organized by Schedule

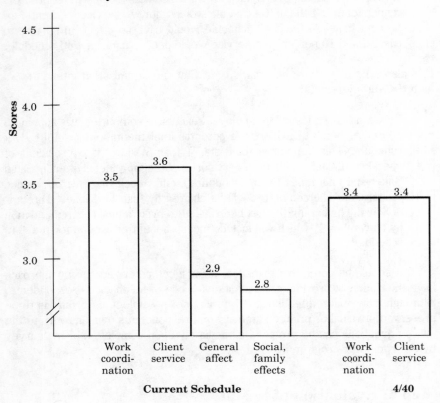

You then move on to the second scale for each schedule and follow this process for each remaining scale. This type of approach would favor the organization of results like those shown in Figure 6–11 and facilitates a more comprehensive and systematic comparison across alternative schedules.

Using either of these approaches, next evaluate the degree to which each schedule can be expected to satisfy the objectives you set forth in Step 1. Back in Step 2 you made your first detailed evaluation of each of the schedules to be included in the survey, basing your evaluation on information from the literature and your own knowledge of the organizational situation. Now you can repeat this evaluation procedure using a much broader base of information—the survey results. We encourage you to fill out the same rating form (Figure 6–5) with the detailed information now at your disposal to help you evaluate your current work schedule and the alternatives under consideration. In Figure 6–12 we provide an example that compares the 5/40 and 4/40 schedules using the objectives-rating

Figure 6–10. *Continued*

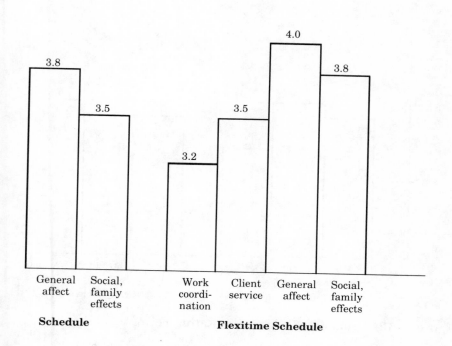

form specified in Step 2. After your comparison you will be able to make a data-based choice for a future work schedule that best (but probably not perfectly) fits your objectives.

After you have selected a new schedule we urge you to evaluate it once using the approach shown in Figure 6–10. This encourages careful examination of its strengths and weaknesses and highlights the fine tuning necessary prior to its implementation. If your analysis suggests that you stay with the current schedule, you will need to decide whether to keep it totally intact or to modify it, depending upon the survey results. If you select an alternative you must determine whether to implement it as originally described in the survey or fine-tune it based on survey results.

Finally, you should prepare a statement like the one shown in Figure 6–13, describing the expected effects of the schedule selected. This statement should include a cost–benefit analysis (where possible) and identify any anticipated

Figure 6–11.   Comparison of Schedules, Organized by Scale

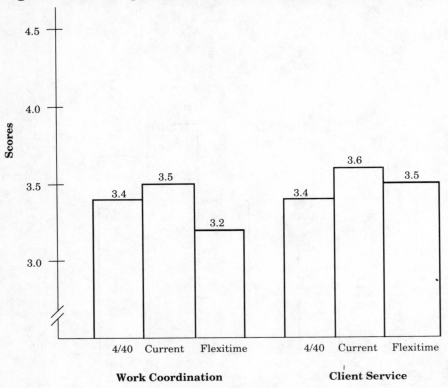

Work Coordination   **Client Service**

Figure 6–12.   Completed Objectives Rating Form

Directions: Each of the alternative schedules listed below could influence each of the four objectives listed on this page. For each schedule, circle the number that best corresponds to the degree to which you expect that schedule would have a positive or negative effect on attaining each objective. If you feel the schedule would neither aid nor hamper reaching the

			Objective 1: Increase satisfaction for at least 75% of employees		
Schedule	*Very Negative Effect*	*Negative Effect*	*No Effect*	*Positive Effect*	*Very Positive Effect*
1. 5/40 fixed, M–F 7:30–4, 30 min. lunch	1	2	③	4	5
2. 4/40 compressed, M–Th	1	2	3	④	5

NOTE: Estimated effects are circled.

Figure 6–11.   *Continued*

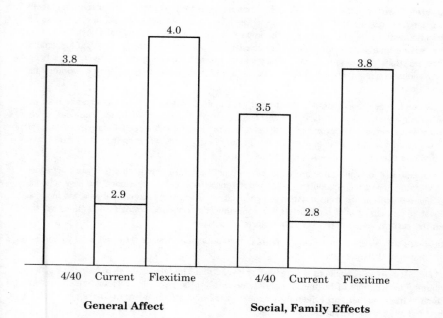

General Affect   **Social, Family Effects**

Figure 6–12.   *Continued*

objective, circle *3* for "no effect." If you feel the schedule would interfere with meeting the objective, circle a *1* or a *2* to indicate how negative you believe its effect will be. If you feel the schedule would help meet the objective, circle a *4* or a *5* to indicate how positive of an effect you expect.

Objective 2: Reduce turnover from 45 to 30% among employees who are young, single parents					*Objective 3: Increase by 25% the number of qualified applicants for entry-level technical job openings*					*Objective 4: Increase by 25% the proportion of candidates who accept job offers*				
Very Negative Effect	*Negative Effect*	*No Effect*	*Positive Effect*	*Very Positive Effect*	*Very Negative Effect*	*Negative Effect*	*No Effect*	*Positive Effect*	*Very Positive Effect*	*Very Negative Effect*	*Negative Effect*	*No Effect*	*Positive Effect*	*Very Positive Effect*
1	2	③	4	5	1	2	③	4	5	1	2	③	4	5
1	2	3	④	5	1	2	3	4	⑤	1	2	3	④	5

Figure 6–13. Description of Schedule and Statement of Expected Effects

Description: The new work schedule will be a four-day, forty-hour schedule. Under this schedule, all employees will work Monday through Thursday from 7:15 A.M. to 5:45 P.M. with a 30-minute lunch break.

Expected Positive Effects: It is expected that approximately 80 percent of current employees will react favorably to the 4/40 schedule. These favorable reactions should be strongest for satisfaction with the work schedule; in the impact of the schedule on family and social activities; and in leisure-time satisfaction. A mild but consistently positive reaction is expected for general worker reactions such as general job satisfaction, satisfaction with company policies and practices, organizational commitment, satisfaction with the work itself, and satisfaction with coworkers and supervision.

Hourly employees are expected to react somewhat more favorably to the new schedule than will salaried employees. The most favorable reactions are expected among relatively young employees who are single parents. (Approximately 30 percent of our hourly work force falls into this category.) It is expected that the turnover rate for this group of employees will drop from its current level of 45 percent per year to 30–35 percent per year.

Certain potential job candidates are expected to react very favorably to the new work schedule, thus allowing use of the schedule as a recruiting tool. It is expected that once the new schedule is publicized applications from qualified job candidates for entry-level technical jobs will increase at least 25 percent. It is also predicted that companywide acceptance rates for job offers will rise from the current level of 40 percent to at least 50 percent.

Employees will realize a 20 percent savings in commuting costs since they will need to come to work only four days per week.

Building Services will be able to reduce heating levels from Thursday evening to Monday morning, requiring one less day of heating. Janitorial services will be needed only four times per week instead of five. Furthermore, the new schedule will allow three uninterrupted days per week for scheduled and corrective maintenance projects.

Expected Negative Effects: It is forecasted that approximately 10 percent of current employees will have indifferent reactions to the new work schedule, and that another 10 percent will clearly dislike it. Even among those who like the new schedule overall, it is anticipated that there will be concerns about the quality of client service provided when the office is closed on Friday. Indeed, for a small number of our clients, this will be a problem. This will, however, be somewhat compensated for by the advantage of the longer work days Monday through Thursday.

For approximately 40 percent of employees it is expected that both physiological and psychological stressors will increase somewhat, leading to a greater fatigue level near the end of the work day. This is expected to be most problematic for older workers in the warehouse and in delivery services.

A few employees (approximately 10 percent) will need to change their transportation arrangements by finding new bus schedules and/or new car pools. A similar number will need to change their child-care arrangements for Monday through Thursday.

Financial Issues: If turnover is reduced as projected, an annual cost savings of $475,000 should be realized.

Anticipated recruiting advantages should save approximately $80,000 per year in direct recruiting costs.

Heating savings should be approximately $22,000. Janitorial savings should be at least $40,000.

By scheduling regular equipment maintenance on Fridays, overtime maintenance costs of $35,000 should be saved.

The costs for consultant help in implementing, studying, and fine-tuning the new schedule will be approximately $20,000.

Overtime wages will need to be paid to two employees who are represented by a union. Our current contract specifies overtime pay for work in excess of eight hours per day. This will cost approximately $5600 during the first year. We will attempt to renegotiate this clause for future years.

future difficulties likely to arise from the schedule. Keep in mind the objectives you set forth in Step 1 while preparing the statement.

Summary

This chapter contained specific instructions for the process of systematically evaluating your current and possible alternative work schedules—*before* making a decision as to which schedule will best meet the needs of your organization. This admittedly time-consuming procedure is imperative if you are to avoid the disappointments, frustration, and often unpredictable consequences that can arise from haphazard or poorly planned changes. To help you gather the information necessary for such systematic planning, the chapter offered directions on how to design, administer, and score a survey. It also discussed the merits of involving affected employees in the data-collection process to gain valuable information and lay a strong foundation of support for the implementation stage. Accompanying the chapter's instructions were sample forms showing how to specify objectives, identify and evaluate potential alternative schedules, organize survey results, reexamine a chosen schedule, and describe its expected effect.

Appendix A provides technical information on the development and validation of the research scales discussed in this chapter. Appendix B illustrates the design, implementation, and evaluation of a field experiment with a 4/40 work schedule.

Endnotes

1. Dunham and Smith discuss the importance of anonymity as well as a variety of other related issues in their book, *Organizational Surveys: An Internal Assessment of Organizational Health* (Glenview, Ill: Scott, Foresman, 1979).

2. Other useful scales include organizational commitment (see L. W. Porter, R. W. Steers, R. T. Mowday, and P. V. Boulain, "Organizational Commitment, Job

Satisfaction, and Turnover among Psychiatric Technicians," *Journal of Applied Psychology* 59 [1974] 603–609); job involvement (see T. M. Lodahl and M. Kejner, "The Definition and Measurement of Job Involvement," *Journal of Applied Psychology* 49 [1965] 24–33); intrinsic motivation (see E. E. Lawler, III, and D. T. Hall, "Relationships of Job Characteristics to Job Involvement, Satisfaction, and Intrinsic Motivation," *Journal of Applied Psychology* 54 [1970] 305–312); and physiological and psychological stress (see M. Patchen, *Participation, Achievement, and Involvement on the Job* (Englewood Cliffs, N.J.: Prentice-Hall, 1970).

3. It is beyond the scope of this book to provide a tutorial for those who are not familiar with statistical techniques. We strongly encourage you to review one of the excellent statistics books now available.

4. If you use the computerized-survey approach, we encourage you to provide respondents with a brief form as well, so that they can make written comments about the work schedules under consideration.

Chapter Seven

←——————————————————————————————————————→

Implementing and
Evaluating Work
Schedules

▶   Good ideas can fail in practice as a result of poor planning and an inadequate implementation process. Similarly, good ideas well implemented must be evaluated or they may soon die from lack of organizational support. It is not sufficient to identify a (potentially) better work schedule—you must also carefully *manage* its implementation and evaluation. A systematic approach to implementation and evaluation can pay substantial dividends. This chapter focuses on the four remaining tasks: (1) implementation planning, (2) implementation, (3) evaluation, and (4) fine-tuning. These follow the four steps of setting objectives, listing alternatives, collecting data, and analyzing the information discussed in Chapter Six.

Step 5: Planning for Implementation

By completing Steps 1–4, you identified a schedule for future use and know its anticipated advantages, disadvantages, and costs. Assuming you have chosen either to modify your existing schedule or to switch to an alternative one, you now need to plan how to implement this change. Among other considerations, you need to decide the following:

- ► Whether to implement the new schedule on a trial basis or permanently
- ► Whether to use the schedule with all employees or a subset of the total employee group
- ► Who is likely to support or resist implementation of the new schedule, and for what reasons
- ► How to develop support for the new schedule and reduce any expected resistance
- ► How to counteract the expected disadvantages identified in Step 4
- ► What the logistical details for implementation will be, including a specific timetable

The following sections address each of these issues in order to provide a basic understanding of the underlying processes.

Trial versus Permanent Implementation

Given the thoroughness of the search for and examination of alternative schedules conducted in Steps 1 through 4, permanent implementation of the new schedule often makes sense. Indeed, evidence that appears overwhelmingly favorable for a schedule can make it difficult to resist permanent implementation. There are several arguments, however, in favor of a trial implementation before making a final commitment.

In a trial implementation, employees are usually told that the new schedule will be tried for a specified period of time (perhaps three to six months) and that no final decision will be made until after the results of the trial are analyzed. Employees are often more willing to accept a new schedule—especially one they have reservations about—if they see a possible escape from it. Similarly, many key decision makers may approve a new schedule for a trial use more readily than if it were requested on a permanent basis.

For those of a cautious nature, a trial seems safer. In fact, a trial can provide a more complete examination of the merits of the chosen schedule for your organization with *your* employees. If two alternative schedules were considered and appear to have very similar merits, for example, a trial of *each* schedule might be appropriate to see which works better "under fire." A trial also might be indicated in a situation where your evaluation of a schedule's expected effects identified a combination of positive and negative by-products or produced other ambiguous expectations. Whether or not a trial is necessary for a final assessment of a schedule's merits, the trial approach can be quite useful for gentle implementation purposes.

All Employees versus a Subgroup _____

In addition to determining whether the new schedule is to be implemented on a trial or permanent basis, you must decide which employees will use it. One common method when conducting a trial is to use one group of employees as the trial group while retaining a similar group of employees on the old schedule. This allows direct comparison of the effectiveness of the two schedules.

You may wish to implement the new schedule using an initial group of employees and gradually phase in the remaining employee groups. Just as use of a trial is more acceptable to some managers and decision makers, gradual implementation is also preferred by many. Implementation with a subset of employees is often a good risk-management technique. No matter how carefully you plan, something unexpected will always occur. Just as fighting a small fire is easier than fighting a large one, so it is easier to address implementation problems in a small group than across the entire organization.

There are, of course, situations where certain subgroups of employees will never be involved with a particular schedule. One such case involved a data-processing company whose managers implemented a 4/40 schedule for system engineers, data-entry employees, and clerical workers but wanted to retain a 5/40 schedule for customer-support personnel who fielded calls and incoming data transmissions from credit unions. If your previous examination of an alternative schedule revealed certain employee groups for whom the schedule would not be appropriate, you will have to decide whether you are willing to use two or more different schedules to meet employee and/or organizational needs.

Anticipating Resistance to Change _____

One of the major factors determining how well a new schedule will work is the degree to which employees support or resist it. Even when employees like the idea of a new schedule, some may resist its actual implementation. Many people believe that resistance to change is irrational and unreasonable; but in reality, most people resist change for logical, rational reasons. Substantial research has identified the primary reasons (see Figure 7–1). In this section we identify and discuss some of these reasons to help you anticipate which of your employees is likely to resist the introduction of a new work schedule— and why. In the next section we discuss techniques to reduce this resistance and develop support for a new schedule.

Fear of Losing Something Valuable.   The most common reason why some people resist change is that they believe the change will cause them to lose something they value. The greater the anticipated loss, the greater the resistance. It is important to note that the fear of loss is based on a person's

Figure 7–1.   Common Reasons for Resistance to Change

▶ Fear of the loss of something of value
▶ Misunderstanding of the change
▶ Lack of trust in management
▶ Disagreement on the advisability of change
▶ Low personal tolerance for the change

perception, without regard to whether this perception is realistic. Common fears of loss when an alternative work schedule is introduced include:

▶ Loss of control over the work schedule
▶ Loss of established working relations with coworkers, superiors, and subordinates
▶ Deterioration in arrangements with external constituents
▶ Interference with personal activities
▶ Loss of the current schedule (which may be valued by some employees).

Even employees who feel they will gain much when the new schedule is introduced often fear the loss of at least some valued things associated with the existing schedule.

Misunderstanding.   Many employees misunderstand the details of a new schedule. Reasons and objectives are often misunderstood, along with the nature of the change itself. Implementation of a schedule may be resisted as employees react negatively to their mistaken perceptions of what the new schedule will entail. Recently, for example, we observed an attempt to introduce a flexitime work schedule in a small local office of a larger organization. Due to poor communication, employees incorrectly assumed that the new flexitime schedule would permit supervisors to assign starting and quitting times to employees on a daily basis. Because of this misunderstanding about the nature of the new schedule, employees resisted quite strongly.

Lack of Trust.   When employees mistrust management, they commonly resist implementation of new schedules. This occurs even when public descriptions of the new schedules match employees' desires. Because of the lack of trust, employees question the honesty and accuracy of the description of the schedule. They become concerned about unknown details and possible implications of the schedule; and they often assume that the new schedule was adopted to take advantage of them rather than to benefit both employees and the organization.

Employees who do not trust their employers may resist even an acceptable change for fear that this will set a precedent for future changes that might be unacceptable to them. Resistance to change due to lack of trust is unique since the reasons for it often have little to do with the specific change in question. Lack of trust frequently combines with other reasons for resistance to magnify the resulting resistance to a new schedule.

Disagreement on Advisability of Change. Employees who feel that the new schedule is a technically unsound idea are likely to resist its introduction. They may believe that the new schedule is not in the best interests of the organization or the employees. A supervisor, for example, might believe that a flexitime schedule would make coordination of work within the work unit more difficult. Disagreement on the advisability of a new schedule can take two forms.

1. Two parties might examine the same set of information and reach different conclusions. This could occur because either the data are ambiguous or the two parties are predisposed to view the options differently.
2. The second type of disagreement occurs when two parties examine different sets of information, leading them to reach contrasting conclusions.

This more common type of disagreement occurs, for example, when one party has read published literature about alternative work schedules but the other party has not, or when one party has access to the survey results concerning this alternative schedule and the other party does not. It is worth noting that resistance for this (second) reason can be good because it sends a signal to an organization that someone has reasons why the new schedule may be a bad idea. If the concerns have merit they should be considered in the design of the work schedule. If the concerns are not worthy of consideration, you probably need to share the missing information with resisters to help them see the merits of the change.

Low Personal Tolerance for Change. Some employees have a lower personal tolerance for the introduction of change than do others. In fact, this type of employee might even agree that a change would be good for both the organization and its employees, yet still resist. Even the reasons behind this type of resistance, however, can often be quite rational. Some employees, for example, might fear that they will become extremely fatigued if asked to work a ten-hour day as part of a 4/40 schedule. Perhaps an employee being placed on flexitime fears that expert advisors will not always be present when needed. In fact, a common and legitimate concern is that change will disrupt interpersonal relationships. Other employees have a low personal tolerance for change because of deeply ingrained attitudes. Their belief that people should work from 9 A.M. to 5 P.M., five days a week, can be difficult to change if they have held that belief for many years.

Certain personality characteristics can also lead to resistance to change. Highly dogmatic or closed-minded employees may resist the new work schedule unless it is consistent with their personal views of the way work should be scheduled. Employees with a strong internal locus of control want to rule their own destinies and thus may resist a new work schedule (or any other change) unless they have participated in its selection. Employees with highly authoritarian personalities tend to support change implemented by an authority figure but resist otherwise. Those with low tolerance for ambiguity may resist even a desirable schedule because they fear the uncertainties that may accompany its start-up or operation. It is critical, therefore, that you systematically anticipate who will resist the new schedule—and why—*before* you implement it. As Harvard change expert Leonard A. Schlesinger would say to the manager who believes that if an idea is good enough, it will work,

> One must recognize that one's ability to successfully introduce change is a function not only of the quality of the change idea but also of the existing levels of dissatisfaction and the process of implementation. These three elements act as the three legs of a stool: without all of them the stool will fall.[1]

Developing Support for Change

As you follow the systematic approach outlined in Chapter Six to design and assess work schedules, you are already taking significant steps to develop support for the changes involved when the new schedule is implemented. In addition to those steps and the preceding discussion of anticipating resistance, there are specific techniques you can use to reduce resistance and develop support (see Figure 7–2). Most managers have consciously or unconsciously developed a personal style for reducing resistance or developing support in change efforts. Your personal style is likely to influence how you will manage the introduction of a new work schedule as well. Effective managers assess the situation and then select the appropriate resistance-reduction technique(s) to match that situation. Let us take a closer look at some of these techniques.

Education and Communication. The best time to use education and communication to develop support is *prior* to the emergence of resistance—

Figure 7–2. Techniques for Developing Support

- ▶ Education and communication
- ▶ Participation and involvement
- ▶ Support
- ▶ Incentives
- ▶ Manipulation and co-optation
- ▶ Coercion

in other words, before you introduce the new schedule. Education and communication about a work schedule should include descriptions of—

1. *What* the change is,
2. *When* it is to be introduced,
3. *How* it will be implemented,
4. *Why* it is needed,
5. The *logic* which supports it, and
6. Its *objectives*.

Education and communication can reduce misunderstandings about the change and can help those with a limited tolerance for change to deal with their personal concerns prior to the introduction of the new schedule. This technique is probably most effective, however, for dealing with those who might otherwise disagree about the advisability of the change.

As with any technique, there are potential drawbacks to this approach. For one thing, education and communication about a new work schedule requires a significant amount of time, effort, and money. You should also be aware that once you have explained the details of a new schedule this information could make your workers realize that they genuinely dislike it and develop more powerful arguments against it. It is also important to note that education and communication best develop support and reduce resistance when a reasonable state of trust exists within an organization. Otherwise organizational members may believe the purpose of your communication is to manipulate them.

Participation and Involvement. Organizational members can be asked to participate at the planning stage and/or at the time you implement the new schedule. Participation and involvement have two powerful potential payoffs. First, participation by organizational members often improves the actual design of a new work schedule. Second, employees' acceptance of and commitment to a new schedule is likely to be enhanced through employee participation.

Participation and involvement are not without disadvantages, though. What will you do, for example, if participating employees help you design a poor work schedule? If you go along with their recommendation you will have to implement a schedule you feel is unwieldy, risky, or inappropriate. If you reject their ideas you risk alienating the very employees you sought to involve. This suggests the importance of carefully defining ground rules before participation begins. If, as a safety mechanism, you intend to ask employees to provide input only, then make sure they understand that their role is to do just this and *not* to make a final decision.

Participation and involvement can be an effective technique for identifying an appropriate alternative schedule inasmuch as the initiator of a new schedule often has inadequate information to do it alone. This technique can also be useful if it leads to a high level of commitment, since it is important to capitalize upon potential positive reactions from employees. If you intend to use this technique you should plan for the fairly large investment of time and energy that it requires.

Support. Introduction of an alternative work schedule can be accompanied by two different types of organizational support, facilitative and emotional. Facilitative support provides appropriate tools, materials, advice, or training to help make a change work effectively. A new scheduling control system might be needed for a flexitime schedule, for example; or new material-handling procedures developed to support a multishift operation. Supervisors sometimes need to be taught how to maintain control when they themselves cannot always be physically present at the work place.

Emotional support addresses personal concerns about the change. This is often best provided by an understanding supervisor or coworker. Emotional support might be needed by employees who are worried about their ability to work extended daily hours as part of a compressed work schedule, or those who are concerned that they will spend too much time working alone on a flexitime schedule.

If an alternative schedule is designed appropriately to begin with, much of the facilitative support is incorporated into its general design. Similarly, if a new schedule has been designed to meet employees' needs, little emotional support will be necessary for most of the employees. This type of support can be directed toward specific troubled individuals.

Facilitative support and emotional support are not without cost (e.g., the cost of developing new procedures and the time taken to provide emotional support) to the organization and neither guarantees success. This is especially true if organizational members have strong personal feelings against the new schedule.

Incentives. Organizational members are more likely to support a new work schedule if they have some incentive for doing so. If an alternative schedule is selected in part because of its attractiveness to employees, the incentive for supporting the change is built into the new schedule itself. Employees are thus motivated to help implement a new schedule because they recognize that it will benefit them personally. The most effective incentives are those that are *intrinsic,* or a product of the change itself.

Compensatory incentives are another way to encourage support for the introduction of a new schedule, even among those who dislike it. An employee being asked to work the second shift, for example, might be paid a shift differential as a compensatory incentive. Supervisors who fear their work load will increase when a new schedule is implemented might be offered new office space as both an incentive and a tool to aid their work. Although compensatory incentives can be quite effective, they do have costs and can be risky. If you provide incentives primarily for those who resist a new schedule, you may actually encourage others to show signs of resistance in hopes that they too will be compensated.

Manipulation and Co-optation.   The use of manipulation for dealing with resistance and developing support is mentioned here primarily to *discourage* you from using this technique. Of all the techniques discussed in this section, this is the only one that is deceitful and perhaps unethical. However, it is a technique that is often used and it can be effective under certain circumstances.

Manipulation involves the intentional control or distortion of information so that the picture presented does not accurately represent reality. An example is omitting information about the fatique older workers might experience as part of the extended work day in a compressed work schedule. Distortion can also include misstatements of facts (lying), as would be the case if supervisors were told that their work loads would not increase during the initial introduction of a flexitime schedule.

Co-optation is a special form of manipulation. One way to co-opt someone who disagrees with a goal is to place the dissenter in a position where he or she acquires a vested interest in meeting the objective. Co-optation can become manipulative if people are assigned positions that appear to be important but in fact have little or no significance. A supervisor with reservations about a 4/40 schedule, for example, might be asked to chair an alternative work-schedule committee. The supervisor could be told that this is a very important position and that his or her opinions on the design of an alternative schedule are valued. This is exactly the same as would be done when using the participation and involvement approach. In manipulative co-optation, however, the chairperson position is simply a meaningless figurehead role. The organization's primary intent is to change the supervisor's mind, or at least prevent resistance to the new schedule. In participation and involvement the organization is genuinely interested in the supervisor's opinions and ideas; in manipulative co-optation there is no such interest.

Manipulative approaches can be easy, relatively inexpensive ways to gain at least short-term support for a new work schedule. There are a number of drawbacks, however, such as the fact that they are deceitful, often unethical, and may even backfire. First, giving someone a figurehead position creates the possibility that the person will use the implied importance of the role to negatively influence others. Second, if manipulation of any kind is detected, it will reduce your ability to use more honest techniques of creating support. Employees who recognize that they have been manipulated or co-opted often react by *increasing* their resistance. Even if they merely suspect an effort to involve them to be insincere, they may react to it as though it were blatant manipulation.

Coercion.   Coercion can be used to convince potential resisters that resistance will lead to punishment. This potent technique for dealing with resistance forces people to go along with a change even when it runs counter to their desires. Coercive threats can be implicit or explicit involving, for example, the loss of a job, promotion, or a valued work assignment. Although coercion can effectively force someone to go along with a new work schedule, there are likely to be undesirable side effects. Employees may appear to accept a new work schedule, for example, but then engage in work slowdowns, sabotage, or general uncooperativeness. Employees who have been forced to accept a new schedule may leave as soon as they find new jobs with a more desirable schedule.

The use of coercion typically produces dissatisfaction, leads to resentment, and reduces the effectiveness of more positive techniques for developing support. If forced to adopt a new work schedule, employees may then be unwilling to cooperate in its implementation and refinement. Although these are potential problems, coercion can be quite effective in situations where change must occur and other techniques for encouraging support are inadequate. We hope you will use this technique selectively because of the many potential negative side effects.

Selecting Techniques

We have discussed six possible techniques for developing support and dealing with resistance to the introduction of a new work schedule. Each is associated with certain advantages and disadvantages. Table 7–1 summarizes some of the pros and cons and some of the situations where each technique is commonly used. When you select the technique(s) you intend to use to develop support for your new work schedule, consider whether you are automatically choosing one that matches your personal style and preferences, or a better one that truly meets the needs of your situation.

Step 6: Implementing a New Schedule

Figure 7–3 summarizes the actions we have suggested to this point as well as those that are still needed. Step 6 deals with the actual implementation of a new schedule. As shown in the figure, implementation involves the classic steps of unfreezing, changing, and refreezing. *Unfreezing* means that you make people aware of the need for the change to the new schedule. This might include presentation of the objectives and a discussion of the weaknesses of the existing schedule. It is here that the techniques you chose in Step 5 to reduce resistance should be put into use.

The change step is when the new schedule actually goes into effect. The cut-off date must be selected, all affected employees carefully informed of the

Table 7–1. **Advantages and Disadvantages of Techniques to Develop Support for Change**

Technique	Useful in Situations Where	Advantages	Disadvantages
Education and Communication	Information is inaccurate or incomplete	Once persuaded, people often help with implementation	Can be very time-consuming
Participation and Involvement	Initiators do not have all the information needed and others have considerable power to resist	People are committed and information they have will be integrated into the change plan	Very time-consuming if participants design an inappropriate change
Support	People resist because of adjustment problems	No other approach works as well with adjustment problems	Can be time-consuming, expensive, and still fail
Incentives	Someone with considerable power will lose out in a change	Sometimes a relatively easy way to avoid major resistance	Can be expensive, alert others to negotiate for compliance
Manipulation and Co-optation	Other tactics do not work or are too expensive	Can be relatively quick, inexpensive	Can lead to problems if people feel manipulated
Coercion	Speed is essential and initiators possess considerable power	Fast, can overcome any kind of resistance	Risky if it leaves people mad at initiators

Modified and reprinted by permission of the *Harvard Business Review.* An adaptation of an exhibit from "Choosing Strategies for Change" by John P. Kolter and Leonard A. Schlesinger (March-April 1979). Copyright © 1979 by the President and Fellows of Harvard College; all rights reserved.

new system, and a set of contingency plans put in place to handle the inevitable (but unpredictable) problems. Open communication is essential here to identify and solve little problems before they become magnified. Further, this is the stage in which the positive techniques for building early support for the change become increasingly useful. If the unfreezing stage was managed properly— and especially if a trial implementation was conducted—the full-scale introduction of a new schedule should proceed smoothly.

Following implementation of the new schedule, *refreezing* is necessary. Order can now be restored to the organization and the new schedule integrated

Figure 7–3.   Summary of Steps for Managing a Change to an Alternative Schedule

1. Specify the objectives for a new schedule.
2. Identify a list of potential alternatives.
3. Collect information.
4. Evaluate information.
5. Plan for implementing the change to a new schedule.
6. Implement alternative schedule.
   A. Unfreezing
      (1) Create the perceived need for the new schedule.
      (2) Minimize resistance to the new schedule.
   B. Changing
      (1) Change the schedule.
      (2) Encourage continuing support for it.
   C. Refreezing
      (1) Reinforce outcomes.
      (2) Make constructive modification(s).
7. Evaluate the success and limitations of the new schedule.
8. Fine-tune the new schedule.

into standard operating procedures. In refreezing, the positive outcomes of the new schedule should be reinforced and any new or continuing resistance addressed. Minor modifications of the schedule can also be made during the refreezing process.

Figure 7–4.   Comparison of Actual Effects to Those Anticipated

Directions: Each of the alternative schedules listed below could influence each of the four objectives listed on this page. For each schedule, circle the number that best corresponds to the degree to which you expect that schedule would have a positive or negative effect on attaining each objective. If you feel the schedule would neither aid nor hamper reaching the

Objective 1: Increase satisfaction for at least 75% of employees

Schedule	Very Negative Effect	Negative Effect	No Effect	Positive Effect	Very Positive Effect
4/40 compressed, Monday-Thursday	1	2	3	(4ᵃ)	5

Satisfaction increased for 68%

ᵃPredicted effects prior to implementation are circled. Actual effects are written in.

Step 7: Evaluating a New Schedule

After a new schedule has been implemented, we strongly recommend that you evaluate its effectiveness. Unfortunately, the evaluation stage of managing work schedules is frequently overlooked. This may be due to the fact that managers (1) have exhausted their energy by the time they have reached this stage, (2) assume that evaluation is simply unnecessary, or (3) fear discovering failures and having to explain them. Evaluation is essential, however, if you are to manage current and future work schedules effectively.

To the degree that you systematically identified the objectives and specified criteria for their attainment, the evaluation step will not be burdensome. It involves a fairly straightforward assessment of the degree to which these objectives were met and the criteria were satisfied.

This evaluation can be accomplished by using the same rating form as that shown in Figure 6–5, this time to evaluate the *actual* effects of the new schedule. It is often enlightening to compare the actual effects to those anticipated during Step 4 so that you can identify areas where expectations have and have not been met. (See Figure 7–4 for a sample.) This analysis of shortfalls should prove useful in Step 8, where possible refinement of the new schedule is considered.

When evaluating a new schedule, many managers readminister the survey initially used to explore several potential alternatives. Typically, the post-

Figure 7–4.   *Continued*

objective, circle *3* for "no effect." If you feel the schedule would interfere with meeting the objective, circle a *1* or a *2* to indicate how negative you believe its effect will be. If you feel the schedule would help meet the objective, circle a *4* or a *5* to indicate how positive of an effect you expect.

Objective 2: Reduce turnover from 45 to 30% among employees who are young, single parents					Objective 3: Increase by 25% the number of qualified applicants for entry-level technical job openings					Objective 4: Increase by 25% the proportion of candidates who accept job offers				
Very Negative Effect	Negative Effect	No Effect	Positive Effect	Very Positive Effect	Very Negative Effect	Negative Effect	No Effect	Positive Effect	Very Positive Effect	Very Negative Effect	Negative Effect	No Effect	Positive Effect	Very Positive Effect
1	2	3	④	5	1	2	3	4	⑤	1	2	3	④	5

Turnover reduced to 26%   *Applications increased by 48%*   *Acceptances increased by 15%*

Part Four

Final Comments

Chapter Eight

← ─────────────────────────────────────── →

Conclusion

A Model of Relationships

▶   For a variety of reasons such as utilization of the organization's facilities; meeting the needs of various external constituencies; or attracting, motivating, and retaining employees, work schedules are an important part of any organization. To be effective, therefore, work schedules must be adapted to a variety of forces. As illustrated in Figure 8–1, the better the match between work-schedule characteristics (A) and these needs and constraints (B), the more effective the organization (H) will be. Effectiveness is due to the performance of individual employees, the coordination of work within and among groups of employees, the degree to which customer or client needs are met by the work schedule, and many other factors in the work environment (F).

In addition to influencing organizational effectiveness directly, work schedules affect reactions of organizational members such as work attitudes, motivation, tardiness, and performance. To be most attractive to employees, a work schedule must meet physiological, psychological, and emotional needs. These needs include personal preferences for the particular time of day to work (C) as well as a good match with each employee's natural physiological rhythms. Employees also have a need for harmony between work and nonwork affairs in order to conduct personal business and interact with friends and family members. There are substantial differences in the degree to which work schedules interfere with these off-job activities or permit a balance between these two worlds.

153

Figure 8–1. Role of Work Schedules and Other Factors in Affecting Organization Effectiveness

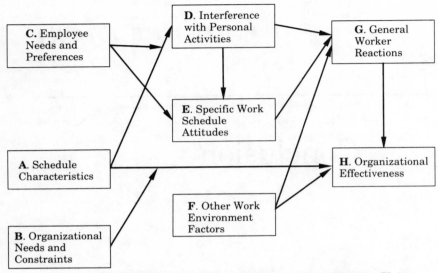

Source: From R. B. Dunham, J. L. Pierce, and M. Castenada, "Alternative Work Schedules: Two Field Quasi-Experiments," *Personnel Psychology* 40 (1987): 215–242.

Given these observations, two relatively direct effects of any work schedule on an organization's employees can be anticipated. The first is the degree to which a work schedule actually interferes with personal activities (D). The second is the affective or attitudinal reaction of employees to the specific characteristics of the schedule (E). Presumably these two types of reactions are related; satisfaction with the schedule is in part a function of the degree to which that schedule interferes with or facilitates personal activities. These two sets of worker reactions each exert a moderate amount of influence on the more general reactions to the work experience such as overall job satisfaction, job involvement, motivation, organizational commitment, and experienced stress (G). Since the general reactions are quite far removed from the characteristics of the work schedule per se, the influence of the schedule on these is considerably less than the influence on the more immediate reactions of perceived interference and satisfaction with the schedule. This could help explain some of the ambiguous and often contradictory findings in the work-scheduling literature.

Although the model shown in the figure is both general and untested, it can aid in the interpretation and integration of the research. It can also serve to guide future inquiry into the social-psychological, organizational, and behavioral consequences associated with work schedules.

Previous research has to a large extent employed a rather haphazard approach to the selection of dependent variables used for the evaluation of the impact of alternative work schedules. Also evident has been a tendency to assume that an alternative schedule will automatically meet many of the needs, preferences, and constraints of both organizations and organizational members. The actual relationships are not this simple.

The model introduced in Figure 8–1 clearly raises a potential dilemma. On the one hand, the characteristics of a work schedule will influence organizational effectiveness only to the extent that it meets *organizational* needs and constraints. On the other hand, the schedule will affect worker satisfaction only to the extent that it meets *employee* needs and preferences. Can both sets of needs be accommodated simultaneously? We believe it is possible.

Unfortunately, alternative work schedules became one of the fads of the past two decades. Many people hoped that the use of alternative work schedules would produce broad benefits for both organizations and their employees. Such early hopes for 4/40 schedules, for example, led one observer to make the following optimistic prediction:

> In my opinion, 4-day will spread, and spread rapidly, because it works well. Firms, by and large, are more efficient on 4-day; and employees, by and large, are better off with a 3-day weekend. It may also be better for the nation: if firms are more productive on 4-day, then 4-day has potential for increasing the GNP.[1]

Despite hopes like these, the potential benefits of alternative work schedules have not always been fully realized. As noted in the comprehensive reviews in Chapters Two to Five, sound empirical support for the individual and organizational benefits of such schedules is limited, fragmented, and sometimes contradictory.

The popularity of alternative work schedules may have been based largely on two naive assumptions made by their advocates. The first is the simple premise that workers prefer alternative schedules. The second is the equally simple conclusion that "the introduction of one will predictably produce broad, powerful, and positive effects on a wide range of worker reactions and on organizational effectiveness."[2] As with all assumptions, these cry out for intellectual examination and empirical evaluation.

In contrast to these assumptions, both our model and the empirical literature in general suggest that the greatest effects of alternative work schedules are to be found in worker attitudes *specific* to work schedules themselves. Strong, broad effects on *general* worker reactions are relatively unlikely, as is a strong impact on organizational effectiveness, due to the many other environmental factors that influence these dependent variables. The model does show a causal linkage from specific reactions to general worker reactions, but these are probably not powerful. Our model also shows a linkage from general worker reactions to organizational effectiveness, which is due to some likely improvements in attendance and retention. But there is limited reason to expect a strong *direct* impact of a schedule on worker effectiveness (the A → H relationship). Unless a desired schedule is offered as a contingent reward for employees who improve and then maintain their performance levels, why would it motivate employees to be more productive? The answers to this question remain to be provided.

To summarize the study reported more fully in Appendix B, we have examined major aspects of the model shown in Figure 8–1. We did so for a group of employees who clearly preferred the 4/40 schedule. The results of this study help us understand the nature and scope of reactions to alternative work schedules.

As expected, given our model and the existing needs, preferences, and constraints of the organization and employees involved, *a 4/40 schedule did make a difference.* It influenced organizational effectiveness, but only to the extent that it met a particular need for client service. It reduced interference with personal activities, but only in the way employees had been experiencing specific difficulties. Perhaps its largest impact, however, was on affective reactions to the characteristics of the schedule itself. A general positive halo (perhaps Hawthorne?) effect was also realized for a wide range of general worker reactions but these were minor. When the employees were returned to the original 5/40 schedule these reactions were for the most part reversed.

Conclusions

In conclusion, we offer the following seven observations and prescriptions for successful management of alternative work schedules:

1. Employee attitudes toward work have changed dramatically in the United States and will continue to do so. One of the more dominant social trends has been the increased desire on the part of many workers to have and enjoy more time away from work for the pursuit of leisure and recreational activities.
2. All of the alternative work-schedule arrangements are complex, multidimensional systems that must blend with other organizational requirements such as cost, technology, and customer-service needs. Potential adopters must understand the many facets of each schedule and attempt to incorporate the most salient ones in order to produce the desired results.
3. There is a powerful expectation of participation among contemporary employees, who feel that they ought to be consulted on many issues important to them. Closely coupled with this is a widespread desire for personal control and the right to exercise options in one's life.

These phenomena are particularly pertinent in the design and implementation of alternative work schedules, where the needs and predispositions of employees are highly individualized.

4. As with any employee benefit, the positive impact of an alternative work schedule may be relatively short lived. Instead of becoming discouraged and prematurely withdrawing a new schedule, organizations are well advised to maintain regular communication programs or systems to ensure that the central features of the schedule remain identifiable and understood by the participants. In addition, as new forms of work schedules are developed in the future, organizations should remain open to modifying their present practices to incorporate any improvements.

5. Organizations are encouraged to conduct systematic evaluations of the effects of their own experiments with alternative work schedules. They should also report the results so that other firms may benefit from the knowledge gained. It is only through this process that the quality of the literature on alternative work schedules can improve and the results can have widespread benefits.

6. Managers interested in adapting their organization's traditional work schedules to the newer forms should thoroughly assess the emerging body of knowledge on those of interest to them. It is particularly important to evaluate the external validity of the available reports from individual firms, so as to ascertain the degree to which the results achieved are transferable to a different group of employees and contrasting organizational context.

7. Both managers and researchers are encouraged to search for better answers as to why an alternative work schedule might work. Better understanding of the processes through which the individual and organizational effects are attained will lead to better predictability of the benefits and more accurate choices from among the alternatives.

Leisure. Multidimensionality. Participation. Communication. Evaluation. Transferability. Understanding. Taken collectively, these seven themes represent the essential keys to improvement in the understanding, design, implementation, and future development of alternative work schedules.

Endnotes

1. R. Poor, ed., *Four Days, Forty Hours: Reporting a Revolution in Work and Leisure* (Cambridge, Mass.: Bursk and Poor, 1970), p. 37.

2. H. Z. Levine, "Alternative Work Schedules: Do They Meet Work Force Needs?, Part 1," *Personnel* 64 (February 1987): 57–62.

Appendices

Appendix A

The Development of Work-Schedule Attitudinal Measures

▶ This appendix reports on the technical development of a set of research scales that can be used to examine worker attitudes toward possible alternative work schedules.[1] The scales were developed and validated in connection with two field experiments, one dealing with a flexible work schedule and the other with a 4/40 arrangement. In addition to a presentation of the items in each of the scales, a discussion of the development and validation of the research scales is provided. The casual reader may want to read only the introduction and discussion sections, skipping the detailed materials (samples, data collection, analyses) in the method section and the study's results.

The Need for Instrument Development

Interest in the specific impact of various work schedules has increased during recent years. Practitioners and researchers alike have examined various configurations of work schedules and attempted to document systematically their strengths and weaknesses. Despite these efforts to understand the effects of the various schedules on workers and their organizations, most of the literature still focuses primarily on a relatively

161

narrow range of workers' *reactions*—job satisfaction, stress, internal work motivation, job involvement, and organizational commitment.

With few exceptions, very little empirical effort has been directed toward examining employees' attitudes regarding *prospective* work-schedule alternatives. This in turn has prevented practitioners from understanding how these attitudes may be used to *design* a successful work-schedule program.

Mahoney, Newman, and Frost developed a set of scales to assess workers' attitudes toward the four-day work week.[2] Their results suggested promise for the assessment of such attitudes. Unfortunately, they did not publish the scale items (they were only described in general) nor did they provide reliability or validity information.

In a more thorough study, Golembiewski, Yeager, and Hilles developed a set of eighteen items for assessing attitudes toward a current work schedule.[3] These items were apparently written to allow their use with a wide range of types of existing schedules. The items were used for a group of workers on a 5/40 schedule and later on a flexitime schedule. This study demonstrated the potential feasibility of systematic assessment of attitudes toward work schedules, although there were several limitations to it. First, the scales appeared to be designed to assess attitudes toward current work schedules only, thus disallowing the possibility of anticipatory reactions to alternative work schedules until the workers actually experienced them. Second, the authors did not describe the development of the items so it is difficult to determine whether the items represented the researchers' perspective, the subjects' perspective, or some other perspective. Finally, identification of the underlying factors from the eighteen items was based on only fifty subjects—at best, a marginal subject-to-item ratio. Thus, although the Golembiewski study demonstrated the importance and feasibility of assessing workers' attitudes toward work schedules, further work was clearly needed.

If an appropriate set of valid, reliable instruments were available to assess attitudes toward *specific* work schedules, organizations would be able to evaluate the strengths and weaknesses of their existing work schedules and then compare them with the anticipated strengths and weaknesses of various alternatives. Such instruments and the resulting data could also be used to aid in the selection, design, implementation, and evaluation of an alternative work schedule.

This appendix presents a set of measurement scales to assess workers' attitudes toward almost any existing or alternative work schedule. These scales were developed during a three-phase research program involving six samples and over 700 clerical, technical, construction, manufacturing, and health-care employees working under a variety of schedules. The date reported here indicate the predictive effectiveness of several sets of variables for anticipating workers' preferences among work schedules.

Research Method

Study Design

In Phase 1 of the three-phase research, the instruments were developed, administered, and tested for reliability and validity. The instruments were then refined in Phases 2 and 3; and further reliability and validity tests were conducted with additional samples.

Samples

Phase 1 utilized three diverse samples (corporate-office workers, traveling construction crews, and local repair crews and office workers) from a large Midwest utility company. The 467 participants consisted of approximately 23 percent supervisory and 77 percent nonsupervisory employees. The employees participating in Phase 2 were office workers from the same utility company and consisted of 28 supervisory and 104 nonsupervisory personnel. At the time of the study, all subjects from Phases 1 and 2 were working under a fixed 5/40 schedule. Phase 3 used samples from two county health departments at two points in time. The 156 nonsupervisory employees included nurses, educators, sanitation workers, clerical workers, and administrators. One of these samples ($n = 57$) worked a flexitime schedule during the entire study period. The second sample ($n = 99$) worked a fixed-5/40 schedule during Time 1 and a 4/40 schedule during Time 2.

Instrument Development

Based upon information from the work-schedule literature and interviews with a wide cross section of sixty workers from the organization involved in Phase 1, an initial set of 100 attitude-based items was constructed. A twelve-member labor–management committee from the utility-company sample and the researchers reviewed and revised the list to obtain sixty-six items. A priori classification identified eighteen items that focused upon attitudes toward current schedules, ten that dealt with attitudes toward alternative schedules, and thirty-eight related to perceived work-schedule interference with personal activities.

In Phase 2, instrument development built upon the findings of Phase 1. Two new items were written and other items were rewritten so that the same set of questions could be used to address existing and possible alternative schedules. Because the results from Phase 2 suggested a need for a more reliable assessment of the impact of work schedules on outside constituents (e.g., customers, clients), three new items were written for Phase 3 in order to gain this information.

Data Collection

Groups of employees (who were given work-release time to participate in the study) completed paper-and-pencil questionnaires to provide data for this study. Subjects participating in Phase 1 answered questions regarding their attitudes toward their current 5/40 work schedule and about its level of interference with personal activities. In addition, each Phase 1 sample group received the following set of alternative work-schedule items: the corporate office workers were asked to react to 4/40, 4½/40, staggered, and flexitime schedules (which were defined for them in terms of core time and areas of choice); traveling construction crews reacted to 4/40 and staggered schedules; and local crews and office workers reacted to 4/40, 4½/40, staggered, and flexitime schedules.

In addition to the work schedule–related items, Phase 1 subjects answered questions relating to age, sex, education level, marital status, number of children at home, personal security, company tenure, job involvement,[4] internal work motivation,[5] job satisfaction (via the short form of the Index of Organizational Reactions),[6] work-schedule discretion,[7] and a direct measure of work-schedule preference.

Phase 2 subjects answered the items dealing with interference with personal activities and the revised attitude toward work schedules for both their existing 5/40 schedule and for a flexitime arrangement. Both samples of Phase 3 subjects completed the interference items and the second revision of the attitude-toward-work-schedule items for both a fixed 5/40 and a 4/40 schedule. Two months later the questionnaire was readministered to both Phase 3 samples.

Analyses

Across the three phases of the research program, various analytic techniques examined the following characteristics of the instruments being developed: dimensionality, similarity of dimensionality across samples and types of schedules, internal consistency, test–retest reliability, and ability to predict actual work-schedule preferences. For a number of reasons (e.g., subject-to-item ratios, appropriateness of specific alternative schedules for particular groups of workers, and the stage of scale development), analytic procedures employed were not always identical for all samples in each phase of the research program.

To identify scale dimensionality at Phase 1, principal component analyses with VARIMAX rotations were employed in an attempt to find relatively pure subdimensions of the general construct. In Phases 2 and 3, OBLIMAX rotations further refined the several moderately correlated dimensions. At all three phases, the underlying number of factors was established through the combined use of both Skree tests and interpretability criteria. Congruency coefficients were calculated to compare the similarity of solutions across samples, types of schedules, and time.[8]

Based on the results of the component analyses, unit-weighted scale scores were constructed. Coefficient alpha estimates were calculated to assess the internal consistency for each scale, and (for Phase 3 samples) test–retest reliability estimates were examined.[9]

As a partial test of the construct validity of the new scales, a nomological network was created including the constructs as measured by the new scales, actual work-schedule preferences, and several other potential predictors of schedule preferences such as personal characteristics, job involvement, work motivation, satisfaction, and current discretion over work scheduling. Using the Phase 1 corporate-office sample, a series of discriminant function analyses with classification analyses and multivariate Omega-squared estimates appraised the nature, strength, and predictive accuracy of each set of variables in the network for the prediction of actual work-schedule preferences.[10]

Results

Attitudes toward Work Schedules

Phase 1. The eighteen items assessing attitudes toward the current work schedule and the ten items directed toward each of the alternate schedules were subjected to component analyses with VARIMAX rotations for the combined sample of 467 and for the two individual samples with sufficient subject-to-item ratios. Each analysis of the current work-schedule attitudes produced a four-factor solution. Factor-congruency estimates used to compare the similarity of the solutions across the samples ranged from .79 to .93 for the first three factors and between .39 and .73 for the fourth. Fifteen of the eighteen items subsequently defined unit-weighted scales interpreted as (1) personal effects, (2) organization effects, (3) coordination of work effects, and (4) perceived uniqueness of work schedule. Coefficient alpha estimates range from .74 to .95 for the first three scales and from .59 to .69 for the fourth scale.

Each analysis of the ten alternative work-schedule attitude items suggested a two-factor solution. Factor congruency estimates for the solutions across samples and types of schedules ranged from .96 to .99 for the first factor and from .97 to .99 for the second. Two of these items were used to define a unit-weighted scale interpreted as work-coordination effects; four items defined a scale interpreted as personal effects; four items played no meaningful role due to low or complex loading. Coefficient alpha estimates for these two factors ranged from .80 to .96.

The results of these analyses identified several shortcomings that led us to revise the instruments. Members of the organization's labor–management committee provided assistance. Of particular concern were low congruency and reliability estimates for the fourth current-schedule scale, the ability to identify only two dimensions for alternative schedules, and a recognition that it would be very advantageous to have a single set of items for assessing attitudes toward both current and alternative work schedules.

Phase 2. As a result of the work done in Phase 1, twenty items were designed to be usable with any current and alternative schedule. In Phase 2, these items obtained reactions to both 5/40 and flexitime schedules. Component analyses with OBLIMAX rotations suggested very similar five-factor solutions for both analyses. Unit-weighted scale scores were formed for these dimensions, which were identified as (1) general affect toward schedule, (2) work-coordination effects, (3) uniqueness of work schedule, (4) family attitude toward schedule, and (5) schedule effects on social and family life. Coefficient alpha estimates were very good for the first three scales, ranging from .77 to .93. The fourth scale had an alpha of .78 for the 5/40 scale but only .60 for the flexitime scale. The fifth scale had low alphas (.40s) for both schedules.

The reliability problems in Phase 2 and the inability of the instrument to identify adequately a dimension dealing with the effects of a schedule on outside constituents led to the second major revision of these items and the research conducted in Phase 3. Phase 3 would also provide an extension of the external validity and stability of the research scales.

Phase 3. The second major revision of the attitude-toward-schedule scales resulted in a twenty-three-item instrument. Two of the items in this set were inappropriate for respondents who were unmarried or living alone: "In general my family would be satisfied with my working . . ." and, "My husband/wife would like me to work. . . ." As a result, these two items were excluded from analyses and future versions of the scales.

Component analyses with OBLIMAX rotations for each of the Phase 3 sample/schedule/time combinations suggested that a six-factor solution was most appropriate.

Table A–1. Final Instrument[a] for Measuring Attitudes toward Work Schedules, and Results of Principal Component Analysis

	Factor					
	1	*2*	*3*	*4*	*5*	*6*
General affect toward schedule[b]						
1. I would be very productive under the _____ method of scheduling.	89	05	−05	03	14	04
2. The _____ schedule would have a favorable influence on my overall attitude toward my job.	80	00	−08	−10	01	08
3. My current work schedule would encourage me to do my best.	78	01	−09	05	−12	−06
4. Taking everything into consideration, I would be satisfied with my life in general while working a _____ work week.	68	09	−02	−25	−04	07
5. I would be dissatisfied with my current work schedule.	−68	00	04	14	−01	03
6. I personally would like the _____ method of scheduling.	62	12	−08	−15	−01	−03
7. A _____ schedule would have an unfavorable influence on my physical health.	54	23	22	09	−20	−14
Service to external constituency						
8. The _____ schedule would improve client access to the services of the department.	05	85	−01	00	00	05
9. The _____ method of scheduling would help the department meet the needs of its clients.	−08	82	−10	−01	−04	−08
10. The _____ method of scheduling would make it easier for me to meet the service needs of the clients.	10	76	−01	−12	01	−02
11. The _____ method of scheduling would hurt the quality of client service.	−09	−53	43	−07	−10	04
Work-coordination effects						
12. The _____ method of scheduling would cause problems in coordinating work with my supervisor.	02	−04	83	07	11	−05

Table A–1. *Continued*

	Factor					
	1	2	3	4	5	6
13. The _____ method of scheduling would cause problems in coordinating work with my coworkers.	−11	−12	81	03	04	05
Schedule effects on social and family life						
14. The _____ work schedule would have an unfavorable influence on my family life.	08	−03	−08	86	05	04
15. The _____ method of scheduling would make it easier for me to coordinate my schedule with the schedules of other family members.	14	09	08	−66	07	−05
16. The _____ work schedule would have an unfavorable influence on my social life.	−38	21	19	51	10	11
Uniqueness of work schedule						
17. Almost none of my neighbors work a _____ work schedule.	−08	13	03	−10	85	12
18. Almost all of my friends work a _____ work schedule.	−11	14	−07	−13	−78	20
Transportation and personal security						
19. Working or leaving the work place at an unusual (early or late) hour would represent a personal-security problem for me under the _____ work schedule.	18	−09	−10	09	−03	89
20. Under the _____ method of scheduling, transportation to and from work would be difficult.	−31	10	25	01	−03	57
Item not used in scales						
21. Overall, the _____ method of scheduling would have more good than bad aspects.	37	53	11	−08	−04	02

[a] Decimal points omitted.

[b] The work-schedule attitude questions are responded to on five-point Likert scales anchored: 1 = strongly disagree; 2 = disagree; 3 = neither agree nor disagree; 4 = agree; 5 = strongly agree.

Of the six factors, four paralleled factors from Phase 2: general affect toward schedule, work-coordination effects, uniqueness of schedule, and schedule effects on social and family life (see Table A–1). In addition, two factors not defined in Phase 2 were identified: transportation and personal security, and service to external constituencies (customers, clients, and suppliers outside of the home organization).

Unit-weighted scales for the six dimensions across samples and types of schedules produced coefficient alphas that were for the most part at acceptable levels (.70s and .80s). The major exception was the transportation and personal-security scale, with alphas ranging from .29 to .90. Test–retest coefficients were also mostly strong (.60s to .80s), with a few exceptions. In particular, schedule effects on social and family life were poor (averaging in the .20s).

Perceived Interference

The thirty-eight perceived-interference-with-personal-activities items were analyzed for the combined sample from Phase 1. The results of the principal component analysis with VARIMAX rotations suggested three underlying dimensions (see Table A–2). Twenty-one of the items defined three scales: (1) interference with activities involving family and friends, (2) interference with access to services, events, and consumer goods, and (3) interference with financial and related activities. With one exception, coefficient alpha estimates for the three scales for the three samples and for the combined sample were very high (.81 to .93).

Prediction of Work-Schedule Preference

In the corporate office–worker sample, several sets of potential predictors of work-schedule preferences were used to predict workers' actual first choice (from a set of five schedules that were under consideration). The sets of predictors included personal characteristics, job involvement and motivation, job satisfaction, current discretion over work schedules, interference with personal activities, and attitudes toward schedules (as measured using the newly developed instruments). A series of discriminant-function analyses determined whether a given set had a significant relationship with schedule preference; identified the percent of variance explained; and assessed classification accuracy using the set of variables to predict schedule preference.

Table A–2. Results of Principal Component Analysis: Interference with Personal Activities

	Factor		
	1	2	3
Interference with activities involving family and friends[a]			
1. Spend time with your children[b]	.84	.33	.14
2. Maintain personal family relations	.76	.30	.22
3. Spend time with your spouse	.76	.29	.24
4. Spend time with friends	.75	.35	.17
5. Take family on recreational outings	.75	.33	.21

Table A–2.   *Continued*

	Factor		
	1	2	3
6. Take part in children's education	.73	.20	.31
7. Attend children's school activities	.68	.21	.35
8. Participate in sports with others	.66	.33	.27
9. Participate in nonwork organizations	.64	.31	.24
Interference with access to services, events, consumables			
10. See a movie	.25	.78	.16
11. Go to a tavern or buy liquor	.19	.75	.07
12. Go to the laundromat	.31	.70	.24
13. Go out to eat	.21	.68	.31
14. Attend a play, concert, or cultural event	.41	.68	.19
15. Watch favorite TV programs	.33	.61	.09
16. Buy groceries	.31	.58	.33
17. Go shopping for clothes	.37	.53	.39
18. Use public transportation	.23	.45	.21
Interference with financial and related activities			
19. Go to the bank	.18	.14	.79
20. Cash a check	.10	.18	.75
21. Go to the post office	.30	.07	.65
Items not used in scales			
22. Attend spectator sports	.43	.47	.29
23. Get hair cut or styled	.38	.33	.43
24. Pay bills	.24	.49	.53
25. Get prescription filled	.23	.47	.63
26. Go to the library	.21	.41	.54
27. Visit doctor or dentist	.38	.14	.62
28. Buy gas	.33	.45	.38
29. Continue your education	.55	.30	.18
30. Have repair work done	.57	.09	.43
31. Visit relatives	.63	.39	.11
32. Do individual sports or hobbies	.68	.34	.31
33. Attend family events	.56	.35	.17
34. Go to the dry cleaners'	.37	.32	.49
35. Attend church or synagogue	.41	.58	.10
36. Do routine work around home	.68	.24	.37
37. Do part-time military activity	.46	.38	.25
38. Spend time alone	.37	.35	.19

[a] Some items are abbreviated in this table. The complete items, as well as a longer version describing the scale development and a more complete set of tables, may be obtained by writing to Randall B. Dunham, University of Wisconsin, Graduate School of Business, 1155 Observatory Drive, Madison, Wis. 53706.

[b] Items were presented by "How easy or difficult is it for you now to . . . ?" Response format was from 1 to 5, very difficult to very easy.

Neither the job-satisfaction nor the job involvement-motivation sets of variables had significant relationships with schedule preference. Personal characteristics accounted for 3 percent of the variance with a 39 percent classification accuracy. Current discretion over the work schedule also accounted for 3 percent of the variance with a 30 percent classification accuracy. Interference from the work schedule explained 12 percent of the variance and had a 23 percent classification accuracy. The set of attitudes toward schedules explained 74 percent of the variance and produced a 67 percent accuracy in classification. The combined set of variables accounted for 85 percent of the variance and provided correct classification in 71 percent of all cases.

Discussion of Results

Scale Development

The previous section reported on the technical development and validation of a set of scales to measure workers' attitudes toward various work schedules. The three-phase investigation created scales to measure six work-schedule attitudes and perceived interference with three sets of personal activities (see Figure A–1).

It was particularly interesting to note that when workers form attitudes toward work schedules they focus not only on personal and family effects but also on the likely impact of a particular work schedule on organizational effectiveness, in terms of both work coordination and service to external constituencies. The interference caused by a work schedule can be in one or more of the three distinct personal or organizational areas. The distinction is made between these three different areas of interference because the managerial actions taken to remedy associated problems may be very different, depending on the particular area(s) in which interference is most severe.

The scales developed to measure each dimension demonstrate adequate validity and reliability. With the possible exception of the uniqueness scale (the measure with the most serious remaining questions about reliability), the scales developed here can be used with a wide range of employee types and/or schedules while maintaining adequate reliability and validity. Since the same scales can be used for many combinations of existing and alternative schedules, direct comparisons can be made for each of the attitudes across types of schedules.

Figure A–1.　Work-Schedule Measurement Scales

Attitudes toward work schedules
1. General affect toward the schedule
2. Service to external constituencies
3. Work-coordination effects
4. Schedule effects on social and family life
5. Uniqueness of work schedule
6. Transportation and personal security

Interference with personal activities
1. Family and friends
2. Access to services, events, and consumables
3. Financial and related activities

In addition to demonstrating acceptable dimensional validity and reliability, placement of the attitude scales into a nomological network provided further evidence of construct validity. Wide differences in preferences toward work schedules could *not* be explained entirely on the basis of employee characteristics or general affective orientation. *Attitudes must actually be measured;* it is not adequate to draw inferences based on employee characteristics. Once schedule attitudes are assessed, work-schedule *preferences* can be predicted with a high degree of accuracy. Classification analyses conducted in these studies were able to predict work-schedule preferences with an overall accuracy of up to 71 percent. The strongest predictors of work-schedule preferences were specific attitudes toward work schedules (primarily affect) followed by personal characteristics, current scheduling discretion, and interference with personal activities. It is these findings that most strongly support the construct validity of the measures developed in these studies.

Practical Applications

The utility of the scales to help plan, implement, and evaluate alternative work schedules is discussed further in Appendix B. Practitioners will find the instruments reported here useful for either designing or modifying work schedules. More complete knowledge of workers' complex work-scheduling attitudes will allow a much more systematic approach to schedule design and redesign than has been possible in the past. The fact that workers' attitudes toward current and alternative work schedules focus on both personal and organizational impacts suggests that *workers' attitudes and opinions can be very useful in designing work schedules beneficial to the organization as well as to the worker.* The scales can help organizations identify the more desirable alternative work schedules, anticipate probable positive and negative aspects, and systematically evaluate the effectiveness of alternative work-schedule interventions.

Endnotes

1. This appendix is adapted from R. B. Dunham and J. L. Pierce, "Attitudes toward Work Schedules: Construct Definition, Instrument Development, and Validation," *Academy of Management Journal* 29 (January 1986): 170–182.

2. T. A. Mahoney, J. M. Newman, and P. J. Frost, "Worker Perceptions of the Four-Day Week," *California Management Review* 18 (1975): 31–35.

3. R. T. Golembiewski, S. Yeager, and R. Hilles, "Factor Analysis of Some Flexitime Effects: Attitudinal and Behavioral Consequences of a Structural Intervention," *Academy of Management Journal* 18 (1975): 500–509.

4. T. M. Lodahl and M. Kejner, "The Definition and Measurement of Job Involvement," *Journal of Applied Psychology* 49 (1985): 24–33.

5. J. R. Hackman and G. R. Oldham, "Development of the Job Diagnostic Survey," *Journal of Applied Psychology* 60 (1975): 159–170.

6. R. B. Dunham, F. J. Smith, and R. S. Blackburn, "Validation of the Index of Organizational Reactions with the JDI, the MSQ, and FACES Scales," *Academy of Management Journal* 20 (1977): 420–432; F. J. Smith, Index of Organizational Reactions (IOR), *JSAS Catalog of Selected Documents in Psychology* 6 (1976): MS. 1265.

7. J. L. Pierce and J. W. Newstrom, "Employee Responses to Flexible Work Schedules: An Interorganization, Intersystem Comparison," *Journal of Management* 8 (1982): 9–25.

8. H. H. Harmon, *Modern Factor Analysis* 3rd ed. (Chicago: University of Chicago Press, 1975).

9. L. J. Cronbach, "Coefficient Alpha and the Internal Structure of Tests," *Psychometrika* 16 (1951): 297–334.

10. M. M. Tatsuoka, *An Examination of the Statistical Properties of a Multivariate Measure of Strength of Relationship* (Urbana: University of Illinois, 1973).

Appendix B

<svg>←————————————————————→</svg>

Implementation and Evaluation of an Alternative Work Schedule: An Experiment

▶ In this appendix we report on the evaluation of a quasi-experimental implementation of a 4/40 work schedule. The employees participating in this field experiment were working under a 5/40 arrangement, which was changed to a 4/40 schedule for four months and then returned to the 5/40. Reactions were evaluated using a model for understanding the impact of work schedules.

A Model of Relationships

Employee work schedules are an important part of an organization. To be effective, work schedules must meet organizational needs and constraints. The better the match between work schedules and these needs and constraints, the more effective the organization will be (review Figure 8–1). Effectiveness arises from the performance of individual employees, the coordination of the work within and among groups of employees, and the degree to which customer or client needs are met by the work schedule.

In addition to influencing organizational effectiveness directly, work schedules also affect several reactions of organizational members, as discussed earlier. To be attractive to employees, a work schedule must meet their needs. These needs involve personal preferences for the particular time of day to work; and personal needs for off-job activities such as conducting personal business and interacting with friends and family members. There are differences in the degree to which work schedules interfere with these off-job activities.

Given these observations, two relatively direct effects of work schedules on employees are anticipated. The first of these is the degree to which a work schedule *interferes* with personal activities. The second is the *affective* reaction of employees to the characteristics of a schedule. Presumably these two types of reactions are related: satisfaction with a schedule is in part a function of the degree to which it interferes with or facilitates personal activities. Each set of worker reactions should exert a moderate amount of influence on more general reactions to the work experience, such as overall job satisfaction, job involvement, motivation, and experienced stress. Since these more general reactions are quite far removed from the characteristics of a work schedule itself, it is expected that the influence of the schedule on these will be considerably less than the influence on the immediate reactions of perceived interference and satisfaction. This could help explain some of the ambiguous findings on these issues in the current work-scheduling literature.

Predictions from the Model

This appendix presents an empirical investigation of the major linkages shown in Figure 8–1.[1] The primary purpose is to illustrate the design, implementation, and evaluation of an alternative work schedule. In the study reported here, the characteristics of employee work schedules were changed and the subsequent effects explored. A group of employees working a 5/40 schedule were placed on a 4/40 schedule for four months, after which they were returned to the 5/40 arrangement. Five research questions, each containing a general directional prediction, were addressed in this study. These predictions were based on previous research and on the model introduced in Chapter Eight. It should be noted that all the predictions were made for employees who had previously indicated preferences for the alternative schedules implemented as part of this study. The following were the questions and predictions of our study:

1. Does the introduction of an alternative work schedule (4/40) influence organizational effectiveness as measured by employee performance, work coordination, and client service? It was predicted that organizational effectiveness would improve.
2. Does the introduction of an alternative work schedule (4/40) influence interference with the personal activities of workers in the following areas?

   a. Interactions with family and friends
   b. Access to services, events, and consumables
   c. Conduct of financial activities

   It was predicted that a change from 5/40 to 4/40 would decrease interference, while movement from 4/40 to 5/40 would increase it. (This presumed, however, that the benefits derived from the new free day would override the personal costs of the extra hours worked on the other four days in the switch to 4/40.)

3. Does the introduction of an alternative work schedule (4/40) influence worker satisfaction with the work schedule? It was predicted that movement from 5/40 to 4/40 would increase satisfaction with the work schedule while the change from 4/40 to 5/40 would decrease satisfaction.

4. Does the introduction of an alternative work schedule (4/40) influence general worker reactions such as overall satisfaction, job involvement, motivation, and stress? It was predicted that movement from 5/40 to 4/40 would cause a small improvement in these reactions while return from 4/40 to 5/40 would cause a small decline.

Organizations are often quite uncertain about the probable effects of the introduction of a particular alternative work schedule. This is understandable in light of the inconsistency of reactions to work schedules reported in the literature, summarized in Chapters Two through Five. Of course it would be very useful to an organization to be able to anticipate worker reactions to alternative schedules prior to the selection of one for implementation. In the present study, information was obtained prior to the introduction of the alternative schedule, which allowed prediction of its probable effects. This allowed comparison of anticipated reactions to subsequent actual reactions to the new work schedule. Thus the final research question was:

5. Do worker reactions toward an alternative work schedule (4/40) obtained prior to experience with it (i.e., in concept) match actual reactions after experiencing it? In other words, can reactions be predicted prior to the introduction of an alternative schedule? It was predicted that reactions could be accurately anticipated.

Based on these five questions, an empirical study was conducted to explore the various impacts of an alternative work schedule (4/40). This field study was better focused than many previous ones in this area due to the guidance of the interrelationships model presented in Figure 8–1. The statistical tests were also more consistent with the specific research questions than has been common in this area of the literature. Much of the previous research was improved upon by using a quasi-experimental field design with repeated measures and by utilizing well-developed and validated instruments (identified and discussed in Appendix A) for assessing the dependent variables. Also important were the tests of the degree to which worker reaction to various work-schedule changes could be accurately anticipated prior to the introduction of the new schedule.

Method

Sample and Study Design

In this experiment, a group of employees working a 5/40 schedule were placed on a 4/40 schedule for four months, after which they were returned to the original 5/40.

This 4/40 field experiment followed a pre–post test, comparison-group design. Data for this natural quasi-experimental study were obtained from two groups of county health-department employees. The employees consisted of county health nurses, health educators, environmental health technicians (e.g., sanitation workers, laboratory technicians), clerical, and administrative personnel. At the first of three data-collection periods, the study's experimental group consisted of ninety-nine employees. Only forty-three were available for participation at all three data-collection periods. The comparison group consisted of forty-one employees. This group was chosen from another county to provide a group comparable to the experimental group. The comparison group worked a 5/40 schedule throughout the study period. Participants were fully informed about the experimental nature of the study and the 4/40 schedule.

Data were collected for the comparison group in conjunction with the first two data-collection periods for the experimental group, before and after the 4/40 manipulation. At Time 1, the experimental group was working a 5/40 schedule. Two weeks later, this group of employees began a 4/40 schedule. Two months following the introduction of the 4/40, employee response and performance data were again collected (Time 2). Four months after the implementation of the 4/40, these employees returned to a 5/40 work week. Time 3 observation of the experimental group was made two months after return to the 5/40 schedule. (Data were not collected from the control group at Time 3.)

Organizational effectiveness measures included five dimensions of worker performance (e.g., quantity, quality, reliability), work coordination, and quality of client service. Performance was assessed with a performance appraisal by supervisors. The four specific performance dimensions assessed were (1) productivity (Produces a volume of work consistent with established standard), (2) quality (Performs duties accurately and effectively), (3) reliability (Performs work on assigned tasks in an efficient, conscientious, dependable manner without close supervision), and (4) reaction to problems (Identifies, analyzes, and acts upon a problem in a constructive, responsible manner). These four scales were combined via an additive model to obtain an overall performance measure. Each of the four performance dimensions was rated by the immediate supervisor on a frequency scale, where performance increments ranged from "0 to 10 percent of the time" to "91 to 100 percent of the time." The work-schedule scales discussed in Appendix A were used to obtain measures of work coordination and client service associated with both 5/40 and 4/40 schedules at each point in time. These measures were obtained from nonsupervisory employees as well as from first- and second-level managers. There were no significant differences as a function of level.

Three dimensions of interference with personal activities were also measured: activities with family and friends; access to services, events, and consumables; and financial activities.[2]

Seven specific work-schedule attitudes were measured. The first of these was time autonomy, which was measured using a five-item scale.[3] Five scales were used to measure attitudes toward both 5/40 and 4/40 at each time point.[4] These scales included: general schedule affect; schedule uniqueness; effects on family and social life; family attitude toward the schedule; and effects on transportation and personal security. Hours-of-work satisfaction were also measured using the FACE scales.[5]

Eight general worker reactions were also measured at each point in time. These included general job satisfaction, which was assessed using the short form of the Minnesota Satisfaction Questionnaire.[6] Leisure-time satisfaction was measured with a second set of FACE scales. Organizational commitment was measured with a fifteen-item scale.[7] Job involvement,[8] intrinsic motivation,[9] and symptoms of physiological and psychological stress[10] were measured by various scales. Finally, a scale for the measurement of fatigue was created for this study.

For those data collected directly from employees, questionnaires were administered to groups of about twenty employees who were given job-release time for data-collection purposes. Participation was voluntary and confidentiality was promised. Employees were asked to place their names or other personalized identifications on each questionnaire to allow matching of participant responses across the multiple data-collection periods.

Cronbach's coefficient alpha was employed to assess the reliability of each multiple-item scale.[11] The reliability estimates are presented in Table B–1. Most reliabilities were at acceptable levels, with some exceptions for the two-item scales. The descriptive statistics (means and standard deviations) are presented in Table B–2.

A set of nested and interaction contrasts (i.e., linear combinations of means where the coefficients add up to zero) were tested within a planned-comparison strategy. Several techniques can be used for a priori identification of the most relevant specific cell contrasts and subsequent analysis of the statistical significance for each of these planned comparisons.[12] One of these techniques, known as the *Dunn-Bonferroni procedure*, allows both one- and two-directional tests or a combination of the two.[13] Significance tests, using the Dunn-Bonferroni procedure, are conducted by calculating a t statistic and then evaluating this (observed) value against its respective critical value. Observed t values are calculated according to the following general formula:[14]

$$t_D = \frac{\hat{\psi}_i}{\hat{\sigma}_{\psi i}}$$

Where:

t_D = denotes the Dunn-Bonferroni t statistic
$\hat{\psi}_i$ = denotes the estimated contrast of interest
$\hat{\sigma}_{\psi i}$ = denotes the estimated standard deviation of the contrast

Critical values of t_D for traditional alpha levels (.01, .05, .10) are available, while the critical values for nontraditional alpha levels may be calculated with an approximation formula.[15]

In this study, three contrasts are required to test the five research questions. Contrasts 1 and 2 address Research Questions 1 to 4, while Contrast 3 tests Research Question 5.

In Contrast 1, observed changes for the experimental group between the pretest and first posttest periods are compared to the observed changes for the control group

Table B–1. Reliability Coefficients (Coefficient Alpha)

	Time 1[a]	Time 2[b]	Time 3[b]
Organizational Effectiveness			
Performance	N.A.	N.A.	N.A.
Work coordination			
5/40	.78	.91	.84
4/40	.85	.87	.94
Client service			
5/40	.63	.79	.81
4/40	.81	.87	.88
Specific Work-Schedule Attitudes			
Time autonomy	.93	.94	.96
General schedule affect			
5/40	.74	.89	.87
4/40	.90	.78	.91
Uniqueness			
5/40	.64	.63	.62
4/40	.58	.72	.70
Family & social life			
5/50	.81	.74	.71
4/40	.72	.86	.90
Family attiude toward schedule			
5/40	.44	.77	.95
4/40	.84	.84	.83
Transportation & personal security			
5/40	.45	.54	.06
4/40	.42	.65	.40
Hours-of-work satisfaction	N.A.	N.A.	N.A.
General Worker Reactions			
General job satisfaction	.83	.84	.82
Leisure-time satisfaction	N.A.	N.A.	N.A.
Organizational commitment	.87	.90	.90
Job involvement	.70	.71	.78
Intrinsic motivation	.72	.80	.85
Fatigue	.65	.65	.61
Physiological stress	.68	.75	.83
Psychological stress	.61	.68	.69

[a] Reliability estimates based on total sample

[b] Reliability estimates based on experimental group

Table B–2. **Descriptive Statistics (Means and Standard Deviations)**

Scale	Time 1 E[a]	Time 1 C[b]	Time 2 E	Time 2 C	Time 3 E
Organizational Effectiveness					
Performance					
Quantity	7.70(1.33)	6.77(1.31)	8.31(0.89)	6.92(0.96)	8.25(0.89)
Quality	7.79(1.34)	7.00(1.15)	8.24(0.91)	7.41(0.88)	8.25(0.75)
Reliability	7.85(1.42)	6.87(1.53)	8.28(1.03)	7.21(0.77)	8.04(1.07)
Reactions to problems	7.49(1.52)	6.77(1.58)	7.97(0.94)	6.92(1.35)	7.61(1.57)
Overall	30.82(4.88)	27.41(4.76)	32.79(3.26)	28.46(3.22)	32.14(3.58)
Work coordination					
5/40	4.54(1.49)	4.29(1.38)	4.12(1.12)	4.50(1.83)	4.07(1.35)
4/40 or flexitime	4.65(1.54)	5.44(1.60)	4.51(1.55)	5.10(1.99)	4.65(1.66)
Client service					
5/40	12.33(2.21)	16.21(1.62)	12.51(2.18)	13.77(3.50)	13.41(2.71)
4/40 or flexitime	13.56(2.90)	12.74(3.31)	13.83(3.02)	13.55(3.68)	13.14(3.06)
Interference with Personal Activities					
Family and friends	31.95(8.41)	31.85(7.31)	26.74(7.38)	32.79(7.94)	28.83(8.10)
Services, events, and consumables	28.95(8.34)	27.29(8.48)	27.88(8.16)	26.68(8.74)	27.88(8.25)
Financial	5.05(2.04)	6.93(1.96)	4.84(1.60)	6.29(2.09)	5.28(1.96)
Specific Work-Schedule Attitudes					
Time autonomy	19.07(6.29)	17.25(6.77)	18.74(6.51)	17.29(7.25)	17.63(5.97)
General schedule affect					
5/40	21.35(3.05)	22.74(3.30)	20.07(3.80)	22.23(4.21)	21.24(3.46)
4/40 or flexitime	23.09(2.66)	23.04(2.55)	24.19(2.80)	25.45(5.14)	24.98(4.19)
Uniqueness					
5/40	5.44(1.45)	5.11(1.60)	5.44(1.72)	4.70(1.37)	5.79(1.59)
4/40 or flexitime	7.74(1.51)	7.93(1.30)	7.16(1.51)	7.66(1.23)	7.77(1.15)
Family & social life					
5/40	4.86(1.47)	4.86(1.76)	5.16(1.38)	4.67(1.61)	4.91(1.45)
4/40 or flexitime	4.56(1.52)	4.30(1.51)	4.33(1.23)	4.55(1.96)	4.63(1.31)

continued

Table B–2. *Continued*

Scale	Time 1		Time 2		Time 3
	E^a	C^b	E	C	E
Specific Work-Schedule Attitudes (continued)					
Family attitude toward schedule					
5/40	10.16(2.10)	10.27(2.20)	9.10(2.71)	10.92(2.48)	10.26(2.78)
4/40 or flexitime	11.20(2.57)	9.92(1.66)	11.17(2.17)	11.15(2.36)	10.61(2.75)
Transportation & personal service					
5/40	4.63(1.31)	3.93(1.27)	4.19(1.20)	3.70(1.34)	4.12(1.25)
4/40 or flexitime	3.93(1.28)	3.79(1.42)	4.00(1.27)	3.75(1.38)	4.17(1.11)
Hours-of-work satisfaction	4.74(1.09)	4.96(1.23)	5.16(1.25)	4.83(1.34)	4.56(1.16)
General Worker Reactions					
General job satisfaction	72.72(7.46)	75.70(10.43)	73.88(7.13)	74.03(9.59)	71.91(7.68)
Leisure-time satisfaction	4.47(1.53)	5.00(1.81)	4.98(1.34)	4.90(1.68)	4.35(1.40)
Organizational commitment	72.58(11.39)	79.46(3.93)	72.40(12.37)	77.32(15.49)	71.72(12.25)
Job involvement	13.23(3.20)	15.29(2.96)	13.30(2.95)	14.58(2.71)	13.09(3.08)
Intrinsic motivation	32.93(3.67)	36.39(3.05)	32.47(4.13)	35.58(3.15)	32.26(4.01)
Fatigue	11.12(2.31)	10.96(3.02)	10.88(2.24)	11.26(3.13)	10.91(2.40)
Physiological stress	8.83(3.43)	9.57(2.57)	8.81(3.24)	9.55(3.52)	9.12(3.21)
Psychological stress	8.29(1.70)	8.26(1.63)	8.49(1.64)	7.94(1.53)	8.47(1.49)

[a] Descriptive statistics based on the experimental group.

[b] Descriptive statistics based on the control group.

during the same period. This tests for effects as the experimental group was moved from a 5/40 to a 4/40 schedule. Contrast 1 may be stated as follows:

Contrast 1: $(E_{T_2} - E_{T_1}) > (C_{T_2} - C_{T_1})$

In Contrast 2, the first posttest levels for the experimental group are compared to the second posttest levels for the same group. This comparison tests for effects as

Endnotes

1. This appendix is based in part on material in R. B. Dunham, J. L. Pierce, and M. B. Castaneda, "Alternative Work Schedules: Two Field Quasi-Experiments," *Personnel Psychology* 40 (1987): 215–242.

2. R. B. Dunham and J. L. Pierce, "Attitudes toward Work Schedules: Construct Definition, Instrument Development, and Validation," *Academy of Management Journal* 29 (1986): 170–182.

3. J. L. Pierce and J. W. Newstrom, "Employee Responses to Flexible Work Schedules: An Interorganization, Intersystem Comparison," *Journal of Management* 8 (1982): 9–25.

4. Dunham and Pierce, op. cit.

5. T. Kunin, "The Construction of a New Type of Attitude Measure," *Personnel Psychology* 8 (1955): 65–78; R. B. Dunham and J. B. Herman, "Development of a Female FACE Scale for Measuring Job Satisfaction," *Journal of Applied Psychology* 60 (1975): 629–631.

6. D. J. Weiss, R. V. Dawis, G. W. England, and L. H. Lofquist, *Manual for the Minnesota Satisfaction Questionnaire* (Minneapolis: University of Minnesota Industrial Relations Center, Work Adjustment Project, 1967).

7. L. W. Porter, R. M. Steers, R. T. Mowday, and P. V. Boulain, "Organizational Commitment, Job Satisfaction and Turnover among Psychiatric Technicians," *Journal of Applied Psychology* 59 (1974): 603–609.

8. T. M. Lodahl and M. Kejner, "The Definition and Measurement of Job Involvement," *Journal of Applied Psychology* 49 (1965): 24–33.

9. E. E. Lawler, III, and D. T. Hall, "Relationships of Job Characteristics to Job Involvement, Satisfaction, and Intrinsic Motivation," *Journal of Applied Psychology* 54 (1970): 305–308.

10. M. Patchen, *Participation, Achievement, and Involvement on the Job* (Englewood Cliffs, N.J.: Prentice-Hall, 1970).

11. L. J. Cronbach, "Coefficient Alpha and Its Internal Structure of Tests," *Psychometrika* 16 (1951): 197–334.

12. R. E. Kirk, *Experimental Design: Procedures for the Behavioral Sciences* (Belmont, Cal.: Brooks/Cole, 1982).

13. M. B. Castaneda, R. B. Dunham, and J. R. Levin, *Application of a Powerful a Priori Multiple-Comparison Technique with Behavioral Data.* Paper presented at the 46th Annual Meeting of the Academy of Management, Chicago, 1986.

14. Kirk, op cit.

15. Ibid.

Appendix C

Comprehensive Work-Schedule Survey

▶ As Chapter Seven suggested, there is substantial merit in allowing employees to participate in the process of designing and selecting the alternative work schedule to be implemented. This can not only provide valuable information but also increase the probability that employees will enthusiastically support the new schedule. A systematic and comprehensive data-gathering approach is recommended for this purpose, and Appendix C provides an illustration of the types of questions that may be useful to explore. This particular survey includes sets of questions to identify key demographic factors that might be important, employee feelings about organizational change in general, opinions and feelings about the current work schedule, projected reactions to an alternative work schedule, and feelings about a range of other work-related factors. Later, of course, it could be readministered in slightly revised form to gain information on reactions to the change and to identify areas for possible refinement.

Section I

1. What is your age? (Circle one.)
   1. under 21
   2. 21–25
   3. 26–30
   4. 31–40
   5. 41–50
   6. 51–60
   7. over 60
2. What is the highest education level you have achieved? (Circle one.)
   1. some high school
   2. high-school graduate or equivalent
   3. some college, but no degree
   4. associate or technical degree
   5. college graduate (Bachelor's degree)
   6. some graduate school
   7. graduate degree (Master's or higher)
3. What is your job classification? (Circle one.)
   1. nonsupervisory clerical
   2. supervisory clerical
   3. nonsupervisory technical
   4. supervisory technical
   5. nonsupervisory production
   6. supervisory production
4. How long have your worked for this company? (Circle one.)
   1. less than 1 year
   2. 1–3 years
   3. 4–8 years
   4. 9–15 years
   5. 16–25 years
   6. over 25 years
5. Where do you work? (Circle one.)
   1. Green Bay
   2. Milwaukee West office
   3. Milwaukee South office
   4. Schaumburg
   5. Cincinnati
   6. Memphis
   7. Denver
   8. Columbus
6. Are you—? (Circle one.)
   1. Male
   2. Female

Section II[1]

	Strongly Disagree	Disagree	Neither Agree nor Disagree	Agree	Strongly Agree
7. More often than not, organizational changes benefit the majority of employees who are involved in the change.	1	2	3	4	5
8. More often than not, organizational changes benefit the organization.	1	2	3	4	5
9. Organizational changes often take advantage of employees.	1	2	3	4	5
10. More often than not, organizational changes are introduced before the details of the changes have been well worked out.	1	2	3	4	5
11. In my opinion, many of the changes introduced in this organization are not good ideas.	1	2	3	4	5
12. I am concerned that I may adapt poorly to the organizational changes to be introduced in the next few years.	1	2	3	4	5
13. I enjoy the changes that occur at this organization.	1	2	3	4	5
14. Working here would be less interesting if things did not change so often.	1	2	3	4	5

Section III[2]

Sometimes a work schedule can interfere with opportunities to do other things. The following questions ask how easy or difficult it is for you to do some common activities under your *current* work schedule.

	Very Easy	Easy	Neither Difficult nor Easy	Difficult	Very Difficult
15. Spend time with your children	1	2	3	4	5
16. Maintain personal family relations	1	2	3	4	5
17. Spend time with your spouse	1	2	3	4	5
18. Spend time with friends	1	2	3	4	5
19. Take family on recreational outings	1	2	3	4	5
20. Take part in children's education	1	2	3	4	5
21. Attend children's school activities	1	2	3	4	5
22. Participate in sports with others	1	2	3	4	5
23. Participate in nonwork organizations	1	2	3	4	5
24. See a movie	1	2	3	4	5
25. Go to tavern or buy liquor	1	2	3	4	5
26. Go to the laundromat	1	2	3	4	5
27. Go out to eat	1	2	3	4	5
28. Attend play, concert, cultural event	1	2	3	4	5
29. Watch favorite TV programs	1	2	3	4	5
30. Buy groceries	1	2	3	4	5
31. Go shopping for clothes	1	2	3	4	5
32. Use public transportation	1	2	3	4	5
33. Go to the bank	1	2	3	4	5
34. Cash a check	1	2	3	4	5
35. Go to the post office	1	2	3	4	5

The questions in this section ask about your opinions and feelings concerning your *current* work schedule. For each statement, circle a number to indicate the degree to which you agree or disagree with the statement.

	Strongly Disagree	Disagree	Neither Agree nor Disagree	Agree	Strongly Agree
36. I am very productive under the current method of scheduling.	1	2	3	4	5
37. The current schedule has a favorable influence on my overall attitude toward my job.	1	2	3	4	5
38. My current work schedule encourages me to do my best.	1	2	3	4	5
39. Taking everything into consideration, I am satisfied with my life in general while working my current work week.	1	2	3	4	5
40. I am dissatisfied with my current work schedule.	1	2	3	4	5
41. I personally like the current method of scheduling.	1	2	3	4	5
42. The current schedule has an unfavorable influence on my physical health.	1	2	3	4	5
43. The current schedule provides good client access to the services of the department.	1	2	3	4	5
44. The current method of scheduling helps the department meet the needs of its clients.	1	2	3	4	5
45. The current method of scheduling makes it easy for me to meet the service needs of clients.	1	2	3	4	5
46. The current method of scheduling hurts the quality of client service.	1	2	3	4	5

	Strongly Disagree	Disagree	Neither Agree nor Disagree	Agree	Strongly Agree
47. The current method of scheduling causes problems in coordinating work with my supervisor.	1	2	3	4	5
48. The current method of scheduling causes problems coordinating work with my coworkers.	1	2	3	4	5
49. The currrent work schedule has an unfavorable influence on my family life.	1	2	3	4	5
50. The current method of scheduling makes it easy for me to coordinate my schedule with the schedules of other family members.	1	2	3	4	5
51. The current work schedule has an unfavorable influence on my social life.	1	2	3	4	5
52. Almost none of my neighbors works the same schedule as I currently work.	1	2	3	4	5
53. Almost all of my friends work the same schedule as I currently work.	1	2	3	4	5
54. Working or leaving the work place represents a personal security problem for me under my current work schedule.	1	2	3	4	5
55. Under my current work schedule, transportation to and from work is difficult.	1	2	3	4	5

56. Use the space below to make written comments on *favorable* aspects of the current method of scheduling work.

57. Use the space below to make written comments on *unfavorable* aspects of the current method of scheduling work.

58. Use the space below to make any other written comments on the current method of scheduling work, including possible variations, etc.

You were just asked a series of questions about your current work schedule. In the next sections, those questions are repeated to see how you feel about an alternative work schedule.

The alternative schedule is known as *flexitime*. Under the flexitime schedule, there would be two blocks of time (core hours) each day during which all employees must be at work. Under this plan, everyone would work between 10 and 11:30 A.M. and between 2 and 3 P.M. On a daily basis each worker would decide when to work the remaining five hours of the work day. Thus you (and all other employees) would be free to choose your starting time, break times, and quitting time as long as you worked a total of seven and a half hours each day and you were present during the core hours.

Sometimes a work schedule can interfere with opportunities to do other things. The following questions ask how easy or difficult it would be for you to do some common activities under the *flexitime* work schedule.

	Very Easy	Easy	Neither Difficult nor Easy	Difficult	Very Difficult
59. Spend time with your children	1	2	3	4	5
60. Maintain personal family relations	1	2	3	4	5
61. Spend time with your spouse	1	2	3	4	5
62. Spend time with friends	1	2	3	4	5
63. Take family on recreational outings	1	2	3	4	5
64. Take part in children's education	1	2	3	4	5
65. Attend children's school activities	1	2	3	4	5
66. Participate in sports with others	1	2	3	4	5
67. Participate in nonwork organizations	1	2	3	4	5
68. See a movie	1	2	3	4	5
69. Go to tavern or buy liquor	1	2	3	4	5

	Very Easy	Easy	Neither Difficult nor Easy	Difficult	Very Difficult
70. Go to the laundromat	1	2	3	4	5
71. Go out to eat	1	2	3	4	5
72. Attend play, concert, cultural event	1	2	3	4	5
73. Watch favorite TV programs	1	2	3	4	5
74. Buy groceries	1	2	3	4	5
75. Go shopping for clothes	1	2	3	4	5
76. Use public transportation	1	2	3	4	5
77. Go to the bank	1	2	3	4	5
78. Cash a check	1	2	3	4	5
79. Go to the post office	1	2	3	4	5

The questions in this section ask about your opinions and feelings concerning the *flexitime* work schedule. For each statement, circle a number to indicate the degree to which you agree or disagree with the statement.

	Strongly Disagree	Disagree	Neither Agree nor Disagree	Agree	Strongly Agree
80. I would be very productive under the flexitime method of scheduling.	1	2	3	4	5
81. The flexitime schedule would have a favorable influence on my overall attitude toward my job.	1	2	3	4	5
82. The flexitime work schedule would encourage me to do my best.	1	2	3	4	5
83. Taking everything into consideration, I would be satisfied with my life in general while working a flexitime work week.	1	2	3	4	5
84. I would be dissatisfied with the flexitime work schedule.	1	2	3	4	5
85. I personally would like the flexitime method of scheduling.	1	2	3	4	5

	Strongly Disagree	Disagree	Neither Agree nor Disagree	Agree	Strongly Agree
86. The flexitime schedule would have an unfavorable influence on my physical health.	1	2	3	4	5
87. The flexitime schedule would provide good client access to the services of the department.	1	2	3	4	5
88. The flexitime method of scheduling would help the department meet the needs of its clients.	1	2	3	4	5
89. The flexitime method of scheduling would make it easy for me to meet the service needs of clients.	1	2	3	4	5
90. The flexitime method of scheduling would hurt the quality of client service.	1	2	3	4	5
91. The flexitime method of scheduling would cause problems in coordinating work with my supervisor.	1	2	3	4	5
92. The flexitime method of scheduling would cause problems coordinating work with my coworkers.	1	2	3	4	5
93. The flexitime work schedule would have an unfavorable influence on my family life.	1	2	3	4	5
94. The flexitime method of scheduling would make it easy for me to coordinate my schedule with the schedules of other family members.	1	2	3	4	5

	Strongly Disagree	Disagree	Neither Agree nor Disagree	Agree	Strongly Agree
95. The flexitime work schedule would have an unfavorable influence on my social life.	1	2	3	4	5
96. Almost none of my neighbors works the flexitime schedule.	1	2	3	4	5
97. Almost all of my friends work the flexitime schedule.	1	2	3	4	5
98. Working or leaving the work place would represent a personal security problem for me under the flexitime work schedule.	1	2	3	4	5
99. Under the flexitime work schedule, transportation to and from work would be difficult.	1	2	3	4	5

100. Use the space below to make written comments on *favorable* aspects of the flexitime method of scheduling work.

101. Use the space below to make written comments on *unfavorable* aspects of the flexitime method of scheduling work.

102. Use the space below to make any other written comments on the flexitime method of scheduling work, including possible variations, etc.

103. My personal preference is to work— (Circle one.)
    1. The current work schedule
    2. The flexitime work schedule
104. The schedule that would be more beneficial to the company in trying to accomplish its work would be— (Circle one.)
    1. The current work schedule
    2. The flexitime work schedule

Section IV[3]

The following questions ask how you *currently* feel about a variety of work-related factors. For each question, circle a number to indicate the degree to which you agree or disagree with the statement.

	Strongly Disagree	Disagree	Neither Agree nor Disagree	Agree	Strongly Agree
105. My physical working conditions make it difficult for me to do my job.	1	2	3	4	5
106. I am satisfied with my physical working conditions.	1	2	3	4	5
107. The example my fellow employees set encourages me to work hard.	1	2	3	4	5
108. I like the employees that I work with a great deal.	1	2	3	4	5
109. Work like mine tends to discourage me from doing my best.	1	2	3	4	5
110. I like the kind of work I do very much.	1	2	3	4	5
111. I am somewhat worried about my future at this company.	1	2	3	4	5
112. Hard work seems fairly worthwhile to me with regard to my future at this company.	1	2	3	4	5
113. This is a good company to work for.	1	2	3	4	5
114. Working at this company encourages me to do my best.	1	2	3	4	5
115. Very few of my needs are satisfied by the pay and benefits I receive.	1	2	3	4	5
116. The way pay and benefits are handled at this company makes it worthwhile for me to work hard.	1	2	3	4	5

	Strongly Disagree	Disagree	Neither Agree nor Disagree	Agree	Strongly Agree
117. The supervision I receive is the kind that tends to discourage me from giving extra effort.	1	2	3	4	5
118. I am satisfied with the supervision I receive.	1	2	3	4	5
119. The amount of work I'm expected to do makes it difficult for me to do my job well.	1	2	3	4	5
120. I am dissatisfied with the amount of work I am expected to do.	1	2	3	4	5
121. During the next three months, I plan to arrive at work on time whenever it is possible to do so.	1	2	3	4	5
122. During the next three months, I expect to miss at least one day of work on a day when it would be possible for me to come to work.	1	2	3	4	5
123. I will probably quit my job with this company sometime during the next two years.	1	2	3	4	5

Endnotes

1. This scale was developed as part of an ongoing research project conducted by R. B. Dunham and J. L. Pierce in conjunction with L. L. Cummings and D. G. Gardner.

2. R. B. Dunham and J. L. Pierce, "Attitudes toward Work Schedules: Construct Definition, Instrument Development, and Validation," *Academy of Management Journal* 29 (January 1986): 170–182.

3. Items 105–120 of this scale were created by R. B. Dunham and have been validated through a comparison to other existing job-satisfaction instruments.

Appendix D

Survey Scoring

Instructions

▶ In this appendix, we identify the scoring procedures to use for each scale score. For illustration purposes, we present an example of a completed survey and calculate a scale score for that example. (No scoring information is provided for Section I, inasmuch as it contains only demographic and organizational-classification questions.)

Section II: Receptivity to Change

	Strongly Disagree	Disagree	Neither Agree nor Disagree	Agree	Strongly Agree
7. More often than not, organizational changes benefit the majority of employees who are involved in the change.	1	2	③	4	5
8. More often than not, organizational changes benefit the organization.	1	2	3	④	5
9. Organizational changes often take advantage of employees.	5 1̷	4 2̷	3	2 ④	1 5̷
10. More often than not, organizational changes are introduced before the details of the changes have been well worked out.	5 1̷	4 ②	3	2 4̷	1 5̷
11. In my opinion, many of the changes introduced in this organization are not good ideas.	5 1̷	4 2̷	3	2 ④	1 5̷
12. I am concerned that I may adapt poorly to the organizational changes to be introduced in the next few years.	5 1̷	4 ②	3	2 4̷	1 5̷
13. I enjoy the changes that occur at this organization.	1	2	3	4	⑤
14. Working here would be less interesting if things did not change so often.	1	2	3	④	5

Receptivity to Change:

$$\text{Scale Score} = \frac{Q7 + Q8 + Q9 + Q10 + Q11 + Q12 + Q13 + Q14}{8}$$

$$\text{Example Score} = \frac{3 + 4 + 2 + 4 + 2 + 4 + 5 + 4}{8} = \frac{28}{8} = 3.50$$

Note: High scores = high receptivity to change.

Section III: Reactions to Specific Work Schedules

A. Interference Caused by Current Schedule ───────────

Sometimes a work schedule can interfere with opportunities to do other things. The following questions ask how easy or difficult it is for you to do some common activities under your *current* work schedule.

	Very Easy	Easy	Neither Difficult nor Easy	Difficult	Very Difficult
15. Spend time with your children	1	2	3	④	5
16. Maintain personal family relations	1	2	3	④	5
17. Spend time with your spouse	1	②	3	4	5
18. Spend time with friends	1	2	③	4	5
19. Take family on recreational outings	1	2	3	④	5
20. Take part in children's education	1	2	3	4	⑤
21. Attend children's school activities	1	2	3	4	⑤
22. Participate in sports with others	1	②	3	4	5
23. Participate in nonwork organizations	1	②	3	4	5
24. See a movie	1	②	3	4	5
25. Go to tavern or buy liquor	1	②	3	4	5
26. Go to the laundromat	1	2	③	4	5
27. Go out to eat	1	②	3	4	5
28. Attend play, concert, cultural event	1	②	3	4	5
29. Watch favorite TV programs	1	2	3	④	5
30. Buy groceries	1	②	3	4	5
31. Go shopping for clothes	1	2	3	④	5
32. Use public transportation	1	②	3	4	5
33. Go to the bank	1	2	3	④	5
34. Cash a check	1	2	③	4	5
35. Go to the post office	1	2	3	4	⑤

Interference with activities with family and friends:

$$\text{Scale Score} = \frac{Q15 + Q16 + Q17 + Q18 + Q19 + Q20 + Q21 + Q22 + Q23}{9}$$

$$\text{Example Score} = \frac{4 + 4 + 2 + 3 + 4 + 5 + 5 + 2 + 2}{9} = \frac{31}{9} = 3.44$$

Interference with access to services, events, consumables:

$$\text{Scale Score} = \frac{Q24 + Q25 + Q26 + Q27 + Q28 + Q29 + Q30 + Q31 + Q32}{9}$$

$$\text{Example Score} = \frac{2 + 2 + 3 + 2 + 2 + 4 + 2 + 4 + 2}{9} = \frac{23}{9} = 2.55$$

Interference with financial activities:

$$\text{Scale Score} = \frac{Q33 + Q34 + Q35}{3}$$

$$\text{Example Score} = \frac{4 + 3 + 5}{3} = \frac{12}{3} = 4.00$$

The questions in this section ask about your opinions and feelings concerning your *current* work schedule. For each statement, circle a number to indicate the degree to which you agree or disagree with the statement.

	Strongly Disagree	Disagree	Neither Agree nor Disagree	Agree	Strongly Agree
36. I am very productive under the current method of scheduling.	1	2	3	④	5
37. The current schedule has a favorable influence on my overall attitude toward my job.	1	②	3	4	5
38. My current work schedule encourages me to do my best.	1	2	③	4	5

	Strongly Disagree	Disagree	Neither Agree nor Disagree	Agree	Strongly Agree
39. Taking everything into consideration, I am satisfied with my life in general while working my current work week.	1	2	③	4	5
40. I am dissatisfied with my current work schedule.	5 / 1̶	4 / 2̶	3	2 / ④	1 / 5̶
41. I personally like the current method of scheduling.	1	2	③	4	5
42. The current schedule has an unfavorable influence on my physical health.	5 / 1̶	4 / ②	3	2 / 4̶	1 / 5̶
43. The current schedule provides good client access to the services of the Department.	1	2	3	④	5
44. The current method of scheduling helps the Department meet the needs of its clients.	1	2	3	④	5
45. The current method of scheduling makes it easy for me to meet the service needs of clients.	1	2	③	4	5
46. The current method of scheduling hurts the quality of client service.	5 / 1̶	4 / ②	3	2 / 4̶	1 / 5̶
47. The current method of scheduling causes problems in coordinating work with my supervisor.	5 / 1̶	4 / ②	3	2 / 4̶	1 / 5̶
48. The current method of scheduling causes problems coordinating work with my coworkers.	5 / 1̶	4 / ②	3	2 / 4̶	1 / 5̶
49. The currrent work schedule has an unfavorable influence on my family life.	5 / 1̶	4 / 2̶	3	2 / ④	1 / 5̶

	Strongly Disagree	Disagree	Neither Agree nor Disagree	Agree	Strongly Agree
50. The current method of scheduling makes it easy for me to coordinate my schedule with the schedules of other family members.	1	2	③	4	5
51. The current work schedule has an unfavorable influence on my social life.	5 ~~1~~	4 ~~2~~	3	2 ④	1 ~~5~~
52. Almost none of my neighbors works the same schedule as I currently work.	1	②	3	4	5
53. Almost all of my friends work the same schedule as I currently work.	5 ~~1~~	4 ~~2~~	3	2 ④	1 ~~5~~
54. Working or leaving the work place represents a personal security problem for me under my current work schedule.	5 ~~1~~	4 ~~2~~	③	2 4	1 ~~5~~
55. Under my current work schedule, transportation to and from work is difficult.	5 ~~1~~	4 ②	3	2 4	1 ~~5~~

General affect toward current schedule:

$$\text{Scale Score} = \frac{Q36 + Q37 + Q38 + Q39 + Q40 + Q41 + Q42}{7}$$

$$\text{Example Score} = \frac{4 + 2 + 3 + 3 + 2 + 3 + 4}{7} = \frac{21}{7} = 3.00$$

Service to external constituents:

$$\text{Scale Score} = \frac{Q43 + Q44 + Q45 + Q46}{4}$$

$$\text{Example Score} = \frac{4 + 4 + 3 + 4}{4} = \frac{15}{4} = 3.75$$

Work coordination effects:

$$\text{Scale Score} = \frac{Q47 + Q48}{2}$$

$$\text{Example Score} = \frac{4 + 4}{2} = \frac{8}{2} = 4.00$$

Effects of current schedule on social/family life:

$$\text{Scale Score} = \frac{Q49 + Q50 + Q51}{3}$$

$$\text{Example Score} = \frac{2 + 3 + 2}{3} = \frac{7}{3} = 2.33$$

Uniqueness of current schedule:

$$\text{Scale Score} = \frac{Q52 + Q53}{2}$$

$$\text{Example Score} = \frac{2 + 2}{2} = \frac{4}{2} = 2.00$$

Transportation and personal security:

$$\text{Scale Score} = \frac{Q54 + Q55}{2}$$

$$\text{Example Score} = \frac{3 + 4}{2} = \frac{7}{2} = 3.50$$

Note: High scores on the transportation and personal-security scale = high security and convenient transportation.

C. Interference Caused by Flexitime Schedule _____

Sometimes a work schedule can interfere with opportunities to do other things. The following questions ask how easy or difficult it would be for you to do some common activities under the flexitime work schedule.

	Very Easy	Easy	Neither Difficult nor Easy	Difficult	Very Difficult
59. Spend time with your children	1	②	3	4	5
60. Maintain personal family relations	1	②	3	4	5
61. Spend time with your spouse	1	②	3	4	5
62. Spend time with friends	1	2	③	4	5
63. Take family on recreational outings	1	②	3	4	5
64. Take part in children's education	1	②	3	4	5
65. Attend children's school activities	1	②	3	4	5
66. Participate in sports with others	1	2	③	4	5
67. Participate in nonwork organizations	1	2	③	4	5
68. See a movie	1	②	3	4	5
69. Go to tavern or buy liquor	1	②	3	4	5
70. Go to the laundromat	1	②	3	4	5
71. Go out to eat	1	②	3	4	5
72. Attend play, concert, cultural event	1	②	3	4	5
73. Watch favorite TV programs	1	2	③	4	5
74. Buy groceries	1	②	3	4	5
75. Go shopping for clothes	1	②	3	4	5
76. Use public transportation	1	②	3	4	5
77. Go to the bank	1	②	3	4	5
78. Cash a check	1	②	3	4	5
79. Go to the post office	1	②	3	4	5

Interference with activities with family and friends:

$$\text{Scale Score} = \frac{Q59 + Q60 + Q61 + Q62 + Q63 + Q64 + Q65 + Q66 + Q67}{9}$$

$$\text{Example Score} = \frac{2 + 2 + 2 + 3 + 2 + 2 + 2 + 3 + 3}{9} = \frac{21}{9} = 2.33$$

Interference with access to services, events, consumables:

$$\text{Scale Score} = \frac{Q68 + Q69 + Q70 + Q71 + Q72 + Q73 + Q74 + Q75 + Q76}{9}$$

$$\text{Example Score} = \frac{2 + 2 + 2 + 2 + 2 + 3 + 2 + 2 + 2}{9} = \frac{19}{9} = 2.11$$

Interference with financial activities:

$$\text{Scale Score} = \frac{Q77 + Q78 + Q79}{3}$$

$$\text{Example Score} = \frac{2 + 2 + 2}{3} = \frac{6}{3} = 2.00$$

D. Attitudes toward Flexitime Work Schedules _____

The questions in this section ask about your opinions and feelings concerning the *flexitime* work schedule. For each statement, circle a number to indicate the degree to which you agree or disagree with the statement.

	Strongly Disagree	Disagree	Neither Agree nor Disagree	Agree	Strongly Agree
80. I would be very productive under the flexitime method of scheduling.	1	2	3	④	5
81. The flexitime schedule would have a favorable influence on my overall attitude toward my job.	1	2	3	4	⑤
82. The flexitime work schedule would encourage me to do my best.	1	2	③	4	5
83. Taking everything into consideration, I would be satisfied with my life in general while working a flexitime work week.	1	2	3	④	5
84. I would be dissatisfied with the flexitime work schedule.	① 5	2̸ 4	3	2 4̸	1 5̸

	Strongly Disagree	Disagree	Neither Agree nor Disagree	Agree	Strongly Agree
85. I personally would like the flexitime method of scheduling.	1	2	3	4	⑤
86. The flexitime schedule would have an unfavorable influence on my physical health.	5 / 1̸	4 / 2̸	③	2 / 4̸	1 / 5̸
87. The flexitime schedule would provide good client access to the services of the Department.	1	2	③	4	5
88. The flexitime method of scheduling would help the Department meet the needs of its clients.	1	2	③	4	5
89. The flexitime method of scheduling would make it easy for me to meet the service needs of clients.	1	2	③	4	5
90. The flexitime method of scheduling would hurt the quality of client service.	5 / 1̸	4 / ②	3	2 / 4̸	1 / 5̸
91. The flexitime method of scheduling would cause problems in coordinating work with my supervisor.	5 / 1̸	4 / ②	3	2 / 4̸	1 / 5̸
92. The flexitime method of scheduling would cause problems coordinating work with my coworkers.	5 / 1̸	4 / 2̸	3	2 / ④	1 / 5̸
93. The flexitime work schedule would have an unfavorable influence on my family life.	5 / 1̸	4 / ②	3	2 / 4̸	1 / 5̸
94. The flexitime method of scheduling would make it easy for me to coordinate my schedule with the schedules of other family members.	1	2	3	④	5

	Strongly Disagree	Disagree	Neither Agree nor Disagree	Agree	Strongly Agree
95. The flexitime work schedule would have an unfavorable influence on my social life.	5 ①̸	4 2̸	3	2 4̸	1 5̸
96. Almost none of my neighbors works the flexitime schedule.	1	2	3	④	5
97. Almost all of my friends work the flexitime schedule.	5 1̸	4 ②̸	3	2 4̸	1 5̸
98. Working or leaving the work place would represent a personal security problem for me under the flexitime work schedule.	5 1̸	4 ②̸	3	2 4̸	1 5̸
99. Under the flexitime work schedule, transportation to and from work would be difficult.	5 1̸	4 2̸	③	2 4̸	1 5̸

General affect toward flexitime schedule:

$$\text{Scale Score} = \frac{Q80 + Q81 + Q82 + Q83 + Q84 + Q85 + Q86}{7}$$

$$\text{Example Score} = \frac{4 + 5 + 3 + 4 + 5 + 5 + 3}{7} = \frac{29}{7} = 4.14$$

Service to external constituents:

$$\text{Scale Score} = \frac{Q87 + Q88 + Q89 + Q90}{4}$$

$$\text{Example Score} = \frac{3 + 3 + 3 + 4}{4} = \frac{13}{4} = 3.25$$

Work coordination effects:

$$\text{Scale Score} = \frac{Q91 + Q92}{2}$$

$$\text{Example Score} = \frac{4 + 2}{2} = \frac{6}{2} = 3.00$$

Effects of flexitime schedule on social/family life:

$$\text{Scale Score} = \frac{Q93 + Q94 + Q95}{3}$$

$$\text{Example Score} = \frac{4 + 4 + 5}{3} = \frac{13}{3} = 4.33$$

Uniqueness of flexitime schedule:

$$\text{Scale Score} = \frac{Q96 + Q97}{2}$$

$$\text{Example Score} = \frac{4 + 4}{2} = \frac{8}{2} = 4.00$$

Transportation and personal security:

$$\text{Scale Score} = \frac{Q98 + Q99}{2}$$

$$\text{Example Score} = \frac{4 + 3}{2} = \frac{7}{2} = 3.50$$

Note: High scores on the transportation and personal security scale = high security and convenient transportation.

Section IV: Job Satisfaction

The following questions ask how you *currently* feel about a variety of work-related factors. For each question, circle a number to indicate the degree to which you agree or disagree with the statement.

	Strongly Disagree	Disagree	Neither Agree nor Disagree	Agree	Strongly Agree
105. My physical working conditions make it difficult for me to do my job.	5 / 1	4 / 2	3	2 / (4)	1 / 5
106. I am satisfied with my physical working conditions.	(1)	2	3	4	5
107. The example my fellow employees set encourages me to work hard.	1	2	3	(4)	5
108. I like the employees that I work with a great deal.	1	2	3	(4)	5
109. Work like mine tends to discourage me from doing my best.	5 / (1)	4 / 2	3	2 / 4	1 / 5
110. I like the kind of work I do very much.	1	2	3	4	(5)
111. I am somewhat worried about my future at this company.	5 / 1	4 / (2)	3	2 / 4	1 / 5
112. Hard work seems fairly worthwhile to me with regard to my future at this company.	1	2	3	(4)	5
113. This is a good company to work for.	1	2	3	(4)	5
114. Working at this company encourages me to do my best.	1	2	3	(4)	5
115. Very few of my needs are satisfied by the pay and benefits I receive.	5 / 1	4 / (2)	3	2 / 4	1 / 5
116. The way pay and benefits are handled at this company makes it worthwhile for me to work hard.	1	2	3	(4)	5

Table E–3. Receptivity to Change and Job Satisfaction: All Company and by Office

	Co. Av.	Office							
		G. Bay	Milw. West	Milw. So.	Schaum- burg	Cincin- nati	Mem- phis	Den- ver	Col'- bus
Change receptivity									
Physical satisfaction									
Coworker satisfaction									
Work satisfaction									
Career satisfaction									
Policy/practices satisfaction									
Pay satisfaction									
Supervision satisfaction									
Amount-of-work satisfaction									

Table E–4. Reactions to Schedules: All Company and by Job Classification

	Co. Av.	Job Classification					
		Nonsup. Clerical	Sup. Clerical	Nonsup. Tech.	Sup. Tech.	Nonsup. Prod.	Sup. Prod.
Current Schedule							
Interference: fam/ friends							
Interference: svcs, etc.							
Interference: fin, etc.							
General affect							
Service							
Work coordination							
Social/family life							
Uniqueness							
Transportation/ security							
Flexitime Schedule							
Interference: fam/ friends							
Interference: svcs, etc.							
Interference: fin, etc.							
General affect							
Service							
Work coordination							
Social/family life							
Uniqueness							
Transportation/security							

Table E–5. Reactions to Schedules: All Company and by Office

	Co. Av.	Office							
		G. Bay	Milw. West	Milw. So.	Schaum-burg	Cincin-nati	Mem-phis	Den-ver	Col' bus
Current Schedule									
Interference: fam/friends									
Interference: svcs, etc.									
Interference: fin, etc.									
General affect									
Service									
Work coordination									
Social/family life									
Uniqueness									
Transportation/security									
Flexitime Schedule									
Interference: fam/friends									
Interference: svcs, etc.									
Interference: fin, etc.									
General affect									
Service									
Work coordination									
Social/family life									
Uniqueness									
Transportation/security									

Table E–6. Reactions to Schedules: Current versus Flexitime

	Current Schedule	Flexitime	Statistical Significance
Interference: fam/friends			
Interference: svcs, etc.			
Interference: fin, etc.			
General affect			
Service			
Work coordination			
Social/family life			
Uniqueness			
Transportation/security			

Notes: $*p < .05$
$**p < .01$

Table E–7. Schedule Preferences: All Company and by Job Classifications (percentages)

	Co. Av.	Job Classification					
		Nonsup. Clerical	Sup. Clerical	Nonsup. Tech.	Sup. Tech.	Nonsup. Prod.	Sup. Prod.
Personal preference is:							
▶ Current schedule							
▶ Flexitime schedule							
Schedule more beneficial to company is:							
▶ Current schedule							
▶ Flexitime schedule							

Table E–8. Schedule Preferences: All Company and by Office (percentages)

	Co. Av.	Office							
		G. Bay	Milw. West	Milw. So.	Schaumburg	Cincinnati	Memphis	Denver	Col'bus
Personal preference is:									
▶ Current schedule									
▶ Flexitime schedule									
Schedule more beneficial to company is:									
▶ Current schedule									
▶ Flexitime schedule									

Index